PSYCHOLOGY PRACTITIONER GUIDEBOOKS

EDITORS
Arnold P. Goldstein, Syracuse University
Leonard Krasner, Stanford University & SUNY at Stony Brook
Sol L. Garfield, Washington University in St. Louis

ANXIETY DISORDERS
IN YOUTH

Titles of Related Interest

Clark/Salkovskis COGNITIVE THERAPY FOR PANIC AND HYPOCHONDRIASIS

Last/Hersen HANDBOOK OF ANXIETY DISORDERS

Matson TREATING DEPRESSION IN CHILDREN AND ADOLESCENTS

Meichenbaum STRESS INOCULATION TRAINING

Saigh POSTTRAUMATIC STRESS DISORDER: A Behavioral Approach to Assessment and Treatment

Warren/Zgourides ANXIETY DISORDERS: A Rational-Emotive Perspective

ANXIETY DISORDERS IN YOUTH
Cognitive-Behavioral Interventions

PHILIP C. KENDALL
Temple University

with (in alphabetical order)
Tamar Ellsas Chansky, Martha T. Kane, Ray S. Kim,
Elizabeth Kortlander, Kevin R. Ronan,
Frances M. Sessa, and Lynne Siqueland

Allyn and Bacon
Boston • London • Toronto • Sydney • Tokyo • Singapore

Copyright © 1992 by Allyn and Bacon
A Division of Simon & Schuster, Inc.
160 Gould Street
Needham Heights, Massachusetts 02194

Printed in the United States of America

10 9 8 7 6 5 4 3 2 1   97 96 95 94 93 92

To all the children and their families who have contributed to our understanding

Contents

Preface   ix

Chapter
1. The Nature of Anxiety and Its Disorders in Youth   1
2. The Cognitive-Behavioral Perspective   12
3. Assessment Strategies and Diagnostic Issues   30
4. Cognitive-Behavioral Strategies Applied to Anxiety
    Disorders in Youth   57
5. Integrated Cognitive-Behavioral Treatment Program
    for Anxiety Disorders   74
6. Clinical Case Illustrations and Research Results   100
7. Dealing With Potential Difficulties   130
8. Working With the Family   144
9. Maintaining Gains   171

Appendix   180
References   187
Author Index   199
Subject Index   205
About the Authors   213

Preface

The Child and Adolescent Anxiety Disorders Clinic (CAADC) at Temple University was founded in 1987 to provide psychological treatment for youth with difficulties associated with distressing levels of anxiety. Acting out and disruptive children routinely receive attention and services; anxious children sometimes go unnoticed and unserved. It remains our intent to study, to better understand, and to effectively treat those children with the quiet quake of disturbing anxiety.

Our goal for this book is to present a clinically sensitive and empirically sound set of procedures for helping youth manage their distressing anxiety. Emerging data from our randomized clinical trial show the promising results of these procedures. However, due to the absence of other published reports of clinical trials with diagnosed cases of anxious youth, the empirical basis for our program rests on the evidence supporting each of the separate components of the treatment as applied with clients of various ages. Variations in the application of our manualized treatment is evidence for and is essential to its clinical sensitivity. It is our intent that this book describe the information necessary to effectively intervene with anxious children.

In the opening chapter we discuss, in general, the defining features of anxiety, its prevalence and normative status, and developmental changes. Our cognitive-behavioral model is introduced in chapter 2, along with consideration of the goals for treatment. As part of our model, the information processing of the child (e.g., expectations, attributions, self-talk), the role of emotionally charged behavioral events, and the impact of the social context are considered. Assessment methods and procedures are described in chapter 3, along with suggestions regarding the use of specific instruments and diagnostic procedures and the integration of diverse sources of data. The coping skills introduced as a part of the anxiety management program and the strategies we use in the intervention process are presented separately in chapter 4. The full program, in its integrated form, including session-by-session descriptions, is provided in chapter 5. To further illustrate the clinical application of the program, four detailed clinical case illustrations are furnished in chapter 6. Also provided in chapter 6 are the results of data analyses of our treatment-outcome project. Those inevitable difficulties that occur in the process of helping others seek behavioral change are given special attention in chapter 7. For example, issues of the denial of anxiety, compliance with treatment, and comorbidity of psychological disorders are addressed. Working with children inevitably involves working, to a degree, with parents and/or family members. Working with family members, as collaborators and as participants in treatment, encompasses chapter 8. Last, chapter 9 relates strategies designed to maintain treatment-produced gains.

This work was a truly collaborative effort. The author team consists of the senior CAADC staff, with each and every individual having been active in the drafting and revising process. Accordingly, the junior author team is listed in alphabetical order. This book and our CAADC would not have been created without the initial support of Temple University's Department of Psychology and research funding from the National Institute of Mental Health (Grant No. 1 RO1 MH 44042-01A1). Many referral sources cooperated with us, and we thank the Counseling or Referral Agency (CORA), the Program of Auxiliary Services for Students (PASS), Elwyn Institute, and District 4 of the Philadelphia Public Schools. The faculty and the staff members of the FitzSimons School also deserve a very special thanks.

The cooperation of the director and staff of the Psychological Services Center at Temple University and the collaboration of faculty and graduate-student colleagues in the Clinical Psychology Doctoral Training Program is appreciated. Special thanks to our clinical and research colleagues Erika Brady, Laura Bross, Michael Friedman, Joellyn Gabrielle, Elizabeth Gosch, Kim Hayden, Bonnie Howard, and Jennifer Panas, and to Sue Gourlay and Beatrice Smith, for their secretarial support.

A book such as this benefits greatly from the empirical reports and theoretical treatises that have preceded it. We note and acknowledge these earlier written contributions: all of those whose labors are cited in our reference list.

Though they appear last, their impact is greatest—we thank our spouses, families, and loved ones: to Sue, Mark, and Reed (PCK), to Phillip (TEC), to Michael, Anna, and Elizabeth (MK), to Tom and Betty Kim (RSK), to Bruce (EK), to the Atkins and Ronans (KR), and to my family and friends (LS).

Chapter 1

The Nature of Anxiety and Its Disorders in Youth

> *You gain strength, courage and confidence by every experience in which you really stop to look fear in the face. You are able to say to yourself, "I lived through this horror. I can take the next thing that comes along." . . . You must do the thing you think you cannot do.*
>
> —*Anna Eleanor Roosevelt*

Anxiety is often defined as: "apprehension, tension, or uneasiness related to the expectation of danger, whether internal or external. Anxiety may be focused on an object, situation or activity that is avoided, as in phobia, or it may be unfocused." Many of the anxieties seen in children and adolescents are fairly common and, usually, transitory. Their appearance and subsequent resolution are normal in the developmental process. In fact, fears can serve as an adaptive response in many situations (Morris & Kratochwill, 1985).

Anxiety, however, can also be so intense or pervasive that it leads to unwanted psychological distress and maladjustment. Childhood anxiety becomes a concern when its severity or duration negatively impinges on the child or those within the family and broader social network (Kendall, Howard, & Epps, 1988). The importance of addressing anxiety disorders early is accentuated by recent findings suggesting that children who suffer from anxiety mature into adults who continue to suffer from anxious symptoms (Last, Phillips, & Statfield, 1987). But before preventive or treatment strategies are implemented for anxious children, normal fears and anxieties must be differentiated from anxiety disorders, so that treatment can be efficiently provided for those children needing services, and unnecessary intervention can be avoided in those cases where children have normal fears (Strauss, 1987).

In order to clarify the distinction between normal and clinical anxiety,

1

two scenarios will be discussed. First is Wendy, an 11-year-old who has always been an average student. Before taking tests, she consistently has "butterflies in the stomach" and worries whether she will pass. However, when given a test, she focuses on the task and completes it. Wendy is by no means a stellar student but performs adequately considering the minimal time and effort she applies to preparing for her assignments. The anxiety she experiences is considered normal—it does not negatively impact on her performance or adjustment.

Scott, on the other hand, has more severe problems than Wendy. He is a bright 12-year-old who has always been a good student. Recently, however, his class was required to present individual book reports. The morning Scott had to present his report, he refused to go to school and locked himself in the bathroom at home. His parents eventually unlocked the door and had to physically carry him to the car. Although kicking and screaming during the drive to school, he calmed down enough to go to class. During class, Scott experienced feelings of nausea and vomited when his teacher told him it was his turn to make his presentation. He has had similar problems when asked to present newspaper articles to the class. Scott's public-performance fear deserves clinical attention, because—unlike Wendy's anxiety—the anxiety Scott experiences is so intense that it has detrimental effects on performance and adjustment.

DEFINING ANXIETY DISORDERS
IN YOUTH

In general, the symptoms associated with anxiety in children resemble those found in adults, including physiological, behavioral, and cognitive manifestations. Childhood anxiety is seen as a multidimensional construct, in which some portion of each of the three response components is experienced.

Physiological symptoms reflect activity in the autonomic nervous system (ANS). The ANS is responsible for the automatic regulation of internal bodily functions. Some physical symptoms appear to have a connection with anxiety in children, including perspiration, diffuse abdominal pain, flushed face, enuresis, trembling, and tics (Barrios & Hartmann, 1988). While these symptoms (see Table 1.1) may be suggestive of an anxiety problem, they do not necessarily indicate anxiety. The relationship of such physical symptoms to anxiety must be based on the demonstration of a cause-and-effect relationship, associated data, or the particular characteristics of the symptom and its history (Werry, 1986). One must also consider other possible explanations for the symptoms.

Behavioral symptoms of anxiety are more public. They involve observ-

Table 1.1. *Select Physical Symptoms of Anxiety in Youth*

- stomach aches, nausea, vomiting
- headache
- muscle tension
- jittery, wiggly behaviors
- heart palpitations
- sweating, especially palmar
- hot flashes or cold flashes
- feelings of suffocation, choking

able behavior resulting from skeletal muscle responses. For instance, these responses include physical attempts to avoid threatening situations or escape behavior, such as running, when avoidance is not possible. However, when avoidance or escape responses are impossible in a threatening situation, other behavioral signs of anxiety are seen, including trembling hands, shaky speech, crying, nail biting, and thumb sucking (Barrios & Hartmann, 1988). Table 1.2 lists behavior characteristics of each of the major childhood anxiety disorders (see Table 1.2). From these behaviors, one might infer that the person is experiencing a state of anxiety.

The cognitive component of anxiety involves the child's mental experience. The child's thoughts about what is happening or how he or she thinks about and reports feeling is part of this experience. For instance, anxious thoughts include, "What is going to happen to me now" or "What if I mess up and make a fool of myself?" (see Table 1.3). Recently, Kendall and Ronan (1990) developed a scale that identifies self-statements characterizing anxious as opposed to nonanxious children. Are these thoughts accurate, reasonable, and/or healthy? Or do they reflect a characteristic pattern of misperceiving the demands of the environment? Kendall (1985) made the distinction between cognitive distortions and cognitive deficiencies in conceptualizing psychopathology. Deficiencies are an absence of thinking where it would be beneficial, while distortions are dysfunctional thinking processes. This differentiation is consistent with other data which suggests that anxious children may not be deficient in information processing, but instead show a distorted information-processing style.

Because anxiety can have physiological, behavioral, and cognitive components, it is often assessed across all three systems. Lang's (1968) tripartite model has great appeal because it stresses the importance of all three components as well as the need for assessing children's anxieties across various methodologies. Clinical interviews, self-report, parent and teacher ratings, behavioral observations, physiological recordings, and family assessment are strategies that have been used to assess expressions of anxiety symptoms across these response channels (Kendall & Ronan, 1990).

Table 1.2. *Some Behavioral Indicators of Anxiety in Youth*

Disorder	Indicator
Overanxious Disorder (OAD)	- avoid doing schoolwork for fear of making errors - can't turn in a school project because it isn't exactly like the teacher's example - are unable to draw a picture due to the excessive erasures and false starts caused by their preoccupation with perfection - frequently visit the school nurse with stomachaches or headaches, or at particular times of the day - watch the other kids or hang back in sports because they question their own ability - ask innumerable questions about upcoming events, often repetitive questions, to the point that adults become frustrated - avoid drawing attention to themselves
Separation Anxiety Disorder (SAD)	- call their mothers frequently from school or stop playing frequently to check on the parent - can't be left with a baby sitter because they protest so strongly - worry frequently about mother's health, to the point of trying to be sure parent has taken medication - stands at the mailbox waiting, crying for the parent to return - refuses to sleep over with friends or go to camp
Avoidant Disorder (AD)	- can't play sports, although they would like to, because they won't go to the initial meeting without knowing anyone else who will be there - sit in the back of the class wishing they could figure out how to make friends with other classmates - kick the soccer ball by themselves on a field where other children are playing soccer - never go to birthday parties - are extremely reluctant to go to any social function, although once there, they may enjoy themselves

There have been, and continue to be, refinements in the definition and classification of the anxiety disorders in children. A new diagnostic category was introduced in the *Diagnostic and Statistical Manual of Mental Disorders-Third Edition* (DSM-III) (American Psychiatric Association, [APA] 1980) that specifically focused on anxiety disorders first arising during childhood or adolescence—Anxiety Disorders of Childhood or Adolescence. This category included three specific disorders, disorders which still exist in the

Table 1.3. *Some Cognitive Features of Anxiety in Youth*

Disorder	Cognitive Feature
Overanxious Disorder (OAD)	- catastrophize, distort, and exaggerate the importance of events or experiences - if they bump a knee, they are sure it is broken; if their shoulder aches, they are sure they have cancer - equate minimal errors with total failure; think that if they get less than a 90, they won't be accepted into college - think that if they can't succeed at a task, such as hitting a tennis ball, in one or two tries that they will never be able to succeed at the task - worry that if they have a spot on their clothes, everyone will notice and laugh at them
Separation Anxiety Disorder (SAD)	- worry that their parents or loved ones are at risk of being kidnapped or killed by some unknown assailant - think that their parents may die of minor illnesses such as a common cold or the flu, or that their parents may disappear and never return for them - think their parents may be injured in the most commonplace of everyday occurrences such as driving to work or cleaning the house
Avoidant Disorder (AD)	- think that they would like to make friends but believe that others would not like to be friends with them - think that others do not even notice them or are purposely ignoring them - worry that there are too many unpredictable situations which may arise at a social event - think that other children's behavior is unpredictable and potentially harmful toward them - assume that no one else shares their interests or enjoys the same activities they do

revised edition: avoidant disorder, overanxious disorder, and separation anxiety.

The most common major anxiety disorder of childhood is the overanxious disorder (OAD). In OAD, the key problem is global worrying. Anxiety is not focused on a specific situation or object. Some characteristics of children with overanxious disorder are excessive worry about future events, an overconcern about one's own performance or evaluation by others, an extreme need for reassurance by others, and marked self-consciousness. Overanxious children are tense much of the time and often have multiple somatic complaints, such as headaches, stomachaches, and fatigue (Strauss, 1988). Although only nascent at this time, there is potential in development of effective treatment procedures for these children based on the adult literature regarding treatment for generalized anxiety disorder (Suinn, 1984).

Separation anxiety has received some fairly systematic research attention (see Klein & Last, 1989). The distress that children experience when separated from the person who cares for them is a normal developmental phenomenon. This leads to some ambiguity about when separation anxiety should be considered a part of normal development and when it should be seen as an indicator of maladjustment. Pathological separation anxiety may manifest itself in several ways. The first and most obvious is extreme distress upon separation. In the severe form of this disorder, distress appears as panic. Second, morbid worries about the potential dangers that threaten family integrity are characteristic of the disorder. Finally, homesickness involving a yearning to be reunited with family members to a degree which goes beyond usual reactions is also symptomatic. These characteristics of separation anxiety can occur concurrently or independently (Gittelman, 1984). Evidence suggests that behavior therapy has been effective in the treatment of separation anxiety (Thyer & Sowers-Hoag, 1988).

The third specific disorder is avoidant disorder. Avoidant disorder is used to refer to children who are abnormally shy and severely inhibited in a variety of social situations. It is important to distinguish avoidant disorder from schizoid disorder. Schizoid children may or may not be anxious in new social situations; they have little interest in social activities and tend to be isolated and socially inept. In contrast, children with avoidant disorders may want to join social groups; they usually have adequate social skills when in familiar settings but become overwhelmed with anxiety in new social situations. It is crucial to make this diagnostic differentiation because the prognosis for these two disorders is quite different—shy children generally have a good prognosis.

Avoidant disorder often overlaps with social phobia, especially with regard to the cognitive features. For instance, examples of cognitive activity seen in children with avoidant disorder and/or social phobia include thinking that others will find their behavior or ideas silly, ridiculous, or laughable; that others will perceive of them as stupid or immature (babyish); that other kids will laugh at their clothing or other aspects of their appearance; that others will laugh if they make a mistake, even a very minor one; or that others actively dislike them and want to humiliate them. Although the current DSM system includes a diagnosis for avoidant disorder, some serious reservations about its existence are in order. According to Gittelman and Koplewicz (1986), no clinical reports of avoidant disorder in children are in the literature. In our clinical experience, we find that it is very difficult to differentiate avoidant disorder from social phobia. In any case, we find avoidant disorder to be rare.

Although several types of anxiety can be differentiated among children, it is not clear whether they represent discrete entities or processes—one could question their distinctiveness because they are frequently found to overlap. Therefore, while diagnostic distinctions provided by the DSM-III-R (Revised; APA, 1987) may help to organize cases, rigid adherence to these different types of anxiety disorders may be premature. Overanxious disorder and separation anxiety disorder show promise, but empirical validation of all of the various affective disorders in youth is an essential goal for future research.

PREVALENCE AND NORMATIVE DATA

Prevalence is a measure of the number of individuals in the population who have a particular disorder at a given time. An important consideration is that true estimates of prevalence can only be obtained by sampling the total population at risk for the disorder rather than sampling treated patients alone. Measures based on treated cases are a problem because they are usually biased. For instance, people who seek treatment are usually higher in socioeconomic status or may represent more severe cases. Therefore, epidemiologic data are best when they come from both treated and untreated samples of the population (Orvaschel & Weissman, 1986).

A number of studies provide estimates of prevalence of childhood anxiety disorders in the general population. Although informative, comparability across these studies is difficult because of variations in methodology and design (Graziano, DeGiovanni, & Garcia, 1979; Orvaschel & Weissman, 1986). In an early report, Lapouse and Monk (1958) explored the frequency and intensity of a number of child anxiety characteristics. They found a 43% prevalence rate of "many fears and worries" in children aged 6 to 12 years. Agras, Sylvester, and Oliveau (1969) provided additional information on the prevalence of fears. In a random sample of both children and adults, a prevalence of 7.7% was found for all phobias. Werry and Quay (1971) obtained data showing 16.5% of children between the ages of 5 and 8 years exhibiting anxiety.

Sampling a younger group of children, Richman, Stevenson, and Graham (1975) reported that approximately 12.8% of 3-year-olds exhibited fears, while 2.6% were worriers. Earls (1980) used similar assessment procedures as Richman et al. (1975) and found 14.0% of 3-year-olds reported fears and 8.0% reported worrying. Finally, Kastrup (1976) and Abe and

Masui (1981) also provide data on the prevalence of childhood anxiety. Kastrup (1976) sampled 5 to 6-year-olds and reported a 4.0% prevalence rate of fears. Prevalence rates reported by Abe and Masui (1981) are less clear. For 11 to 12-year-olds, fears range from 2 to 43%, while worries range from 4 to 33% of the population. Gittelman (1986) provided a summary and comparison of the previously discussed prevalence rates (see Table 1.4).

Many of the fears and anxieties reported by children are a normal part of development. In an early study, Jersild and Holmes (1935) found that mothers reported an average of approximately five specific fears in their young children. McFarlane, Allen, and Honzik (1954) found that 90% of the normal children they studied between the ages of 2 and 14 reported at least one specific fear. Normative data show that the content of these fears change over development because of the child's growth experience, increasing cognitive differentiation, and increased perception of reality (Campbell, 1986).

In addition to developmental differences, sex differences in the number of childhood anxieties appear to exist. Rather consistent findings report fears as generally being more numerous for girls than for boys (e.g., Bauer, 1976; Houston, Fox, & Forbes, 1984; Ollendick, Matson, & Helsel, 1985; Pratt, 1945). Actual gender differences may account for the discrepancies in the number of fears reported. An alternative and possibly related explanation may revolve around sociocultural factors including those that allow girls to admit more freely to their fears (Ollendick et al., 1985), while also allowing parents to report more fears in girls than boys because fearful behavior is seen as more acceptable in girls (Harris & Ferrari, 1983). Additional normative data for different ages would facilitate the differentiation of normal from clinical levels of anxiety in both boys and girls.

DEVELOPMENTAL CHANGES

Developmental issues, alluded to above, are important when investigating or treating fears, phobias, and anxieties in youth. As fears are common in normal child populations, assessing inappropriate fears for a child's developmental level is crucial in determining the severity of the disturbance and the potential need for an intervention (Miller, Barrett, & Hampe, 1974). Caution must be used, however, in assessing these fears because individual differences in the way children express their fears occur with development. Behavioral responses alone may be a poor index of fear (Campbell, 1986). Despite such problems, behavioral observations are useful in cataloguing qualitative changes in children's fears across the age range. Young infants have been found to fear sudden, loud, and unpredictable stimuli, loss of support, and heights (Ball & Tronick, 1971). As infants

Table 1.4. *Studies Reporting Prevalence of Anxiety in Children*

Study	Lapouse & Monk (1958)	Agras, Sylvester, & Oliveau (1969)	Werry & Quay (1971)	Richman, Stevenson, & Graham (1975)	Earls (1980)	Kastrup (1976)	Abe & Masui (1981)
			Design				
Location	US	US	US	UK	US	Denmark	Japan
Sample source	Community	Community	School	Community	Community	Community	Community
Sample size	482	325	1753	705	100	175	2500
Age of sample	6–12 years	Children and adults	5–8 years	3 years	3 years	5–6 years	11–12 years
Informants	Mother	Subject or mother	Teacher	Mother	Mother	Parent	Subject
			Results				
Fears and/or worries	43%	7.7%	16.5%	12.8% (fears) 2.6% (worries)	14.0% (fears) 8.0% (worries)	4.0%	2%–43% (fears) 4%–33% (worries)
Separation concerns	41%					13.7%	
Other anxieties			18.0% (tension) 18.0% (nerves)			8.0% (nightmares)	

Note. From *Anxiety Disorders of Childhood* (p. 67) by H. Orvaschel and M. M. Weissman, 1986, New York: Guilford Press. Copyright 1986 by Guilford Press. Reprinted with permission.

9

approach the end of their first year, they commonly fear strange people and novel objects (Bronson, 1972). They also show distress at separation from their primary caretaker (Bowlby, 1969). These fears are concrete and connected to the infant's daily experience (Campbell, 1986).

As cognitive abilities develop, children's fears begin to change. For instance, early preschoolers commonly fear animals, the dark, and imaginary creatures. The presence of these types of fears demonstrates an ability to anticipate frightening events that are not directly experienced in the immediate environment. As children mature, these fears of animals, the dark, and frightening objects systematically decrease (Bauer, 1976; Maurer, 1965). Replacing them, we see more specific, realistic fears such as those involving social acceptance and school achievement (Bauer, 1976). Most authors agree that increasing age witnesses the declining fears of such things as the dark and supernatural phenomena, only to see them replaced by more internalized anxieties during adolescence and adulthood. Thus, from the bulk of preliminary data, the maturational sequence of the content of children's fears appears to move from global, undifferentiated, and externalized fears to those which are increasingly differentiated, abstract, and internalized (Kendall & Ronan, 1990). The sequence of these fears appears to be relatively constant up to adolescence (Miller, 1983).

Factor analyses have yielded further information on the organization of the content of these fears. For example, Ollendick, Matson, and Helsel (1985) found a five-factor structure: (1) Fear of Failure and Criticism, (2) Fear of the Unknown, (3) Fear of Injury and Small Animals, (4) Fear of Danger and Death, and (5) Medical Fears. Alternatively, Miller, Barrett, Hampe, and Noble (1972) reported a three-factor structure: (1) Factor I contained fears of injury and personal loss, (2) Factor II consisted of fears of natural and supernatural events, and (3) Factor III emphasized "psychic stress and tension" including fears of exams, making mistakes, being criticized, school and social events, and doctors and dentists. Miller et al. (1972) reported these results as a corroboration of earlier work (e.g., Scherer & Nakamura, 1968).

In addition to changes in the content of fears, quantitative changes also occur with development. Fears appear to peak between 2½ and 4 years of age, then start to decline. However, older adolescents (16–18) still report an average of 11.6 fears (from a list of 80 potential fears) compared to an average of 14.2 fears in 7 to 9-year-olds (Ollendick, Matson, & Helsel, 1985). This demonstrates that the decrease in fears is not as great as expected because earlier fears are replaced by new fears that are associated with particular developmental levels (Kendall & Ronan, 1990).

The origins and developmental changes in children's fears may be explained by a combined ethological cognitive-developmental approach. The essential organizing factor implicated in both of these approaches is that of adaptation to the environment. Adaptation may be enhanced by innate, biologically determined factors. For example, humans respond with fear to naturally occurring cues of danger (e.g., loud noises). In this way, some fears might be seen as biologically adaptive—leading the child to avoid potential hazards in order to increase the chances of survival. Proximity to older, familiar members of the same species is one example of a behavioral system (i.e., attachment) thought to enhance survival. Thus, the fear of strangers and separation anxiety (or protest) may well have ethological, and thus adaptive, roots. Additionally, some fears—including infants' fear of strangers and separation protest—are often viewed as not possible until the advent of certain cognitive abilities. In the one-year-old, then, these fears may be paramount; however, by the age of three, strangers may be processed as merely interesting or irrelevant. At another level of cognitive processing, adolescents—by virtue of their ability to reason abstractly and think about their own and other's thoughts—may be more likely to experience panic and agoraphobic concerns (i.e., the fear of fear) than younger, more concrete-oriented children (Nelles & Barlow, 1988).

Future research in developmental issues of childhood anxiety would be valuable. Although cross-sectional methodologies have been used, longitudinal research has been almost nonexistent. This type of research would be helpful to answer such questions as whether early forms of anxiety develop into difficulties later (Sroufe, 1983). More information on the role of cognitive developmental differences and the development of anxiety disorders would no doubt prove valuable to mental health professionals. Also, the impact of family factors on childhood fears must be studied. It would be both useful and interesting to examine the effects of child-rearing practices, parental anxieties, and family structure on the development of anxieties and fears in youth. At the present time, given the empirical evidence available, we advocate a developmental perspective when investigating both normative and maladaptive fears and anxieties in childhood (see also Barrios et al., 1981; King, Hamilton, & Ollendick, 1988). Children often appear to experience relatively short-lived, transitory, and developmentally appropriate fears and anxieties generally not in need of clinical services. However, what is considered a normative fear for a young child may be seen as potentially inappropriate and maladaptive for an older child or adolescent. However, we want to stress that, given this developmental backdrop, differential experiences can lead to individual differences existing in the content, frequency, and intensity of each child's particular discomfort and, consequently, in the decision whether or not clinical services are indicated. For example, some children may have better coping strategies and, in turn, manifest less subjective discomfort and behavioral avoidance than other children who routinely process information in a distorted and maladaptive fashion.

Chapter 2

The Cognitive-Behavioral Perspective

In the discovery of secret things and in the investigation of hidden causes, stronger reasons are obtained from sure experiments and demonstrated arguments than from probable conjectures and the opinions of philosophical speculators of the common sort.

—*William Gilbert*

Cognitive-behavioral approaches to psychological difficulties have been described in texts, applied in clinical settings, and evaluated systematically in research investigations. Although there are several features that may be considered common across most of the therapies labeled cognitive-behavioral, there are also some differences (see Kendall & Kriss, 1983). Some of the distinctive features are most pronounced when working with children and adolescents, where the reasons for referral are typically parent discontent rather than the child's self-reported need for help. To clarify the nature of the cognitive-behavioral treatment that we are offering herein, we first discuss the basic theoretical tenets of the cognitive-behavioral perspective. Next, in an effort to provide a clearer understanding of how the therapist and client interact, we provide a description and discussion of the posture (mental attitude) of the therapist. A cognitive-behavioral model specific to childhood anxiety disorders is then proposed. Last, a statement of reasonable expectations about treatment and its effects is offered. While the present description does not preempt later description of the actual intervention procedures, this chapter sets the stage for the more detailed coverage and illustrations that follow.

BASIC TENETS

Reviews of cognitive-behavioral therapies often offer lists of the premises believed to be held in common by various cognitive-behavioral ap-

12

proaches. Different authors have focused on different themes, but there appear to be a number of core principles that parsimoniously capture the basic tenets of cognitive-behavioral interventions. The following points are adapted from Kendall, Vitousek, and Kane (in press), Kendall and Hollon (1979), Mahoney (1977), and Mahoney and Arnkoff (1978):

1. The client responds primarily to cognitive representations of the environment rather than to the environment per se.
2. Most human learning is cognitively mediated.
3. Thoughts, feelings, and behaviors are causally interrelated, with no implication of primacy assigned to any one over the others.
4. Client attitudes, expectancies, attributions, and other cognitive activities are central to producing, predicting, and understanding therapeutic interventions.
5. Cognitive processes can be integrated with behavioral paradigms, and it is possible and desirable to combine cognitive treatment strategies with enactive techniques and behavioral-contingency management when treating disturbed youth.
6. The task of the cognitive-behavioral therapist is to act as a diagnostician, educator, and technical consultant who assesses maladaptive cognitive processes and works with the client to design learning experiences that may remediate these dysfunctional cognitions and the behavioral and affective patterns with which they correlate.

In this chapter, along with consideration of other related themes, we provide an overview of a cognitive-behavioral perspective in which behavioral events, associated anticipatory expectations and postevent attributions, ongoing cognitive information processing, and emotional states combine to influence behavior change. The approach is problem-solving oriented, deals largely with cognitive information processing, incorporates social, familial and interpersonal domains, and emphasizes *in vivo* exposure and performance-based interventions.

Problems occur ("stuff happens"), and problem solving is an essential ingredient to adequate adjustment in childhood. Different developmental challenges face different youth, and children vary in their ability to recognize a problem in need of a solution. Furthermore, their ability to generate alternatives and competently evaluate each option will influence the quality of their psychological health. Teaching children how to identify emerging problems and to generate and evaluate alternative courses of action facilitates their transition into an adulthood in which they can function as independent, autonomous individuals. Solutions to problems do not materialize from thin air, nor are they handed to someone carte blanche. Rather, successful solutions emerge from the use of a problem-solving process involving cognitive strategies. These strategies are not transmitted through genetic codes but are instead learned through observations and through interactions with others. Teaching problem-solving strategies can be maximized through planned intervention. For anxiety disordered youth, styles of information processing can have profound effects on how one makes sense of the world and one's experiences in it. The dysfunctional information processing that is linked to anxiety requires attention and modification before effective problem solving can emerge.

Mental health professionals and educators are interested in their child-client's effective coping in social situations. Stated differently, the problems in need of solutions are typically social and interpersonal ones, not *im*personal problems. It is the social domain in which the individual interacts reciprocally (Hartup, 1984) and which provides the basis for later experiences and relationships.

Interventions that intend to teach skills and/or remediate skill deficits find that it is through behavioral performance-based procedures that such goals are best reached. Practice of new skills, along with encouragement and feedback, leads to further use and refinement of those skills. Proper contingencies are implemented to shape involvement, to firm up intrinsic interest, or to promote motivation in otherwise disinterested participants. As will become evident, the cognitive-behavioral theory that guides this volume places greatest emphasis on integrating the modification of cognitive information processing of interpersonal and social contexts with behavioral practice-oriented strategies, while concurrently paying attention to the affective tone and involvement of the participant youth.

TOWARD A GUIDING DEFINITION

Interventions designed to facilitate child and adolescent adjustment stem from different treatment philosophies. The present cognitive-behavioral approach can be described as a rational amalgam: a purposeful attempt to preserve the demonstrated positive effects of *in vivo* exposure and performance-based approaches, while incorporating the cognitive activities of the client into the efforts to produce therapeutic change. Accordingly, cognitive-behavioral strategies use enactive performance-based procedures as well as cognitive interventions to produce changes in thinking, feeling, and behavior.

The cognitive-behavioral analyses of child and adolescent disorders and adjustment problems, as well as related analyses of treatment-produced gains, include consideration of both the child's internal and external environment and represent an integrationist perspective (e.g., Meichenbaum, 1977). The model places greatest emphasis on (a) the learning process and the influence of the contingencies and models in the environment, while (b) underscoring the centrality of the individual's mediating and information-processing style in the development and remediation of psychological distress. The tag "cognitive behavioral" is not a direct insult to the contribution of affect and the social context. Rather, the term cognitive-behavioral is a hybrid representing an integration of cognitive, behavioral, affective, and social strategies for change. Abandoning an adherence to a singularly behavioral model, the cognitive-behavioral model includes the relationships of cognition and behavior to the affective state of the individual and the functioning of the individual in the larger social context.

Consider the family. Because behavioral patterns in the external world and cognitive interpretations in the internal world pertain to social and interpersonal contexts, the cognitive-behavioral perspective must consider the importance of the social context. For children and adolescents the centrality of the family and peers as the social context must be underscored. Indeed, satisfactory relations with peers is a crucial component of a child's successful adjustment, and an understanding of peer relationships is required for meaningful assessment and intervention. The role of the family need not be contested, for this social microcosm sets many of the rules and roles for social interaction.

Acknowledgments of peer and family contributions to psychopathology, however, far outweigh the research data base that is currently available, and the need for further inquiry in these areas cannot be overemphasized. Indeed, parents are presently involved in the programs designed for children, despite the lack of empirical data on the nature of their influence. For example, parents serve as consultants when they provide input into the determination of the nature of the problem and when they assist in the implementation of program requirements. Parents are also involved in their child's treatment to the extent that their own cognitive and behavioral functioning is maladaptive and/or contributing to the child's distress. Changes in the family system should be used in conjunction with the skill building that is provided for the child. Cognitive-behavioral interventions assess, consider, and incorporate social and interpersonal matters into their programs.

SUBDIVIDING COGNITION

Many psychologists, educators, and mental health professionals have, in the past, viewed cognition as inaccessible. True, cognition refers to a complex system that is internal to the individual, but the various facets of the system can be subdivided for increased understanding. For instance, it has been suggested (Ingram & Kendall, 1986, 1987; Kendall & Ingram, 1987, 1989) that the broad concept of "cognition" be subdivided into cognitive content (events), cognitive processes, cognitive products, and cognitive structures. The idea being that cognition is not a singular or unitary concept, and that interventions need to attend to these various features of cognitive functioning.

Cognitive *structures* can be viewed as memory and the manner in which information is internally represented in memory. Cognitive *content* refers to the information that is actually represented in memory—the contents of the cognitive structures. Cognitive *processes* are the procedures by which the cognitive system operates—how we go about perceiving and interpreting experiences. Last, cognitive *products* are the cognitions that result from the interaction of information, cognitive structures, content, and processes (e.g., attributions). Childhood anxiety disorders can be related to problems in any or all of these areas, and effective therapy includes consideration of each of these factors for each individual client.

Consider the experience of stepping in something a dog left on the lawn. Your first reaction ("Oh, _____") is probably a self-statement that reflects dismay. Because of the nature of this cognitive content most people say it to themselves. Individuals then proceed to process this experience. Some might begin to assess the potential for social embarrassment ("Oh my goodness, my shoe is going to stink. Everyone will notice—what will they think of me?"); some might become self-denigrating ("I'm so stupid, why didn't I pay attention?"); while others might be inattentive to processing environmental cues and may simply keep walking. The manner of processing the event contributes to the behavioral and emotional consequences. After the unwanted experience (i.e., stepping in it) conclusions are reached regarding the causes of the misstep—cognitive products, such as causal attributions which vary across individuals. Some may attribute the misstep to their inability to do anything right; such a global, internal, and stable attribution often characterizes depression (Abramson, Seligman, & Teasdale, 1978). An angry individual, in contrast, might see the experience as the result of someone else's provocation ("Whose dog left this here—I bet the guy knew someone would step in it!"); attributing the mess to someone else's intentional provocation is linked to aggressive retaliatory behavior. Cognitive content, processes, and products are involved in each individual's making sense of environmental events.

Cognitive structures, or templates, are an accumulation of experiences in memory and serve to filter or screen new experiences. The anxious child brings a history of experiences to new events: the memory of this past—also referred to as a schema—influences current information processing and events. Consistent with cognitive views of adult anxiety disorders (e.g., Beck & Emery, 1985), a dominant schema or structure for anxious children and adolescents is threat—threat of loss, criticism, or harm. (See Dodge, 1985, for a discussion of cognitive bias in aggressive youth.) An individual who brings an anxiety-prone structure to the misstep experience noted earlier would be inclined to perceive the threat of embarrassment, the potential of criticism from others, and the risk of germs, and process the experience accordingly. Such anxious cognitive processing might include self-talk such as: "What if somebody notices the bad smell. . . . They'll think I'm dirty"; "I feel so foolish—others will laugh at me"; "What if germs get into my shoes and then to my socks and my feet? Should I throw these shoes away?"

Cognitive structures serve to trigger automatic cognitive content and overlearned information processing about behavioral events. Attributions about the event reflect the influence of the preexisting structure as well as contribute to the schema brought to the next behavioral event. While the literature has not as yet identified inaccuracies in the attributional styles of anxious youth, one must still be aware of the other features of the child's making sense of his world. Cognitive-behavioral interventions seek to provide treatment experiences that attend to cognitive content, process, and product, such that the child and or adolescent builds a structure that will have a positive influence on future experiences. Cognitive-behavioral interventions also provide an arena to challenge preexisting anxious structures. Knowing that we all, figuratively, step in it at times, what is needed is a structure for coping with these unwanted events when they occur. Our program is designed to build cognitive structures that enable successful coping.

Not all dysfunctional cognition is the same. Understanding the nature of cognitive dysfunction for specific disorders has important implications for treatment. A central issue for children and adolescents concerns the differentiation between cognitive deficiency and cognitive distortion. Deficiencies refer to an absence of thinking (lacking careful information processing where it would be beneficial), whereas distortions refer to dysfunctional thinking processes. Anxiety and depression, for example, are typically linked to misconstruals or misperceptions of the social and interpersonal environment. There is active information processing, but it is distorted (illogical, irrational, crooked). In a series of studies of depressed children, for example, depressed youngsters viewed themselves as less capable than did nondepressed children when, in fact, teachers (the source of an objective outsider's judgment) saw the two groups of children as nondistinct (Kendall, Stark, & Adam, 1990). In the teachers' eyes, the depressed children were not less competent across several dimensions. It was the depressed children who evidenced distortion through their misperception (underestimation) of their actual competencies.

Hyperactive and impulsive children, in contrast to the anxious and depressed youngsters, are often found to act without thinking and perform poorly due to the lack of forethought and planning. Here, cognitive defi-

ciencies are implicated. These children are not engaging in careful information processing and their performance suffers as a result. Consider the case
of a small group of youngsters playing soccer. Twelve players are on the
field—some kicking at the ball, others looking around and talking, while
others are standing still. An anxious nonparticipating child sits on the
sidelines and, when asked why he isn't playing, replies, "I don't know,
what if I get hit with the ball? I don't want to get hurt." In reality, the child
could easily participate in the game and he would not be seriously hurt if
hit with the soccer ball. His comments indicate that he thinks he shouldn't
play to avoid pain—pain that is not likely to occur. The anxious child's
perceptions are distorted, and such thinking is tied to his feeling fearful,
nervous, and alone. Contrast this overly fearful style with that of the
impulsive child who runs directly onto the soccer field and starts after the
ball. He is kicking and running, but does not yet know what team he is
on, who is on his team, or which goal he is going for. His difficulties emerge
more as a result of failing to stop and think (cognitive deficiency) than
from active but distorted processing of information.

Youth with anxiety disorders have an information-processing style
laced with fear, threat, and uncertainty. It is as if the structure—seeing the
world through eyes that anticipate threat—bends one's perceptions, appraisals, and interpretations to the extent that the perceived reality, while
not in fact the same as objective reality, has the dominant influence on
affect and behavior. Interventions that are successful in remediating childhood anxiety are those that correct the information-processing distortions
and build in their place cognitive structures that allow for nondistorted
processing—recognizing problems and engaging in a problem-solving,
coping-focused plan of action.

THE THERAPEUTIC POSTURE

Using the term "posture" to refer to the therapist's manner, style, and
mental attitude, we can describe the posture of the cognitive-behavioral
therapist working with children and adolescents. We choose to describe
the three characteristics of the therapist's posture using the terms (a)
consultant, (b) diagnostician, and (c) educator.

Therapist as Consultant

By consultant we refer to the therapist as a person who does not have
all the answers but who has some ideas worthy of trying out and some
ways to examine whether or not the ideas have value for the individual
client. Telling a child and/or adolescent exactly what to do is *not* the idea;
giving the client an opportunity to try something out and helping him or

her to make sense of the experience is the idea. The therapist as consultant strives to develop skills in the client that include thinking and his or her own moving toward independent, mature problem solving and coping. The consultant (therapist) is a problem-solving model working with the client. When the client asks, "Well, what am I supposed to do?" the therapist might reply, "Let's see, what do you want to accomplish here?" and then, "What are our options?" or "What's another way we could look at this problem?" The exchange is geared toward facilitating the process of problem solving, instead of providing the child with a specific solution. The youngster and therapist interact in a collaborative problem-solving manner.

Therapist as Diagnostician

The term diagnostician might suggest the sole task of labeling an individual as a consequence of the use of a diagnostic system (e.g., *Diagnostic and Statistical Manual of Mental Disorders-Third Edition-Revised* [DSM-III-R]), but, while such diagnostic efforts are not being criticized here, diagnostic labeling is also not the thrust of the term's meaning when used here to describe the therapist's posture. The mental attitude associated with "diagnostician" is one of going beyond the verbal report and/or behavior of the client and his or her significant others. The diagnostician integrates data and (judging against a background of knowledge of psychopathology, normal development, and psychologically healthy environment), makes meaningful decisions. Consider the following example: Suppose that you win a brand new Jaguar automobile. Driving it around for two days, you notice a "clug-clug" sound in the front when making a right-hand turn. There is no noise when you go straight or when you turn left. You contact a special mechanic and tell him about the noise and that the front tie-rod ends need repair. The next day you leave the car for repair and pick it up at the end of the day. Your tie-rod ends are repaired. Would you be satisfied?

Our answer is a definite "no." What do you know about tie-rod ends? You just won the car, you are not a mechanic, and you should not be diagnosing the problem. The auto mechanic is the expert and he should be making the determinations—he should look under the hood! He should not fix what you say is wrong as you are not the expert. He can use your ideas as helpful information but should nevertheless make his own determination.

Similarly, mental health professionals and educators cannot let others tell us what is wrong and what needs to be fixed—we listen and integrate the input, but we have the experience working with children and adolescents with psychological problems, and we make the determination. For example, a parent or teacher report of excessive fears in a child is not sufficient to initiate a cognitive-behavioral therapy or a medication regime. The fact that a parent or teacher suspects an anxiety disorder in a child is useful information, but there are rival hypotheses that must be considered. For example, the child's behavior may be within normal limits: appearing as troubled only when judged against inappropriate parental or teacher expectations about child behavior. There is also the possibility of alternative disorders—anxiety may be the term used by the referring adults, but the wiggly, fidgety behavior could indicate Attention-Deficit Hyperactivity Disorder (ADHD). ADHD may be a better description in terms of mental health professionals' understanding and the optimal approach in treatment. Also, the child's identified problem (excessive fears) may be a reflection of a dysfunctional family-interaction pattern, with the parenting styles needing the greatest attention, not the child per se. In a nutshell, the cognitive-behavioral therapist serves as a diagnostician by taking into account the various sources of information and—by judging these data against a background of knowledge—makes a determination as to the problem's nature and the optimal strategy for its treatment.

Therapist as Educator

The third term used to describe the therapeutic posture of cognitive-behavior therapists is *educator*. The use of the term educator here is intended to communicate that we are talking about interventions for learning behavioral control, cognitive skills, and emotional development, and that we are talking about optimal means of communication to help someone learn. A good educator stimulates the students to think for themselves. An active and involved coach is a good educator. Consider a tennis coach.

What does a good educator or coach do? He or she gets you out on the court and watches you play—observing how you hit the ball and determining for him or herself (diagnostician) if your serve is weak or your backhand slow. The observations would take place on different occasions, against different partners, and under both easy and difficult conditions. Then there would be some feedback regarding strengths and weaknesses and some discussion of possible alternative solutions (consultant). For example, the coach might inform you that your serve is inconsistent and that you might want to do serve drills, tossing the ball in the air over and over, until it becomes almost automatic that you toss it to the right height. Videotaping might be used, along with modeling of service styles, and group lessons could be integrated as well.

A good educator or coach does not make all players play the game the same way. A good coach observes how the student is playing and helps to maximize strengths while reducing thoughts or actions that hinder performance. If a player uses two hands for a backhand, and the rules do not disallow it, then there is no reason to force the player to hit a backhand with one hand or in a way that matches the other players'. Individualized attention means that individuals can and should do things differently. A good educator or coach also pays attention to what the learner is saying to him or herself, as this internal dialogue can be interfering with performance. An effective therapist, just as an effective teacher or coach, is actively involved in the learning process.

The posture, or mental attitude, of the cognitive-behavioral therapist working with children and adolescents is one that has a collaborative quality (therapist as consultant), integrates and decodes information (therapist as diagnostician), and teaches through experiences with involvement (therapist as educator). A high-quality intervention, be it provided by a psychologist, psychiatrist, school counselor, special educator, classroom teacher, or parent, is one that alters how the child client makes sense of experiences and the way the child will behave in the future. Such correction in thought and action places the child on track toward improved adjustment.

COGNITIVE-BEHAVIORAL MODEL OF CHILDHOOD ANXIETY

Research continues to document the role of cognitive concepts such as expectations, attributions, self-statements, beliefs, and schemata in the development of both adaptive and maladaptive behavior patterns and in the process of behavior change. However, the interrelationships of these and other cognitive factors themselves have yet to be fully clarified. How are the functional effects of self-statements similar to or different from those of attributions? How does an individual's maladaptive schema relate to his or her level of irrational beliefs? Do inconsistent or anxious self-statements reduce interpersonal cognitive processing and problem solving? Quite simply, we know only a modest amount about the organization and interrelations of the cognitive concepts receiving clinical and research attention. A model with potential utility for understanding childhood anxiety disorders is one built along a temporal dimension. The model takes into account and reflects the cognitions associated with behavior across time (e.g., cognitions that occur before, during, and after events). Because events do not occur in a vacuum and because behavior is determined by multiple causes, the model allows for the feedback that results from multiple, sequential behavioral events. That is, cognitions before an event vary depending on the outcomes of previous events. The model also allows for fluctuations in preevent cognitions associated with the different outcomes (e.g., successful, unsuccessful) of prior events. Moreover, because repetitions of cognitive-event sequences result in some consistency in cognition, the model highlights the development of more regularized cognitive processing and the development of cognitive structures.

A proposed model is presented in Figure 2.1. The figure illustrates the flow of cognition across behavioral events of different emotional intensity. The starting point is the initial behavioral event (BE), and our discussion will move from the BE point on Figure 1 (at the left) to the cognitive consistency that results (at the right). A behavioral event of import for the development of a child's anxiety disorder may be associated with parental rejection. It may or may not be the case that the parent is intentionally rejecting the child, and it may or may not be the case that an objective outsider would view the experience as one of rejection, but—as perceived by the child—the behavioral event is one where the impact is that of rejection by the parent(s). In the child's experience, this behavioral event (BE) may have a highly negative emotional valence. Because of its heightened emotional intensity, the behavioral event has a greater impact on the development of the cognitive structures that will later serve as a filter for new experiences. We will return to this discussion later.

Attributions are the cognitive concepts often studied at the culmination of a behavioral event. How do children disambiguate the causes of behavior once it has already taken place? Stated differently, of all possible explanations for behavior that can be proposed, how do youth explain their own and others' behavior to themselves? Attributions are temporally short lived in that their occurrence is at the termination of an event. One could, however, assess an attribution long after an event, although numerous factors (e.g., recall from memory) may interfere with accurate recall. Whereas differences in attributional styles have been identified in depressed adults and, to a lesser extent, depressed children, there is as yet no consistent evidence that children with and without anxiety-related problems show characteristic differences on measures of attributions. It has been suggested that when attributional differences are observed they may be a result of association between anxiety and depressive disorders (Kendall & Ingram, 1989).

Repetition of behavioral events (multiple BEs in Figure 2.1) and the related cognitive processing result in consistency in both behavior and cognition. The figure illustrates that cognitive consistency (i.e., cognitive structures) results from cognitive processing of multiple events. These cognitive variables (consistencies over time) are more stable than a single cognitive event. Stable cognitive-style variables may be more predictive in a general sense but are less predictive in specific situations than the actual cognitions at the time of the specific behavioral event. An anxious child

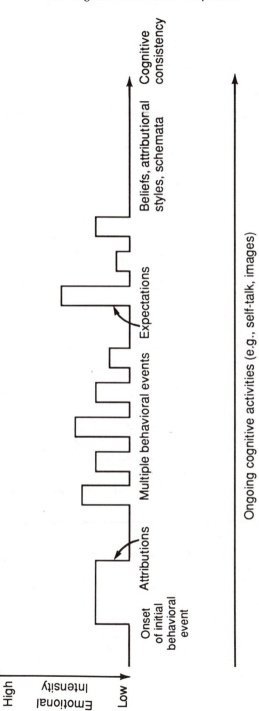

FIGURE 2.1. A temporal model of the flow of cognition and development of cognitive structures across behavioral events of different emotional intensity.

who has on several occasions avoided a situation out of fear that something terrible will happen has built a cognitive structure that will continue to influence the child's view of similar situations in the future. It may not be true in reality, but the child's perception that nothing terrible happened as a consequence of his or her avoidance will only perpetuate the avoidance. One important feature of this model is that it highlights the role of individuals' self-explanations for what actions did and did not have an influence on their emotional state. When a child with an anxiety disorder believes that his or her avoidance has been successful, it is functional in maintaining the avoidance. This is the case despite that the avoidance actually works against successful coping in the future.

Upon the accumulation of a history of behavioral events and event outcomes, the child or adolescent comes to entertain more precise anticipatory cognition (i.e., expectancies). Expectancies have been described, for example, as outcome expectancies and self-efficacy expectancies (Bandura, 1977). Other anticipatory cognitions include intentions, plans, and commitments. These latter variables may be more stable and consistent over time than situationally specific expectancies. Anxious children seem to hold expectations that are more critical, potentially harmful, and generally catastrophic, relative to nonanxious youth. Moreover, their specific expectations that situations are especially anxiety provoking are distorted. For example, the anxious child, prior to a meeting of a small discussion group at school, might be thinking: "What will I say? What if what I say is stupid? Everyone will laugh. What can I do if they all laugh at me?" Expecting that others will be critical in evaluating performance may be an accurate reflection of the child's cognitive structure (and therefore, past experiences), but such an expectation is, in a probabilistic and realistic sense, very far from the most likely outcome. Anxious children's inaccurate expectations are in need of performance-based experiences that correct their distorted processing of the experience so that they can proceed toward new situations with a more reasoned set of expectations. In addition to the cognitions mentioned thus far, other cognitive variables have been demonstrated to be important in a cognitive-behavioral analysis— imagery, self-statements, and cognitive problem-solving skills. These factors occur at all points along the temporal flow depicted in the figure and assessments of these factors (e.g., self-talk) can prove valuable in understanding and treating anxious children and adolescents.

Emotional intensity is represented vertically in the figure. The higher the bar indicating a behavioral event (BE), the more emotionally intense the behavioral event. The more emotionally intense the experience, the greater the impact on the development of a cognitive structure. Thus, a minor event, in terms of anxious arousal, may have a limited influence on future expectations and memory, whereas an emotionally significant event will have greater impact on the development of a schema and on future thinking. One would want therapy to include genuine anxious arousal (*in vivo* experience) *and* be an emotionally positive and involving experience. Such emotionally charged situations, with therapist-guided corrective efforts to modify the cognitive processing, can have positive influences on the development of processing. Therapy helps to reduce the support for dysfunctional schemas and construct a new schema, through which the child can identify and solve problems. An effective intervention capitalizes on creating behavioral experiences with emotional involvement, while paying attention to the cognitive activities of the participant. The therapist guides both the youngster's attributions about prior behavior and his or her expectations for future behavior. Thus, the youngster can acquire a cognitive structure for future events that includes the adaptive skills and accurate cognition associated with adaptive functioning.

GOALS OF TREATMENT

To what end does the cognitive-behavioral therapist working with overanxious youth aspire? What are the goals set before us as worthy of conscientious effort? In answering these questions we consider (a) the trajectory of normal development, (b) rational therapist expectations about behavior change, and (c) theoretical models that detail the nature of our goals.

Building on Normal Development

From birth, the individual is set on a course of development that, in general, moves toward the acquisition of coping skills, self-direction, autonomy, and satisfaction in life. When these developmental trajectories are not deflected, an individual moves toward a satisfying self-determined role. Assuming such a normal developmental trajectory, what place do cognitive-behavioral interventions serve?

Interventions for children and adolescents can be therapeutic, preventative, or enhancement focused. Ameliorative interventions (therapy) are designed to help youth overcome problems that already exist, whereas prevention attempts to forestall problems before they emerge. Interventions designed as enhancements are aimed at the improvement of the quality of life for individuals not currently or necessarily at risk for maladaption. The bulk of our cognitive-behavioral interventions have been therapeutic, though our program could easily be preventative and enhancing.

As clients, children and adolescents require that the therapist give special consideration to treatment goals. For instance, to what extent does the therapist strive to help the child make a better adjustment to present life situations? To what extent does the therapist strive to help the child to alter his or her life situation? When family members or schools are involved in the anxiety disorder, the matter becomes even more complicated. Adjusting to a life situation that is psychologically unhealthy would not be advised, yet one cannot always alter a family or school situation as dramatically as might be desired when thinking of optimal adjustment for the child. A resolution offered by the cognitive-behavioral approach is one that focuses on individual coping, via problem solving, as a goal. The child is given skills that can, within limits, be used to make self-determinations and skills that are in natural agreement with a trajectory toward autonomy. Problem-solving skills allow for individual choices that are unique to the client and optimal for the individual at the time. A child or adolescent client is supported through the thinking processes, encouraged to consider alternative solutions, rewarded and encouraged for effort, and helped to practice the skills needed for future challenges to adjustment. In this manner, the child or adolescent is guided through the process of becoming an active participant in a problem-solving process that does not dictate which answers to choose but allows for choice and self-determination. Helping to identify options, to think through options in a careful manner, and to guide the testing and evaluation of options are goals of cognitive-behavioral therapy.

Psychologically healthy adjustment, as it unfolds along a natural trajectory, builds on resolutions to prior challenges. If one were on a fault-free course of adjustment, interventions would not be necessary. However, when prior challenges have not been met with complete success, new skills are needed; to the extent possible, generic skills that can be applied to a multitude of new challenges are most promising. By demonstrating, teaching, and honing problem-solving skills, the cognitive-behavioral therapist links with normal development in providing skills for use in later challenges to adjustment. The goal is a better-prepared individual—prepared for the inevitable difficulties of life with a set of skills that can facilitate problem resolution.

Rational Therapist Expectations

The best hitter in major league baseball hits approximately .340, professional bowlers do not bowl 300 routinely, and not every play executed in football leads to a score; yet we, as mental health professionals and educators, often carry expectations that we (and our therapies by implication) are expected to help almost all of our clients. To expect such a success rate is irrational.

Rational therapist expectations include the belief that interventions will be helpful in the movement toward successful adjustment and the belief that individuals who acquire the skills communicated in therapy will at some time experience the benefit of those skills. What is irrational is to expect that any child, with any problem, can be "fixed" using psychotherapy—cognitive behavioral or otherwise. The notion that therapy provides a "cure" is a troublesome and misleading belief (see Kendall, 1989).

Children and adolescents do not automatically evidence benefit from therapeutic interventions. And even in cases where some success is obvious, the chance of relapse remains. If relapse does occur, was the therapy ineffective? Should therapy be expected to prevent all relapse as a part of the "cure" of an anxiety disorder? A rational expectation for therapists to hold is that treatment does not cure the disorder. Therapy does provide help, but the help is of the form of a strategy for the *management* of a disorder and distress. The anxiety-disordered adolescent will not receive a treatment that will totally remove all perceptions of situations as anxiety provoking, but he or she will, due to therapy, be able to employ newly acquired strategies in the management of anxious arousal when it does occur. Relapse, or the task of dealing with relapse, is a part of life. Even our most successful clients will be challenged by situations that create anxious arousal. Our goal is not "to have all the anxiety go away forever," but rather to improve upon the trajectory that was evident before treatment began. To *alter* a nonadaptive trajectory is to produce therapeutic gains, and such an expectation is very rational.

Therapists working with children and adolescents with detrimental anxiety often notice comorbidity with depression. Youth with these emotional problems have, as part of the comorbidity, maladaptive processing of their world. As is true with adult clients suffering from these same disorders, cognitive-behavioral interventions strive to rectify the distorted information processing that is linked to the emotional distress. Unfortunately, some have over-promoted the "power of positive thinking." Do we want our clients to become 100% big-time positive thinkers? Is such a goal a rational and desired outcome of treatment? As it turns out, theory suggests and some research evidence supports the idea that it is not so much the power of positive thinking that is related to emotional adjustment or improvement in treatment, as it is the reduction in negative thinking. Kendall (1984) has elsewhere referred to this as "the power of nonnegative thinking."

Youth who talk to themselves in *only* positive terms are not psychologically healthy. We all experience life events that have negative features, and a rational individual considers and attends to these inevitable difficulties. One would not want to be thinking only positive thoughts in a difficult situation. What then should therapists hold as a rational expectation for the outcome of interventions designed to reduce the negative self-critical styles of thinking of the anxious and depressed child?

The ratio of positive to negative thinking that has been found to be associated with adjustment is .62:.38 (see Kendall, Howard, & Hays, 1989; Schwartz & Garamoni, 1989). These findings are reported for college-age samples, but the concept likely holds true for younger persons as well. Generally speaking, this 2:1 ratio suggests that positive thinking occupies two thirds of the thinking, whereas negative thinking occupies one third of the thinking in individuals who are not maladjusted. Depressed cases, identified psychometrically and clinically, show a 1:1 ratio: the 50–50 split indicating an equal frequency of positive and negative thinking. How does this affect the expectations to be held by therapists? We suggest that knowing that an optimal ratio of positive to negative thinking is 2:1 serves as a guide for the therapist. Overly optimistic thinking is not necessarily healthy, and shifting too much toward a 1:1 ratio is unhealthy as well. It is healthy to acknowledge that certain unwanted stressful situations can elicit a negative thought or two; it is then healthy to proceed to counter the negative aspects with some positive thinking. Positive thinking helps overrule negative thinking, but negative thinking should not be totally eliminated.

Models of Change

Children and adolescents with the behavioral and emotional difficulties of anxiety disorders have associated maladaptive cognitive information processing. Theoretically speaking, how might we conceptualize the needed changes? How best to describe the nature of the cognitive changes that are a part of the goals of treatment?

As noted earlier, cognitive distortions require modification. New experiences, with guided processing of the experiences, will help to correct detrimental thinking. What is being suggested is that the existing cognitive structure is not erased, but that new skills and means of construing the world are built, and these new constructions come to serve as new templates for making sense of future experiences. Therapy does not provide a surgical removal of unwanted cognitive structures but offers to help to build new schemata with new strategies that can be employed in place of the earlier dysfunctional ones. Existing cognitive structures are incorporated into the new schemas providing the child with response alternatives. Therapy offers exposure to those behavioral events that had been avoided, with modification of the concurrent cognitive processing. Positive emotional tones can increase the potency of the experience and add to its impact on the new schema. As these new schemas are incorporated into the child's view of the world and his or her place in it, future experiences are construed differently (less maladaptively). Using the newly constructed schemata, the individual moves forward to confront new challenges with the skills needed to manage former maladaptive tendencies.

One of the main challenges facing the developing organism is the movement toward autonomy and independence. Central to this movement is the family, specifically the parents, and their supportive or constraining styles. Child and adolescent clients are not fully capable, as yet, to be entirely independent, and family, school, and other contextual influences must be considered. Indeed, while the thrust of our treatment is on individual change, multiple influences have been considered and incorporated (see later chapters).

Our discussion of the cognitive-behavioral perspective has included little mention of topics such as trust, respect, and relationship factors as part of the therapeutic process. It is not because these matters are unimportant. Quite the opposite is true—they are essential to all forms of therapeutic intervention. Suffice it to say that factors which contribute to a strong relationship are enthusiastically encouraged, as are therapists' behaviors that clearly communicate mutual respect and trust. The cognitive-behavioral perspective outlined herein is one that complements and contributes to basic clinical wisdom about positive adult-child interactions and building an open and trusting relationship.

Chapter 3

Assessment Strategies and Diagnostic Issues

> *The union of the mathematician with the poet, fervor with measure, passion with correctness, this surely is the ideal.*
>
> —*William James*

The diagnosis and assessment of anxiety in youth are relatively new and developing domains within the field of child psychopathology and psychotherapy. Although many of the strategies employed in adult diagnostic work can be used with children, the assessment of childhood anxiety, like that of other childhood disorders, presents a unique challenge. The psychological and behavioral assessment process of children must address the extensive developmental changes occurring during this life stage. Despite such a distinction, the goals of assessing children and adults are similar; assessment is generally conducted for purposes of research, classification, and treatment.

This chapter will focus on the importance of assessing and diagnosing anxiety for purposes of treatment. In this regard, the assessment process has two primary goals. First, mental health professionals must decide if treatment is appropriate. In order to make this judgment, they may assess whether a child meets diagnostic criteria for a clinically or empirically validated syndrome. The first half of this chapter will discuss the diagnosis of childhood anxiety from the perspective of clinically derived and factor-analytic classifications. The second goal of the assessment process is to determine the general areas of dysfunction as well as the specific maladaptive behaviors and cognitions that could be modified through treatment. The second half of this chapter will discuss the assessment strategies most frequently employed with children which can help to identify target behaviors and cognitions.

CLASSIFICATION AND DIAGNOSIS

Many classification schemes for childhood anxiety have been proposed (Barrios & Hartmann, 1988). Generally, they can be grouped into two categories: those that are derived empirically and those that are derived clinically. From factor-analytic studies of childhood disorders, two broadband classifications of behavior problems have emerged: overcontrolled and undercontrolled behaviors (Achenbach, 1985; Achenbach & Edelbrock, 1978; Quay, 1972; 1977). The nature of anxiety merits its classification as a problem of overcontrol. More specifically, Quay (1979) has identified a class of childhood behavior problems that he refers to as "anxiety-withdrawal." The affective manifestations of this classification are tension, inferiority, depression, and worthlessness; and the behavioral manifestations are timidness, withdrawal and hypersensitivity (Barrios & Hartmann, 1988).

The most widely used, clinically derived classification system for childhood anxiety disorders comes from the Diagnostic and Statistical Manual of Mental Disorders (DSM). The third edition of the DSM (DSM-III; American Psychiatric Association [APA], 1980) represented the first formal acknowledgment by mental health professionals that childhood anxiety may not be manifested identically in children and adults (Gittelman, 1985). Thus, in the most recent edition of the DSM (DSM-III-R; APA, 1987), there is a subclass of diagnostic categories, referred to as Anxiety Disorders of Childhood and Adolescence, which includes three disorders: Separation Anxiety, Avoidant, and Overanxious. Other disorders listed in the section of adult anxiety disorders can also be diagnosed in children, including simple phobia, panic disorder, agoraphobia, social phobia, and obsessive-compulsive disorder.

The hallmark of *separation anxiety disorder* is excessive anxiety concerning separation from those to whom the child is significantly attached. As parents are most commonly the child's major attachment figures, "parents" will be used interchangeably with "major attachment figures." According to the DSM-III-R, this anxiety disorder can be manifested in a number of ways. Children with separation anxiety may express an unrealistic and persistent worry that some calamitous event will befall their parents or themselves, resulting in permanent separations. Often these children are preoccupied with morbid fears that they will be kidnapped or killed, or that serious accidents or illness will befall them or their major attachment figures. These children may also persistently avoid being alone. They may exhibit extreme reluctance to go to school or other places in order to stay with their parents or to stay at home; and they may be unable to go to sleep without a parent being in the room or in bed. Frequently, children diagnosed with this disorder won't accept invitations from friends to sleep over at their houses and may be found, in extreme cases, sleeping by the door to their parents' bedroom. They may experience repeated nightmares about being separated from their parents. Separation anxious children often "shadow" their parents around the house. For example, a child may cling to a parent, following him or her from room to room. When separated from their parents, or even when anticipating such separation, these children may complain of physical symptoms such as headaches, stomachaches, or nausea and may exhibit temper tantrums, begging and pleading with their parents to stay. Often, they appear despondent when separated from their parents and want to call home frequently or return home as soon as possible.

Avoidant disorder of childhood or adolescence is characterized by an excessive shyness with unfamiliar people that is of sufficient severity to interfere with appropriate and expected social interactions. Although they generally avoid contact with people they do not know, they do exhibit a desire for social interaction with people they know well, such as family members or peers, and can experience warm and satisfying relationships with these individuals. Children diagnosed with avoidant disorder often appear isolated, socially withdrawn, and timid. In even the most minimal social interactions with unfamiliar people, they may become easily embarrassed and excessively anxious.

The adult diagnosis of *social phobia* is closely related to avoidant disorder of childhood and adolescence. According to the DSM-III-R, social phobia is characterized by a persistent fear of specific or general situations in which an individual may be evaluated by others. The social phobic fears that he or she may do or say something humiliating or embarrassing. The evaluative nature of the fearful situations involved in the diagnosis of social phobia is absent from the explicit criteria of avoidant disorder of childhood and adolescence.

The hallmark of *overanxious disorder* is generalized excessive and unrealistic worry. Overanxious children may worry about the future, such as an upcoming test or doctor's appointment, or the past, such as whether or not they behaved appropriately or made the correct decisions about what to wear or with whom to play. They can be concerned about personal competence in athletic, social, or academic domains, and are often markedly and excessively self-conscious. They may have an excessive need for reassurance, perhaps being unable to complete homework or classwork assignments without being told persistently that they are "doing a good job." The physical manifestations of overanxious disorder may take the form of psychosomatic headaches, stomachaches or nausea (generally attributed to and associated with excessive worry) or marked feelings of tension and an inability to relax.

The nature of overanxious children's worries, such as needing to meet deadlines, adhering to rules, keeping appointments and their excessive inquiry about the discomforts or dangers of situations, often creates the illusion that these children are quite mature. This "pseudo-maturity" may be appealing to many adults but can mask the distress that these children are experiencing. It is also not uncommon for overanxious children to have perfectionistic tendencies. The overt behavioral manifestation of these tendencies may be seen in the child who spends excessive hours completing homework or who procrastinates on school assignments for fear of failure. Children with overanxious disorder may be dubbed as the "teacher's pet" for their strict adherence to regulations and their overzealous need for approval, especially from adults.

Simple phobia is characterized by a persistent and excessive fear of a circumscribed object or situation which interferes with an individual's usual and appropriate functioning. For example, a 13-year-old boy's fear of traveling in airplanes forced him and his family to take a bus from Pennsylvania to Florida in order to see Disney World. The adult diagnoses of panic disorder, agoraphobia and obsessive-compulsive disorder can also be applied to children. However, because their incidence is extremely rare, they will not be described here.

RELIABILITY AND VALIDITY OF DIAGNOSING CHILDHOOD ANXIETY DISORDERS

Given the recent emergence of the category of Anxiety Disorders of Childhood and Adolescence within the past decade, there have been few published studies examining the reliability and validity of these diagnostic groupings. Reliability refers to the accuracy with which a diagnosis can be made, either over periods of time (test-retest reliability) or when different raters are making a diagnosis (interrater reliability). The validity of a diagnosis refers to the extent to which it actually captures the phenomenon that one is trying to describe.

Much of the research on this topic to date has employed the DSM-III (APA, 1980) criteria as opposed to the revisions introduced in 1987 with the DSM-III-R. These revisions included changes in the diagnostic criteria which raised the threshold for diagnosis and enabled older children to meet criteria (APA, 1987).

The reliability of the DSM-III category of childhood anxiety disorders ranges from poor to good, with Kappa coefficients ranging from .25 to .85 (Last, Hersen, Kazdin, Francis, & Grubb, 1987b; Mezzich & Mezzich, 1985; Strober, Green, & Carlson, 1981). The large differences found in these studies can be attributed in part to variations in experimental design. Some studies assessed diagnostic reliability according to information gained through interviews (both structured and unstructured), while others used information from either oral or written case histories. The issue of reliability will be addressed further when specific assessment instruments are presented.

There is even less published data on the validity of childhood anxiety diagnoses than on their reliability. Last (1988) reports that there is evidence from case studies to provide support for the "face" validity of diagnoses of separation anxiety and overanxious disorders. The dearth of research on the validity of these diagnoses reflects the nature of our current knowledge of the topic. Childhood anxiety is still an evolving domain, and as this chapter and others will attest to, much of our work is exploratory. Currently, mental health professionals, both clinical and research oriented, are working to refine the diagnostic, assessment, and treatment strategies designed for anxious children.

CONSIDERATIONS FOR ACCURATE ASSESSMENT AND DIAGNOSIS

The assessment and diagnosis of childhood disorders present a unique challenge. First, differences in developmental level may affect the child's reporting of symptoms and the normative, age-appropriate behavioral standards. Second, children are rarely the ones to present themselves to mental health professionals for treatment. More commonly, a child's parents or teachers will decide whether or not a child's behavior is appropriate for a given context and will refer the child for treatment. Finally, the diagnosis of anxiety in children is continuing to be refined and modified. The comorbidity of childhood anxiety with other disorders has not been well-established, and the ongoing debate concerning whether factor-analytic or clinically derived classification systems are more appropriate attests to the exploratory nature of the field. This section will address these issues and how they affect our ability to assess and diagnose childhood anxiety.

Developmental Considerations

Kendall, Lerner, and Craighead (1984) describe three essential features of child development that influence the assessment and therapeutic process. First, the child can be conceived of as a *structure* which can reciprocally influence others through social interactions. Second, the child is a *processor* with a rapidly changing ability to interpret, respond to, and represent the stimuli in his or her environment. Finally, the child is an *organizer* of his or her environment. A child can actively make choices that shape his or her world and create opportunities. The competencies and skills with which a child makes these decisions are progressively modified over time. Conceptualizing a child simultaneously as a structure, processor, and organizer acknowledges the active and rapid developmental process that progressively transforms children into adolescents and then adults. Others have recognized the significance of incorporating these features into our paradigm for understanding childhood psychopathology (e.g., Cicchetti, 1984; Sroufe & Rutter, 1984).

During childhood and adolescence, remarkable cognitive, socio-emotional, and biological changes occur. In very obvious ways, one can describe how a 3-year-old differs from a 10-year-old along these domains of change. Although the differences between a 10-year-old and a 12-year-old may be less obvious, they are present and can be quite significant to the assessment process. Indeed it is more accurate and relevant to the assessment process to categorize children and adolescents according to their developmental level in cognitive, emotional, and biological domains. For example, the biological changes associated with puberty introduce a clear distinction between prepubertal, pubertal, and postpubertal individuals. Not only do these changes affect the individual, but there is evidence that they affect the way others interact with him or her (e.g., Hill & Holmbeck, 1986).

Further, expected age-appropriate behaviors change with developmental maturation, requiring mental health professionals to use normative data, against which behaviors can be judged developmentally appropriate. Statistical norms document the characteristic behaviors expected for different developmental levels. It may be more acceptable for a 6-year-old to exhibit some mild features of separation anxiety than for a 14-year-old who is expected to be functioning more autonomously. Not only do the nature of children's anxieties change with developmental maturation, but the incidence of fears and anxieties also change. As noted in an earlier chapter, there is ample evidence indicating that young children have numerous fears; however, the frequency of these fears tends to decline with increasing age (e.g., Graziano, DeGiovanni, & Garcia, 1979; Morris & Kratochwill, 1983; Miller, Barrett, & Hampe, 1974; Rachman, 1968). Given this information, it would not be surprising if during the assessment process a 5-year-old child reported having several fears (see Maurer, 1965; Ollendick, 1983, for average number of fears reported per age group). A 14-year-old adolescent presented with the same fears during the assessment process, would likely be considered to be exhibiting developmentally inappropriate behavior and, depending on the severity of interference, intervention may be indicated.

Manifested symptoms of anxiety vary with developmental level. Strauss, Lease, Last, and Francis (1988) found that older children (12 to 19 years) diagnosed with overanxious disorder were much more likely to express an unrealistic concern about the appropriateness of past behavior than younger children (5 to 11 years old) with a diagnosis of overanxious disorder. The older children also more frequently met criteria for a coexisting major depression or simple phobia; the younger children were more likely to be diagnosed concurrently with separation anxiety or attention deficit disorder.

Corresponding to changes in children's cognitive development are changes in children's expressive and comprehension abilities that influence the suitability of certain assessment strategies (Barrios & Hartmann, 1988). For example, during the assessment process, a 9-year-old girl reports that she is experiencing no distressing fear or anxiety, despite her mother's report that she is extremely shy and withdrawn. There are several explanations for the contradiction between the mother and child's reports. The mother may not be accurately assessing the situation; the child may be reluctant to discuss such an unsettling topic as her fears and anxieties (especially with the assessor who is essentially a "stranger") and be denying what she is actually feeling; or, the child may not yet have developed the cognitive capacity to express what she is feeling. Strauss, Lease, Last and Francis (1988) found that older children (12 to 19 years old) referred to an anxiety clinic tended to report a greater number of anxious symptoms than younger children (5 to 11 years old).

If a child reveals distressing anxiety that is not confirmed in the parent report, consider weighting the child's report more heavily. It may be that the child is not confiding in the parent and revealing his or her concerns for fear of upsetting the parent, and the child may admit to that if questioned. For example, a very bright 13-year-old girl with overanxious disorder and multiple simple phobias was able to orchestrate her daily life so as to cope with her generalized worry and to avoid the feared situations. Due to her fear of upsetting her mother and her perception that her mother could do nothing to help her, she never confided in her mother; though she occasionally discussed her difficulties with an aunt and with school personnel.

If the child presents with anxious symptoms but the parent does not confirm the presence of excessive anxiety, evaluate the child's report for coherence to a pattern of anxiety symptoms. For example, the child who presents with frequent nausea and vomiting when faced with stressful situations might also report worries about separation from parent, perfectionism, social acceptance, or other anxiety-based concerns. Otherwise, the child may be using the nausea as a means of attempting to assert control over others.

Evans and Nelson (1986) noted that there is an "imperfectly developed correspondence between word and deed" (p. 604) at early levels of cognitive development. Verbal expressive abilities may be limited as well as comprehension abilities. It is unclear whether the differences between "never worried," "rarely worried," "sometimes worried," and "often worried" represent the same meaning for children at different stages of cognitive development or if children at different cognitive levels are even capable of making such fine distinctions. A younger child or a child with limited verbal expressive and/or receptive skills may not understand the concepts inherent in a discussion of his or her symptoms. He may only be able to provide information about more concrete symptoms, such as his somatic responses to anxiety. For example, a nine-year-old girl with a learning disability denied that she had any worries or other behaviors that would be associated with anxiety, although she acknowledged that she felt shaky all over at times and suffered with numerous headaches. Both parent and teacher reports indicated significant levels of anxiety. In light of the clear report from the parent and teacher, the assumption was made that the child did not comprehend the questions or had limited insight into her experiences. Her limited report was given less relative weight. Craighead, Meyers, Craighead, and McHale (1983) also found developmental differences in children's performances on several cognitive tasks, including response to verbal instructions.

Some investigators have used pictorial assessment instruments instead of verbal ones to address this problem. For example, there is a "fear thermometer" to assess degree of fear of the dark (Sheslow, Bondy, & Nelson, 1982) and an aggression scale that assesses degree of anger by matching one's feelings to one of four stick figures with varying facial expressions (Finch & Montgomery, 1973; Stein, Finch, Hooke, Montgomery, & Nelson, 1975).

Referral by Others

Unlike adult clients, most child clients do not seek the services of mental health professionals on their own. Most often, they are referred for assessment and treatment because some adult, a parent or a teacher, has evaluated their behavior to be maladaptive or dysfunctional. There is speculation that parents cannot consistently evaluate their child's behavior objectively (Harris & Ferrari, 1983); they may hold distorted perceptions or unrealistic expectations of their child's behaviors.

The assessor's inability to rely completely on a parent's report of a child's behavior presents a particular challenge for the assessment of anxiety, especially given the anxious child's tendency to present in a timid and/or perfectionistic manner. The assessment session is perceived as very stressful to an already tense child, and the child may be reluctant to reveal information to the assessor. To the anxious child who fears failure and is concerned with being "perfect," the assessment session can be misperceived as an evaluation where there are right and wrong answers. In his or her attempt to "get the answers right," the child compromises the reliability of the information he or she presents. It is not infrequent that a child referred to a clinic is partly unaware of the reason for their coming to the assessment, and the overanxious child, concerned with following rules and behaving appropriately, may feel as though he or she has done something wrong.

Children who are referred to a clinic by school personnel may not demonstrate the same severity of symptoms at home. Parents may even be surprised by the level of distress their children demonstrate at school. For example, a child who worked diligently on his schoolwork at home rarely said anything to his parents about the level of concern he felt about doing well. However, he demonstrated a marked degree of perfectionism at school, frequently asking questions and requesting reassurance from the teacher about the quality of his work. In such a case, teacher report may present a more accurate picture of the child than initial parent report.

There are anxious children who want to succeed at school, work hard, are model students, and are nice to everyone. They do not draw attention to themselves and they make every effort to succeed. Teachers may miss the signs of distress that signal high levels of anxiety in these youngsters. For example, a 10-year-old boy who had overanxious disorder and simple phobia experienced significant levels of somatic distress and worried excessively about doing well in school. He also had many concerns about health-related matters. In school, however, he was a model student, and he demonstrated superior social skills; the teacher was almost completely unaware of the level of distress he experienced. Her report was therefore inaccurate and given less weight in consideration of his diagnosis.

The nature of anxiety as an overcontrolled behavior can mislead parents and teachers. These adults are less likely to be aware of the more subtle symptoms of childhood anxiety and may not refer a child who needs treatment. Further, when the behavioral symptoms of anxiety, such as fidgeting, appear troublesome to adults, they may be mislabeled as symptoms of undercontrolled behavior. An anxious child may be referred to an inappropriate clinic, such as one treating attention deficit disorders, and be subjected to unnecessary assessment sessions that may be perceived as especially stressful.

An Evolving Diagnostic Category

The diagnostic category of Anxiety Disorders in Children and Adolescents is new and unfolding, with emerging reliability and validity. The manifestation of anxiety disorders and their associated behaviors and cognitions in children are not yet fully known. The adult literature has found considerable overlap between the symptoms, assessment, and treatment of anxiety and depressive disorders (Beck & Emery, 1985; Kendall & Watson, 1989), questioning our ability to reliably distinguish between these disorders of affect. Several studies with child samples have also found such similarities between these two disorders. Last, Hersen, Kazdin, Finkelstein, and Strauss (1987a) found a relationship between the incidence of overanxious disorder and major depression among children (see also Finch, Lipovsky, & Casat, 1989); and Brent, Kalas, Edelbrock, Costello, Duncan, and Conover (1986) noted an association between suicidality and anxiety.

These findings suggest that clinically derived classifications of childhood anxiety disorders do not capture the complete diagnostic picture. Unfortunately, classification systems derived from factor-analytic strategies also create uncertainty as to what is being assessed when a child presents for the treatment of "anxiety." Factor-analytic diagnostic categories can be constrained by methodological and conceptual issues. There may be a limited number of items entered into the analyses; potentially important manifestations of anxiety may be omitted from factor analysis by the investigator's item-selection process. Also, the labeling and description of factor-analytic diagnostic categories have a subjective component.

There is also overlap among the behavioral manifestations of childhood anxiety disorders and externalizing behavior problems that may obscure the assessment process and cause misleading treatment recommendations. Preliminary investigations have found that approximately 9% of children diagnosed with overanxious disorder (Last et al., 1987a) or school phobia (Last, Strauss, & Francis, 1987) met DSM-III criteria for a concurrent behavior disorder. It is possible that the fidgeting and distractibility of the overanxious child can be largely attributed to a preoccupation with worries. There is a qualitative difference between the attention-deficit hyperactive child who appears distracted during class and the overanxious child who appears similarly distracted; in the latter case, the child is more likely to be distracted by constantly saying to him or herself, "what if she calls on me and I don't know the answer?." Similarly, the school phobic child is more likely to be noncompliant about attending school because of issues surrounding separation from parents or fear of some aspect of school, rather than because of oppositional behavior.

Summary of Considerations

The assessment of anxiety in youth requires sensitivity to at least three factors: the developmental challenges of childhood and adolescence, the infrequency of children presenting themselves for treatment, and the continuing refinement of the diagnostic category. These considerations constrain the assessment process as there is no single approach to the assessment of childhood psychopathology that simultaneously addresses these issues. Consequently, the assessment process should try to include multiple methods (questionnaires, interviews, and observations) and multiple perspectives (parent, child, and teacher) in multiple settings (school and home) (Achenbach, McConaughy, & Howell, 1987). The information gathered from these sources is then compared to developmentally sensitive normative data. The next section will review the most widely used child anxiety assessment methods and outline a comprehensive assessment battery.

ASSESSMENT METHODS

Lang's (1968) tripartite model of fear and anxiety has cognitive, behavioral, and physiological components and an accurate assessment of childhood anxiety that would provide the comprehensive representation of the disorder necessary for treatment needs to address the subjective, motor, and physiological manifestations of the disorder (Barrios & Hartmann, 1988). Clinical interviews, self-report measures, behavioral observations, physiological recordings, and family assessments are strategies that can be employed to elicit expressions of anxiety across all response channels.

Clinical Interviews

The clinical interview is one of the most common methods for assessing childhood anxiety (Miller et al., 1974). Numerous interview schedules, designed for administration to both children and parents, have been developed and empirically tested. They range from a highly structured format to an unstructured one and have the advantage of gleaning information about the child's developmental history from both the child and parent's perspectives. Further, interviews with the child permit the potential for establishing a relationship that helps to maintain the child's interest and provides a situation in which ambiguous responses or misunderstandings can be clarified (Edelbrock & Costello, 1988; Morris & Kratochwill, 1983). The interviewer can modify his or her style and rephrase questions to adapt to the developmental level of the child and, to a degree, to the child's pathology. An anxious child is often timid, reticent, and fearful during the interview and will require support and encouragement to respond. Anxious children are better able to respond to specific rather than to open-ended questions (Ollendick & Francis, 1988). Unfortunately, the strength of unstructured interviews is also their principal disadvantage: the flexibility of the interviewer to be developmentally sensitive to the child may introduce bias and/or obscure the standardization of the interview.

Most of the structured clinical interviews, including the Schedule for Affective Disorders and Schizophrenia for School-aged Children (K-SADS; Puig-Antich & Chambers, 1978), the Diagnostic Interview for Children and Adolescents (DICA; Herjanic & Reich, 1982), Schedule for the Assessment of Conduct, Hyperactivity, Anxiety, Mood, and Psychoactive Substances (CHAMPS; Mannuzza & Klein, 1987), the Diagnostic Interview Schedule for Children (DISC; Costello, Edelbrock, Kalas, Dulcan, & Klaric, 1984), and the Anxiety Disorders Interview Schedule for Children (ADIS-C; Silverman, 1987; 1991), set diagnoses according to established classification systems (e.g., the DSM system and the Research Diagnostic Criteria [RDC]; Spitzer, Endicott, & Robins, 1985). The ADIS-C was developed specifically to assess childhood anxiety disorders; the others were designed to ascertain the presence of psychopathology in general. In Table 3.1, sample questions from the ADIS-C are reproduced. Using a structured interview (the ADIS-C), we have found diagnostic reliability (interrater agreement) to be acceptable.

For diagnosis in general, concordance between parent and child report during the clinical interview ranges from moderate to good, but concordance for the diagnosis of anxiety disorders is lower (Chambers, Puig-Antich, Hirsch, Paez, Ambrosini, Tabrizi, & Davies, 1985; Edelbrock, Cos-

Table 3.1. *Sample Questions from the ADIS (Children's Version)* *

Overanxious Disorder

Do you think you worry more than most children (adolescents) your age about things before they happen, such as starting school in the fall, a test, or going to the doctor?

Does it seem like you are always worrying about little things that you have done in the past, such as something you've said that might have been taken the wrong way?

Do you worry a lot about whether you are good enough at something, like sports or school?

Separation Anxiety Disorder

Do you usually feel really bad or worried when you are away from mom and dad, and do you want to go home or call them?

When you are not with your parents do you worry a lot that something bad might happen to them, like they might get sick or hurt and die, or that they will leave and never come back?

Do you worry that something bad might happen to you, like getting kidnapped or killed, so that you couldn't see your parents or someone else again?

Do you refuse to sleep over at other kids' houses because you do not want to be away from your parents?

Note: *Silverman, 1987; Reprinted by permission of Graywind Press.

tello, Duncan, Conover, & Kalas, 1986; Edelbrock, Costello, Duncan, Kalas, & Conover, 1985; Hodges, McKnew, Burback, & Roebuck, 1987). Given the internal nature of the disorder, it is not surprising that children tend to report more anxiety symptoms than parents (Edelbrock et al., 1986; Strauss, 1988), and parents tend to report more overt symptoms of behavioral disturbance such as aggression, disobedience and school problems (Herjanic & Reich, 1982).

The highest agreement between child and parent report is found on questions concerning factual, unambiguous, and concrete information (Herjanic, Herjanic, Brown, & Wheatt, 1975; Herjanic & Reich, 1982) and lowest on questions concerning subjective information and internalizing symptoms related to depression and anxiety (Herjanic & Reich, 1982; Herjanic et al., 1975; Verlhulst, Althaus, & Berden, 1987). Developmental differences have also been shown to affect the reliability of parent and child report during clinical interviews. The reliability of children's report of symptoms associated with overcontrolled behaviors tends to increase with age, and, conversely, the reliability of parent report of their child's overcontrolled symptomatology tends to decrease with increasing child's age (Edelbrock et al., 1985).

Interrater reliability for the diagnosis of childhood anxiety disorders through *un*structured interviews has been disappointing. One study (Chambers et al., 1985) found unacceptable reliability for all anxiety disorders, except separation anxiety for which there was minimally acceptable reliability ($r=.53$). Others (Hodges et al., 1987) have also found greater interrater concordance for separation anxiety ($K=.49$) than for overanxious disorder ($K=0$). An interesting contributor to the low interrater reliability found in the Chambers et al. (1985) study was confusion surrounding obsessive-compulsive rituals associated with pathology and repetitive games that are under volitional control. Many children referred to our Child and Adolescent Anxiety Disorders Clinic at Temple University have reported unusual, ritualistic behaviors that are controllable, of a brief duration, and related to a superstition. For example, a 10-year-old boy reported frequently crossing his fingers before leaving his home for school during a 2½ month period, and an 11-year-old girl occasionally repeated behaviors three times "for luck." In both cases, the obsessive-compulsive tendencies were not of sufficient severity to merit a DSM-III-R diagnosis of obsessive-compulsive disorder.

Self-Report Scales

The most widely used method for assessing childhood anxiety is the self-report inventory. Many inventories have been developed and shown to have adequate reliability and validity (see Barrios & Hartmann, 1988, for a comprehensive review). Some assess specific fears or worries (e.g., the revised Fear Survey Schedule for Children, FSSC-R; Ollendick, 1983); and some assess more general worries and anxieties (e.g., the Revised Children's Manifest Anxiety Scale, RCMAS; Reynolds & Richmond, 1978; and the State-Trait Anxiety Inventory for Children, STAIC; Speilberger, 1973). Tables 3.2 and 3.3 provide sample items from each of these scales to illustrate differences between assessing specific and general fears or worries.

Self-report measures have the advantage of being economical in both time and expense but are limited in several ways. They often do not adequately address the situational specificity of childhood anxiety disorders and may not capture the fears and anxieties specific to the child (Kendall & Ronan, 1990). This limitation is a potentially serious one because without such information treatment cannot be individualized or address what may be a child's unique problem. Kendall and colleagues have devised a questionnaire to address this limitation. The "Coping Questionnaire" (see Table 3.4) assesses a child's ability to cope with his or her individual anxiety-producing situations. In the form of a paper-and-pencil measure, the assessor presents the child with three situations that were found, during the parent and child clinical interviews, to be disturbing. To each of these situations, the child is asked to note the degree to which he or she is "able to make him or herself feel less upset." The child makes this judgment on a seven-point Likert scale from "not at all able to feel less upset" to "able to make myself comfortable." The Coping Questionnaire also provides a baseline for the target behaviors addressed during treatment.

Table 3.2. *Assessing Specific Fears and Worries*

Sample items from the Fear Survey Schedule for Children Revised (FSSC-R)

Instructions to child: A number of statements which boys and girls use to describe the fears they have are given below. Read each fear carefully and put an X in the box in front of the words that describe your fear. There are no right or wrong answers. Remember, find the words which best describe how much fear you have.

1. Giving an oral report . . . . ☐None ☐Some ☐A lot

10. Getting lost in a strange place . . . . ☐None ☐Some ☐A lot

15. Being sent to the principal . . . . ☐None ☐Some ☐A lot

17. Being left at home with a sitter . . . . ☐None ☐Some ☐A lot

31. My parents criticizing me . . . . ☐None ☐Some ☐A lot

40. Failing a test . . . . ☐None ☐Some ☐A lot

45. Dark rooms or closets . . . . ☐None ☐Some ☐A lot

Note: FSSC-R (Ollendick, 1983). Reprinted by permission.

Table 3.3. *Assessing General Fears and Worries*

Sample items from the Revised Children's Manifest Anxiety Scale (RCMAS)

Instructions to child: Here are some sentences that tell how some people think and feel about themselves. Read each sentence carefully. Circle the word "yes" if you think it is true about you. Circle the word "no" if you think it is not true about you. Answer every question even if some are hard to decide. Do not circle both "yes" and "no" for the same sentence. There are no right or wrong answers. Only you can tell us how you think and feel about yourself. Remember, after you read each sentence, ask yourself "Is it true about me?". If it is, circle "yes". If it is not, circle "no".

11. I feel that others do not like the way I do things . . . .   Yes   No

14. I worry about what other people think of me . . . .   Yes   No

15. I feel alone even when there are people with me . . . .   Yes   No

34. I am nervous . . . .   Yes   No

37. I often worry about something bad happening to me . . . .   Yes   No

Sample items from the State-Trait Anxiety Inventory for Children (STAIC)

Assessing state anxiety -

Instruction to child: A number of statements which boys and girls use to describe themselves are given below. Read each statement carefully and decide how you feel *right now*. Then put an X in the box in front of the word or phrase which best describes how you feel. There are no right or wrong answers. Do not spend too much time on any one statement. Remember, choose the word which seems to describe how you usually feel.

I feel . . . .   ☐very worried ☐worried ☐not worried

I feel . . . .   ☐very terrified ☐terrified ☐not terrified

I feel . . . .   ☐very calm   ☐calm   ☐not calm

Assessing trait anxiety -

Instructions to child: A number of statements which boys and girls use to describe themselves are given below. Read each statement and decide if it is *hardly ever,* or *sometimes,* or *often* true for you. Then for each statement, put an X in the box in front of the word that seems to describe you best. There are no right or wrong answers. Do not spend too much time on any one statement. Remember, choose the word which seems to describe how you usually feel.

I am secretly afraid . . . .   ☐hardly ever ☐sometimes ☐often

I worry about things that may happen . . . .   ☐hardly ever ☐sometimes ☐often

I worry about making mistakes . . . .   ☐hardly ever ☐sometimes ☐often

---

Note: RCMAS (Reynolds & Richmond, 1978), STAIC (Spielberger, 1973). Reprinted by permission.

The present inability of self-report inventories to address developmental differences is another disadvantage; many anxiety inventories are not modified for variations in children's ability to comprehend the items. The consistency of children's self-reported anxiety is also questionable; there may be little correspondence across responses in the cognitive, behavioral, and physiological domains or between the child and parent or teacher's responses.

Table 3.4. *Sample of the Children's Coping Questionnaire*

Instructions for completing this questionnaire are given to the child verbally and a practice item is administered to help the child understand how to respond to the questions. Following the practice question, the child responds to item where the individual anxiety-producing situation has been entered.

Practice item: When you go to a restaurant with your parents and you want to order your favorite meal but you find out they don't have it. Are you able to help yourself feel less upset?

1	2	3	4	5	6	7
not at all able					able to help myself feel comfortable	

Sample item: When you are _____.
Are you able to help yourself feel less upset?

1	2	3	4	5	6	7
not at all able					able to help myself feel comfortable	

Reprinted by permission.

A relatively unexplored though promising area of self-report in childhood anxiety concerns cognitive activities. Cognitive contents, schemata, processes, and products have been implicated in the maintenance and etiology of childhood anxiety but have received little empirical attention (Kendall, Howard, & Epps, 1988). Further, researchers examining the cognition of "anxious" children have not targeted clinic-referred anxious populations; instead, they have worked primarily with test-anxious and fearful school children (Francis, 1988).

Preliminary investigations of "think aloud" tasks and thought-listing techniques with anxious children have shown differences between the cognition of anxious and nonanxious children as well as among the cognition of nonpsychiatric children with differing levels of anxiety (Prins, 1986; Zatz & Chassin, 1985). For example, relative to their fifth and sixth grade peers, high test-anxious children exhibited more task-inhibiting cognitions, including more negative self-evaluations and off-task thoughts and fewer positive self-evaluations (Zatz & Chassin, 1985). Interestingly, the high test-anxious children also reported more on-task thoughts and more coping self-statements. This latter finding might suggest that the ruminative quality associated with anxiety can generally interfere with performance (see Kendall & Chansky, 1991).

Recently, self-report measures assessing cognition in anxious children have been developed to explore this relatively unknown domain and are being piloted with samples of children referred for the treatment of anxiety disorders. Francis (1988) has noted ongoing preliminary research to develop a self-report measure (Worry Scale) to examine the cognitive differences between separation anxiety disorder and overanxious disorder. Data on the reliability and validity of this measure have not yet been published.

Kendall and colleagues are piloting the Children's Anxious Self-Statement Questionnaire (CASSQ; Kendall & Ronan, 1990; Ronan, Rowe & Kendall, 1988), designed to assess the content of anxious children's cognitions. (Table 3.5 provides sample items from the CASSQ.) Preliminary analyses assessing the reliability and validity of the CASSQ's ability to differentiate among anxious and nonanxious groups of nonpsychiatrically referred children between 8 and 15 years old have been favorable. Anxious children scored higher on a factor assessing Negative Self-Focused Attention and lower on a factor assessing Positive Self-Concept and Expectations. Interested readers are referred to Figure 3.1, where cartoons with blank thought bubbles are used to assess children's self-talk.

Because negative self-statements are associated with other internalizing disorders, such as depression in adults (Kendall & Ingram, 1989), more research is needed to determine the specificity of these new cognitive assessment scales' ability to assess anxiety. We echo Francis's (1988) acknowledgment that "the need for future research [examining the cognitions of anxious children] is paramount" and that "an especially important area for future study is that which focuses on establishing the psychometric properties of cognitive assessment procedures" (p. 276).

Behavioral Observations

Direct behavioral observations are considered important components of the assessment process, though they are often overlooked. The behavioral assessment of childhood anxiety encompasses many structured and unstructured observational techniques, ranging from informal observations made during clinical interviews to standardized Behavioral Avoidance Tasks (BATs). There are several observational coding systems available, such as the Observer Rating Scale of Anxiety and the Behavior Profile Rating Scale (see Johnson & Melamed, 1979, for a review). A sample of the overt behaviors that anxious children often exhibit include: fidgeting, fingernail biting, avoiding eye contact, speaking softly, trembling, stuttering, and crying.

An advantage of the structured observation strategies, including the BATs and direct observation by trained raters in naturalistic settings (such as in school and on the playground), is that an assessor can observe a child's reactions to multiple stimuli in different settings (Strauss, 1988). The treatment implications of this information are that the gamut of a child's coping style—before, during, and after confronting stressful situations—is identified. This knowledge provides the therapist with target behaviors to address and with a baseline from which to assess the efficacy of treatment.

Table 3.5. *Sample Items from the Children's Anxious Self-Statement Questionnaire**

Instructions to the child: Listed below are some of the thoughts that pop into children's heads. Please read each thought and mark how often, if at all, the thought came into your mind over the past week. Please read each item carefully and then circle your answer on the sheet in the following way:

$$1 = \text{not at all}$$
$$2 = \text{sometimes}$$
$$3 = \text{fairly often}$$
$$4 = \text{often}$$
$$5 = \text{all the time}$$

- I feel great about life	1	2	3	4	5
- I feel sick to my stomach	1	2	3	4	5
- When I took my test, I thought I would fail	1	2	3	4	5
- I was shaking	1	2	3	4	5
- I thought I was going to do something wrong	1	2	3	4	5
- Things will turn out great	1	2	3	4	5
- I wish I could do things right	1	2	3	4	5
- I feel like screaming	1	2	3	4	5

Note: *Kendall & Ronan (1989). Reprinted by permission.

The utility of behavioral-observation techniques are hindered by several potential disadvantages. The observation techniques, coding systems, and instructions vary across studies. Clinical or research settings tend to use individualized, specific techniques that are not comparable. Researchers have also identified problems with the reliability and validity of these techniques, observer coding drift, and poorly defined criteria (Foster & Cone, 1986; Morris & Kratochwill, 1983). Given these problems and the fact that no single behavior is pathognomonic to childhood anxiety, observation strategies may have more value to the therapeutic, rather than to the assessment/diagnostic process.

Parent and Teacher Rating Scales

Parent and teacher rating scales comprise a subset of behavior-observation techniques because they assess children's observable symptomatology in different settings, albeit through less systematic observation. Although many of the rating scales were not designed to assess the general expression of anxiety in children (Morris & Kratochwill, 1983), several contain an anxiety-withdrawal dimension that corresponds to the DSM-III diagnosis of overanxious disorder (Quay, 1986), including the Conners' Teacher Rating Scale (Conners, 1969), the Child Behavior Checklist (CBCL; Achenbach & Edelbrock, 1983), and the Revised Behavior

FIGURE 3.1. An example of a social situation with blank thought bubbles used to elicit children's self-talk. Artist: Peter J. Mikula

Problem Checklist (Quay & Peterson, 1983). Table 3.6 highlights some of the items on the CBCL associated with anxiety.

These rating scales are economical to administer and provide easily quantifiable data. Numerous studies have supported their reliability and validity; and normative data that is developmentally sensitive exists. For example, the CBCL has been standardized separately for boys and girls,

Table 3.6. *Sample Items Assessing Anxious Behaviors From the Parent—CBCL**

Instructions to parents: Below is a list of items that describe children. For each item that describes your child now or within the past 6 months, please circle the 2 if the item is very true or often true of your child. Circle the 1 if the item is somewhat or sometimes true of your child. If the item is not true of your child, circle the 0. Please answer all items as well as you can, even if some do not seem to apply to your child.

0	1	2	Too fearful or anxious
0	1	2	Feels too guilty
0	1	2	Worrying
0	1	2	Cries a lot
0	1	2	Feels he/she has to be perfect
0	1	2	Self-conscious or easily embarrassed
0	1	2	Can't get his/her mind off certain thoughts, obsessions
0	1	2	Fears certain animals, situations, or places
0	1	2	Fears going to school
0	1	2	Nervous, highstrung, or tense
0	1	2	Trouble sleeping

Note: *Parent CBCL (Achenbach & Edelbrock, 1983). Reprinted by permission.

ages 4 to 5, 6 to 11, and 12 to 16. For each of the subscales of the CBCL (e.g., obsessive-compulsive, aggressive, depressed, social withdrawn, internalizing, externalizing), normalized T scores can be derived and compared to the scores of clinic and nonpatient normative samples. Unfortunately, rating scales are limited by some disadvantages (Saal, Downey, & Lahey, 1980), including the retrospective nature of the observations, the lack of explicit training for the raters (i.e., parents and teachers), and the potential confound of rater bias.

Physiological Recordings

Although the physiological manifestation of anxiety in adults has been explored extensively (Borkovec, Weerts, & Bernstein, 1977; Himadi, Boice, & Barlow, 1985; Lick & Katkin, 1976), similarly extensive work has not been completed with children. In a more limited fashion, three types of physiological measures have been used with children:

1. Cardiovascular—heart rate, blood pressure, peripheral blood flow
2. Electrodermal—skin conductance
3. Electromyography—electrical activity in the skeletal muscles

As is the case with adults, the physiological correlates of anxiety are not consistent across studies (Johnson & Melamed, 1979). Some investigators have provided evidence that heart rate and electrodermal changes can be reliably measured and correlate with the presentation of fear-inducing stimuli among children (Beidel, 1988; Melamed, Yurcheson, Fleece, Hutcherson, & Hawes, 1978). Others, however, have not found a correlation between physiological measures and self-report or observer ratings of anxiety in children (e.g., Darley & Katz, 1973).

In addition to the inconsistent research findings, opponents of physiological assessment of anxiety in children have cited the large imbalance between the extensive cost in time and money of gathering such information and its relative yield (Barlow & Wolfe, 1981). Further, many of the physiological-assessment techniques lack adequate normative data for children. Children also appear to show idiosyncratic patterns of response during physiological assessment (Werry, 1986); and these measures are highly sensitive to the incidental motoric and perceptual activity (Wells & Virtulano, 1984) that children are likely to exhibit.

Despite these somewhat daunting limitations, the physiological assessment of childhood anxiety should not be abandoned. Given that the expression of anxiety has biological as well as behavioral and cognitive components (Lang, 1968), a comprehensive assessment and treatment process should include each of these domains.

Family Assessment

Despite the existence of assessments designed to assess anxiety in an individual child, there are no specific assessment devices for measuring anxiety in a family. And while there are "family-assessment" tools available, their direct relevance to anxiety disorders in children remains to be demonstrated.

In deciding how to assess families with anxious children, the researcher or clinician needs to consider several important factors. What are the main characteristics of anxious children and how might the family be involved in the etiology and maintenance of such characteristics (e.g., perfectionism, fear of separation, poor coping with stress)? What is the assessor's particular theoretical conception of anxiety disorders in children? Many methods of family assessment are grounded in a particular theory of family functioning (e.g., systems, structural, psychodynamic, behavioral). Finally, what are the specific questions to be answered by the family assessment? Is the purpose of assessment mainly research oriented—to gain a greater understanding of the characteristics of the families of anxious children? Or is assessment geared toward a more clinical purpose with families being assessed solely to guide specific interventions (Grotevant & Carlson, 1989)?

Assessing families is quite complex. As Jacob and Tennenbaum (1988) pointed out, family assessment involves investigation of the individual, the relationship of two or more family members, and the relationship of the family to the extrafamilial environment. Moreover, the use of self-report inventories for assessment represents only one assessment method:

families might also be assessed through observational means (both naturalistic and laboratory), and information may be gathered via clinical interviews or log books (Grotevant & Carlson, 1989; Jacob & Tennenbaum, 1988). Because it is not within our present scope to describe and evaluate the family-assessment measures that have been proposed, we instead provide only information about the nature of various approaches to family assessment and only briefly consider potentially useful information that may be gathered through family assessment. Much of the information in the present review has been gathered from Grotevant and Carlson (1989) and Jacob and Tennenbaum (1988). For more thorough reviews of specific family-assessment measures, the reader is referred to these sources as well as the relevant journal articles.

Types of Family Assessment. Two types of family assessment—observational methods and self-report instruments—will be discussed.

Observational Methods. Observational methods of assessment include (a) coding and (b) rating systems. Coding systems focus on the interaction between family members. Coding may occur at a microanalytic level of specific behaviors or at a macro level in which rates of various behaviors at the microanalytic level are combined into various broader behavioral constructs. For instance, Grotevant and Carlson (1989) noted that Baldwin, Cole, and Baldwin (1982) created the molar construct of "warmth" by combining the microanalytic level of behaviors "helping one another" and "expressed approval," "hugging," "teasing," and "joking" (p. 15). Moreover, Grotevant and Carlson, citing Gottman (1979) and Jacob (1975), point out that while microanalytic coding has the advantage of providing moment-to-moment information about the contingencies of family behavior, this approach might miss the broader patterns of the relationships of family interactions which may be important for providing empirical support for various theories of family function (Gottman, 1979). Drawbacks concerning family coding systems include limited data on the psychometric properties of the systems, and many have been used in only one or two studies.

At present, there are no specific coding systems designed to study families of anxious children. However, the dimensions tapped by various systems may provide potentially useful information for understanding and helping these families. Among these are self-assertion, separateness, interdependence (very autonomous to very submissive), approval, disapproval, dependency, and compliance. (See Grotevant & Carlson, 1989; Jacob & Tennenbaum, 1988, for reviews of specific measures that tap these as well as other potentially useful dimensions.)

In deciding upon a system the researcher or clinician working with anxious children needs to consider several factors. First, some coding systems are designed for use with adolescents (e.g., Constraining and Enabling Family Coding System, Hauser, Powers, Weiss-Perry, Folansbee, Raja-park, & Greene, [unpublished manuscript]). Thus, though the system may tap dimensions that appear relevant for understanding families of children diagnosed with an anxiety disorder (e.g., judgmental/dogmatic, accept-ance, or problem solving), the age appropriateness of the system may be questionable. Second, the psychometric qualities of these measures vary greatly, and any decision must include a consideration of reliability, valid-ity, and strength of the measure's theoretical foundations. Finally, some coding systems (e.g., Expressed Emotion, Vaughn & Leff, 1976) have been designed for use with particular clinical populations, such as families of individuals diagnosed as schizophrenic. It may be that characteristics of families having a child diagnosed with a clinical disorder overlap, so that one might expect that such measures would be applicable. At the same time, such overlap might prevent analysis of specific characteristics of families with children diagnosed with an anxiety disorder. In considering the use of coding systems, the potential user is warned that the collection and analysis of data is often extremely complicated and time consuming.

In contrast to coding systems, rating systems are designed to assess *patterns* of family functioning along various psychological dimensions (e.g., warmth, control, supportiveness). The emphasis is more on complex pat-terns of family behavior than on frequencies of specific behaviors. Proce-dures used when gathering information on rating scales include (a) directed family interaction (e.g., discussion of a particular topic), (b) semistructured interviews in which there are no specific instructions for what to discuss (although certain topics, e.g., conflict resolution, are encouraged), and (c) structured tasks such as a Q-Sort procedure.

A wide range of psychological dimensions that may be useful for under-standing families of anxious children are covered by rating scales. These include parent-child coalitions, internal boundaries, freedom of expres-sion, involvement, problem solving, and behavior control. Additionally, ratings can be made of very specific communication patterns, such as topic change, support, and attack, as well as ratings of extrafamilial relation-ships, such as norms and values (Grotevant & Carlson, 1989). Grotevant and Carlson warn that different constructs often have the same names on different rating scales (as well as other family-assessment measures), and this should be considered when choosing a measure to use with anxious families. Moreover, the dimensions range from those that are rather sub-jective on the part of the rater (e.g., autonomy) to other, objective con-structs (e.g., topic change in communication); and these differences require consideration. Finally, while a number of rating scales would appear to be useful in the study of families with a child who has been diagnosed with an anxiety disorder, these rating scales have psychometric limitations in one or more areas.

Self-Report Inventories. Self-report questionnaires form another important type of measure used in family assessment that may be potentially useful for working with families of anxious children. Questionnaires tap a wide range of information about the individual's perception of him or herself within a family, as well as perceptions of other family members and various areas of general family functioning. The following are some dimensions covered and scales included in family-assessment questionnaires that may be useful for understanding families of anxious children: independence; achievement orientation; control; family boundaries; affective involvement; different parenting styles (e.g., protective, disciplinarian); children's perception of parental behavior (e.g., instilling persistent anxiety, possessiveness); psychological autonomy; areas of family stress and coping, such as events over the previous year (illness and work transitions); and general family cohesion. (See Grotevant & Carlson, 1989; Jacob & Tennenbaum, 1988, for a review of questionnaires.)

While information across a wide range of family functioning is important for understanding families of anxious children, it may be particularly useful to understand parent-child perceptions of each other as well as their roles within the family. Among the dimensions tapped from the adult perspective are child rearing attitudes, parenting style, perception of parental roles, parenting stress, and perceptions of the child's behavior, such as independence versus dependence and acceptance versus rejection. Among the dimensions by which children may be measured are their perception of parental accepting or rejecting behavior, their perception of the magnitude of problems they may have with a parent, their perception of the quality of attachment, their perception of autonomy and control, and their perception of achievement pressure (Grotevant & Carlson, 1989).

From our cognitive-behavioral approach to treating anxiety, one of the central focuses in treatment is the anxious individual's perception of events and others. Either in the individual child or the family, measures of *perception* may be especially valuable. Thus, while measures that tap actual family behaviors are certainly valuable, they may fail to provide the very important information about the *perceptions* within the family that are contributing to distressing anxiety. For example, how do parents of anxious children perceive their own role in the family? It may be that the perceptions (misperceptions) that the parent holds strongly influence his or her behavior toward the child, contributing in turn to the child's anxiety. For example, does the parent believe that in order to be effective he or she must be very controlling and therefore discourages the child's movement toward independence? This style may then manifest itself in excessive dependency and inhibition on the child's part, which the parent had not initially intended. While this process currently remains at the level of speculation based on our clinical observations, solid measurement of child and parent perceptions of one another and their roles in the family would be very valuable in clarifying the picture of family functioning.

Finally, there are self-report measures specifically assessing family stress and coping. Given the anxious child's difficulty with situations that are perceived as stressful, it may be particularly useful to gather information about any difficulties that his or her family has with stress and coping. Measures of family stress and coping have been developed to assess family responses to both intrafamilial events (e.g., life cycles) and extrafamilial events (e.g., financial and business strains). Also, there are measures to assess the family's ability to acquire support from outside the family (see Grotevant & Carlson, 1989).

In our work we are currently investigating characteristics of the parents of children diagnosed with an anxiety disorder. Parents complete a number of established inventories (e.g., State-Trait Anxiety Inventory, Beck Depression Inventory) as well as new questionnaires designed to assess specific coping abilities (or lack thereof) in their children and the expectation that parents hold regarding their child's coping. This assessment is geared, in part, toward the development of future interventions, in which parents are also treated as part of their child's therapy.

SUMMARY

Because no individual assessment strategy is sufficient, the assessment of anxiety in children requires a multimethod approach, drawing information from multiple sources across several settings. Assessments that account for the distinctive nature of childhood anxiety, including considerations of a child's developmental history, the source of referral for treatment, and the imprecision of the disorder's diagnostic classification, are needed. Further, since it can be argued that the treatment of childhood anxiety is most effective when target behaviors and cognitions are addressed, a comprehensive assessment of the specific cognitive and behavioral features of the disorder for an individual child is also necessary.

An outline of a recommended assessment battery is presented in Table 3.7. This battery permits developmental considerations by its use of a semistructured clinical interview (ADIS-C) and parent and teacher ratings that can be compared to developmentally sensitive normative data (e.g., CBCL). The parent and teacher CBCLs allow a comparison of the child's anxious behavior across settings—at home and in the school. Self-report measures of anxiety, both specific (FSSC-R) and general (RCMAS and STAIC), are administered, providing two views of the child's self-perception of his or her emotional condition. Our coping questionnaire, designed to assess the child's response to personally anxiety-producing situations, is completed by both the child and his or her parent. These data, directly

Table 3.7. *Sample Childhood Anxiety Assessment Battery*

Anxiety Disorders Interview Schedule-Children (parent and child)
Revised Children's Manifest Anxiety Scale
State-Trait Anxiety Inventory for Children
Fear Survey Schedule for Children—Revised
Coping Questionnaire (parent and child)
Children's Depression Inventory
Child Behavior Checklist (parent and teacher)
Behavioral Observation Task
Children's Anxious Self-Statement Questionnaire
Thought Listing Task

---

linked to treatment and its outcome evaluation, are considered an important component of the assessment package. A self-report measure of depression (Children's Depression Inventory; CDI; Kovacs, 1981) is included to assess potential comorbidity between anxiety and depression among children referred for the treatment of anxiety. These data, too, have implications for effective intervention.

The assessment process can be videotaped so that behavioral observations can be coded. In addition, children can be asked to talk spontaneously about themselves for several minutes while looking into a camera. They might be told that the purpose of this task, coined "Tell Us About Yourself," is to provide them with the opportunity to share any information about themselves that they think is important. As we employ it, the children are encouraged to speak about topics that were not addressed during the interview or to emphasize and expand on issues that were raised at that time. Raters, blind to the child's diagnosis, can then code the child's behaviors during this brief task. Anxious behaviors typically coded by raters include gratuitous verbalization (e.g., "um . . . you know . . . uh . . . well"), trembling voice, fingers in or near mouth, gratuitous body movement (e.g., swaying, fidgeting), rigidity, task avoidance (e.g., sitting down, walking out of view of the camera), and an absence of eye contact. At present, additional research is needed before specific behavioral-observation codes can be considered valid indicators of the presence of an anxiety disorder.

For the assessment of children's cognitions, the child completes a self-report measure—the CASSQ. A "thought-listing" strategy could be employed, asking questions such as "when you felt the most nervous, what thoughts came to mind, what did you say to yourself?", or "what strategy did you use to help yourself feel less nervous?" These assessments of cognitions not only assist us in our quest for a better understanding of the child's emotional distress, but also facilitate the individualized application of the treatment.

Given the inconsistent and inconclusive information currently available about physiological measures of anxiety, we do not recommend that such assessment procedures be included in clinical settings. It is presently impractical to clinically employ such assessment strategies: the time, technological, and financial costs of such procedures do not, at this time, contribute meaningfully to differential treatment. However, we do encourage and endorse collecting data on heart rate, blood pressure, and/or electrodermal response in research settings to provide more information on childhood anxiety that would be clinically relevant.

Chapter 4

Cognitive-Behavioral Strategies Applied to Anxiety Disorders in Youth

Fear cannot be banished, but it can be calm and without panic; and it can be mitigated by reason and evaluation.

— Vanneavar Bush

Although a great deal of research effort has been directed to adult anxiety disorders during the past several decades, relatively little attention has been paid to childhood anxiety, until recently. As in the description of the nature of childhood anxiety disorders, researchers and practitioners have drawn from the adult anxiety literature in order to develop treatments for childhood anxiety. For example, various forms of behavioral and cognitive-behavioral therapy have been demonstrated successful in the treatment of generalized anxiety and agoraphobia in adults (Barlow, 1988; Barrios & Shigetomi, 1979; Michelson & Marchione, 1991). In addition, the adult anxiety literature continues to underscore a cognitive component to anxiety (Beck & Emery, 1985; Kendall & Ingram, 1989) that is important in treatment.

Through the synthesis of behavioral and cognitive treatment approaches, with appropriate integration of developmental considerations, therapeutic change may result for the anxious child. In this chapter we first describe several elements of the coping template that the child can employ to reduce unwanted and distressing anxiety. Later, we describe the strategies that the therapist uses in helping the child to develop a coping template. These skills and strategies are integrated into a workbook, the *Coping Cat Workbook* (Kendall, 1990), for use by the children.

ELEMENTS OF THE COPING
TEMPLATE

A variety of skills that are useful for coping with and managing anxiety are included in cognitive-behavioral treatment for anxiety in children and adolescents. This chapter presents an overview of the elements and procedures which are then described as part of our integrated cognitive-behavioral therapy in the next chapter. The coping skills taught to anxious youth include relaxation, imagery, problem solving, and self-rewards, and we also help them to use superhero characters, corrective self-talk, and a coping template.

Relaxation

For some, it is fishing, going for a walk, or participating in a recreational sport. For others, reading, movies, or music are important. What are we referring to here? We are talking about how people take special time to relax. To be stressed and pressured at all times is unhealthy, and to be unable to relax is unhealthy as well. Anxious individuals are typically tense and unskilled in the practice of relaxation. As part of the treatment of psychological distress associated with unwanted anxiety, we offer exercises and opportunities to build skills in the area of relaxation.

In relaxation training, major muscle groups of the body are progressively relaxed through systematic tension-release exercises (see also, King, Hamilton, & Ollendick, 1988). By tensing and relaxing various muscle groups, the individual learns to perceive sensations of bodily tension and to use these sensations as the cues for them to relax. Anxious children and adolescents are not known for their ability to recognize cues for tension or for their skill in relaxing. In helping them to become more sensitive to these cues, it has been recommended that children learn a maximum of three muscle groups each training session and practice the relaxation exercises twice daily at home (Strauss, 1988).

Another method called cue-controlled relaxation is introduced to the client. This process involves a repeated association of the relaxed state with a self-produced cue word, such as "relax" or "calm." While the client is totally relaxed, the cue word is subvocalized with each exhalation. As a result, the cue word can be used as a reminder to relax and/or to combat feelings of anxiety.

When teaching these progressive and cue-controlled relaxation techniques, relaxation training scripts are usually incorporated. Although most of the scripts have been written for adults (Bernstein & Borkovec, 1973; Rimm & Masters, 1974), formats for children have also been developed (Ollendick & Cerny, 1981; Koeppen, 1974). An example of such a relaxation script is provided in the appendix (pp. 180–185).

Does teaching relaxation skills to children have beneficial effects? Although there are only a small number of studies that directly address the specific effects of relaxation training, the data are fairly consistent in supporting the beneficial results of teaching children and adolescents how to relax. For example, Weisman, Ollendick, and Horne (1978) demonstrated the effectiveness of muscular relaxation procedures with normal six- and seven-year-old children. They found that the procedures of both Ollendick and Cerny (1981) and Koeppen (1974) resulted in significantly reduced muscle tension levels. Although both groups were superior to an attention-control group, they did not differ from one another, suggesting that both muscular relaxation procedures can be effective with young children.

Imagery

Children can and often do have active and playful imaginations, and it is beneficial to use imaginal activities to promote coping. Imagery procedures are not used alone but are tapped by the therapist as needed to facilitate coping. For illustrative purposes, let's consider how imagery can help in relaxation training. Because we teach relaxation for the various different muscle groups, our description of various images will be separate for these different muscle groups. When done in a playful and fun manner, the images not only help the child to remember how to relax, but also make for a relaxed session.

Examples of images that are useful in helping children achieve overall body relaxation include (a) a river that begins at the top of the head and flows down through the body carrying all the tightness and tension away through the soles of the feet and (b) a warm glow that begins in the abdomen and gradually overtakes the body parts one by one until the entire body feels warm and relaxed.

Images are helpful when teaching children how to tighten and relax specific muscle groups. For example, when asked to tighten and relax their abdominal area, children can imagine that an elephant is walking along, minding his own business, and doesn't see the child sleeping. His foot just misses stepping on the child's stomach because he pulls it in tight and tense. Then, after the elephant has passed, he can relax his muscles. Boys can imagine a wrestling match where, when you are trying to keep from being pinned down, you tense all your muscles and push upward against the pressure of your opponent. After the match, you can relax all your muscles. Images useful when training relaxation of facial muscles include (a) asking the child to wrinkle his nose so tight it looks like a monkey's nose and then to relax it so that it looks like an elephant's trunk or (b) to make a scary face to frighten away a monster and then to relax it when the monster leaves in a panic.

When working toward relaxed upper arms, the child can be asked to imagine that she is a police officer standing in the middle of a busy intersection holding out her arms to stop all the traffic so that a small puppy can cross the street. She has to hold her arm straight out for several minutes, but then she relaxes when the puppy jumps up into her arms. Or, a boy can imagine that he is a muscle builder posing in a competition, who then relaxes completely before striking the next pose. Also, for relaxing the upper arms, shoulders, and neck, the child can imagine that he or she is a turtle pulling his head deep into his shell only to stick it out fully when the danger is gone. For the legs, the child can stiffen both legs firmly enough to leave a footprint on the carpet—pushing down as hard as one can. After the footprint is visible, the legs relax. Relaxation can be individualized by making an audiotape that draws on the child's preferred imagery and by problem solving with the child about when would be the best time to rehearse the relaxation skills. Relaxation is an important skill for overly anxious youth, and activities with playful images can make the learning of relaxation skills a relaxing and fun experience.

Correcting Maladaptive Self-talk

Cognitively oriented therapies work from the assumption that maladaptive thinking is related to maladaptive behavior. By changing faulty cognitive functioning, thoughts can be realigned so that they serve to help the client function more effectively, rather than contribute to the client's dysfunction. This process is sometimes referred to as "restructuring." Through various strategies that seek to produce cognitive restructuring, faulty cognitions can be modified in order to effect constructive behavior change.

The role of self-talk in childhood anxiety disorders is not as clear or well established as it is for adults. The generalized anxiety seen in adults is more routinely linked to self-reports of anticipated catastrophes and expected misfortunes (most likely unrealistic). These self-reports can be produced spontaneously by adult clients or are sought and identified by therapists questioning and/or use of questionnaires (e.g., Kendall & Hollon, 1989). With children and adolescents, however, you must consider the influence that the level of cognitive development has on the client's ability to recognize and report on internal "thinking," and one must be cautious not to assume the absence of faulty thinking, simply because the client does not volunteer such information. Relatedly, one cannot assume that such thinking exists without some evidence.

Addressing the self-talk of children during stressful situations can have positive effects on their performance. Although there exists the popular phrase "the power of positive thinking," it is not always the case that what is needed is a dose of positive self-talk. Often, and data from research on young adults supports this view, clients who are suffering from undue distress benefit from a reduction in their negative thinking. That is, while they engage in some positive thought, they also engage in a detrimentally high frequency of negative thought that detracts from and undermines their positive thinking. It has been suggested that identification and remediation in the area of self-talk is best focused on reducing excessive negative thinking.

One demonstration of the efficacy of an intervention that sought to modify maladaptive self-talk was reported by Ollendick (1979). In this study, a 16-year-old anorexic male was treated with systematic desensitization and cognitive-restructuring procedures. Although systematic desensitization was effective in reducing his excessive fear of eating and gaining weight, its effects were short lived, resulting in substantial weight loss when treatment was withdrawn. Self-defeating self-statements (e.g., "I can't eat, I'll get fat again") were identified and treated to be more realistic and adaptive (e.g., "If I gain weight, it is true that some kids might not like me. Other kids will like me, however. Besides, what difference will it make whether they like me or not. I will feel better"). The cognitive component was linked to weight gain that was maintained over a 2-year period.

The following is a transcript from a therapy session in which the therapist facilitates less negative self-talk in a child:

Therapist: All righty, how about when you fell down? Why, OK, you knew that, that you were getting scared cause you couldn't breathe. That's a pretty good sign isn't it? Yea. OK. What were you thinking to yourself?

Client: I was thinkin', maybe, oh my God, I broke it, I broke it. I kept thinking I broke it cause I couldn't move it.

Therapist: Mmm Hmm.

Client: I couldn't walk on it.

Therapist: Mmm Hmm.

Client: Oh my God. What am I gonna do? Am I gonna go to the hospital?

Therapist: Mmm Hmm.

Client: And are they gonna give me anesthetics or anything?

Therapist: Will I get a shot?

Client: Yea.

Therapist: I bet that one crossed your mind. OK, what could you have said to yourself? That might have made you feel a little better about it?

Client: Cause as I said, even if I broke it at least I'll go to the hospital
   and maybe, maybe like it'll stop and be able to make it feel better.
Therapist: Yea, people do heal from broken legs, it's not the end of the
   world. What else could you have said to yourself?
Client: I could have said, it may not have just been broken. I could
   just be thinkin' that.
Therapist: You could just what?
Client: I could just be imagining that I broke it.
Therapist: Right, exactly, you could be just sort of making it worse
   than it really was. But maybe you just sprained it or something less
   severe than actually breaking it. OK, that's good Joey. Those are
   very good entrees into your journal. Let me give you your points
   here.
Client: Yea!

Problem Solving

The experience of unwanted and interfering anxiety is often a source
of concern and a prompt for avoidance among youth with anxiety disorders. Instead of avoiding such emotionally arousing situations, the child
needs to consider what solutions to the problem are available. When an
anxiety-provoking situation is approached from the perspective of a problem to be solved, it is not that the anxiety is unmanageable nor the end
of the world. Rather, a problem-solving focus simply identifies the anxious
experience as one that requires some thoughtful consideration of the several options that are available to more effectively cope with the unwanted
fear. For example, a child who was frightened to walk home without a
parent was asked to identify what was frightening about the walk. She
claimed that if she fell and got hurt, no one would know what had happened to her. She also worried about passing a bar that was on her way
(a ruffian might hit her), and she worried about getting lost. In discussing
it, she was asked about each concern and what she could do to address it.
She indicated that she could walk home with a friend who lived in the
neighborhood, that there were alternative routes around the bar, and that
she could practice the route with an adult until she was certain she remem-
bered it. Each problem seemed to have possible solutions. The therapist
also challenged the distortion that she might fall and become so seriously
injured that she could not walk home by asking her if that had ever
happened before to her or to anyone she knew and by reassuring her that
even if she did fall, she would be able to get home.

Our cognitive-behavioral approach to problem solving follows a sequential process (see D'Zurilla, 1986; Nezu, Nezu, & Perri, 1989; D'Zurilla
& Goldfried, 1971). Although it may not always be necessary to have every

child go through each and every problem-solving step, it is worthwhile for the therapist to be aware of these steps as they help to guide effective use of the problem-solving process. Also, when individual children demonstrate a lack of knowledge about how best to proceed when trying to solve an interpersonal problem, the steps can be taught and used to work through solutions to illustrative dilemmas. In the first stage of the problem-solving process, the individual focuses on a "general orientation," beginning to prepare for the solution of a problem (D'Zurilla & Goldfried, 1971). During the second stage, the individual works on "problem definition and formulation," describing the problem and the major goals. Then, the individual can "generate alternative solutions." After this stage, the process of "decision making" takes place. Once a choice is made, the alternative is implemented with later "verification" of the success of this choice (Kendall & Siqueland, 1989). Through this process of working with a problem until reaching a resolution, children and adolescents achieve an understanding of how to cope with and master future problems.

A 13-year-old child worried excessively about failing tests and prepared for many hours before taking them. When she came to a therapy session worried about an upcoming test and stressed by the demands she was placing on herself, the therapist asked her to problem solve about how she might reasonably make her preparations. With support, she generated numerous ideas, including checking with other students about how long they planned to spend preparing for the test, planning to spend a limited amount of time studying each night for several nights prior to the test and asking her mother to help keep track of the time, and reminding herself that any score above 80% indicated mastery of the material.

Kleiner, Marshall, and Spevack (1987) conducted a study to evaluate the ability of problem solving to prevent posttreatment relapses of anxiety disorders in adults. Twenty-six agoraphobic patients were randomly assigned to either an *in vivo* exposure treatment or *in vivo* exposure plus a problem-solving skills training program. All of the patients improved significantly after 12 treatment sessions. However, while the group in the *in vivo* procedure alone either failed to show further gains at follow-up or relapsed, the group receiving training in problem solving showed further improvements at follow-up assessment. This study illustrates that problem solving may facilitate the maintenance of therapeutic gains from treatment strategies such as *in vivo* exposure (e.g., Jannoun, Munby, Catalan, & Gelder, 1980; Arnow, Taylor, Agras, & Telch, 1985).

Managing Rewards

One of the hallmarks of behaviorism is its emphasis on the consequences of behavior and the resultant increase or decrease in the likelihood of that behavior recurring again in the future. Indeed, it is often the case that through systematic application of contingent rewards, specific behaviors are modified. Within a cognitive-behavioral approach, therapists make use of contingent consequences for behavior.

The managing of rewards is an integral ingredient in our cognitive-behavioral approach to the treatment of anxiety disorders. This technique involves a number of treatment procedures derived from the principles of operant conditioning. For instance, according to operant theory (Skinner, 1966), the individual emits an action to which the environment reacts. Whether the individual response is repeated depends on the environment's reaction to the response. Operant procedures include positive reinforcement, shaping, stimulus fading and extinction, and have been employed effectively with a wide variety of behavioral problems in children. Positive reinforcement, as applied to anxiety and fear, involves providing some reward for approach behavior toward the feared stimulus. Assuming a noncatastrophic experience, the reward increases the frequency of the desired behavior. Reward systems have been useful in reducing fearful behaviors such as school phobia, nocturnal anxiety, social withdrawal, toilet phobia, and separation anxiety (Strauss, 1987).

Shaping involves providing a reward following successive approximations of the desired behavior, because the actual targeted behavior is either too difficult or complex to perform. Shaping has been found to be effective in alleviating separation anxiety and fear of riding in a school bus (Neisworth, Madle, & Goeke, 1975; Luiselli, 1978), and its basic principle, rewarding graduated success, is applied within many therapies.

Stimulus fading is an operant procedure that might be useful when a fearful child can perform nonfearful behavior in some settings or conditions but not in others. This procedure teaches the child to perform nonfearful responses in the difficult settings by gradually shifting the characteristics of a comfortable setting, while also providing regular reinforcement. Since few studies have investigated stimulus fading, generalizations about the relative effectiveness of this procedure must be made with caution (Morris & Kratochwill, 1983).

Extinction has been used to eliminate certain anxious behaviors in children. Following on the assumption that some children's anxiety or fear is maintained because they are reinforced for it, it may be possible to reduce such behavior by not reinforcing the child. Strauss (1988) noted that, in most instances, extinction in combination with positive reinforcement for nonfearful behavior has been used.

We use and encourage others who work with anxious children to use rewards to shape and maintain behavioral improvements. However, the rewards must be individualized and specific to each child's preferences. Our experience suggests that there are a wide variety of rewards that are readily available. For example, rewards that have been a part of our clinic have included (a) time to pursue a favorite sports activity like skateboarding, (b) time spent with a favorite adult or peer, and (c) allowing themselves to leave a nonessential task unfinished and spending that time involved in something more interesting. One 13-year-old male rewarded himself by baking brownies, an activity that he had wanted to try for some time but felt uneasy about attempting. In other words, he rewarded himself for coping with anxiety by allowing himself to try something that would previously have been anxiety provoking.

Researchers and clinicians who work with children and adolescents have become increasingly aware of the merits of teaching self-evaluation. For example, impulsive children seem to benefit from being taught to slow down and engage in self-evaluation as a part of their development of greater self-control (Kendall & Braswell, 1985; 1986). Depressed children, in contrast, have been found to be overly critical in their self-evaluation (Kendall, Stark, & Adam, 1990) and benefit from being taught more realistic and positive ways to self-evaluate (Stark, 1990). Anxious children, too, appear harsh in their judgments about themselves and can benefit from more realistic appraisals of their abilities and the demands that the environment places on them.

Self-evaluation tends to be something anxious children do almost spontaneously, although the evaluation of their own performance tends to be uncertain and nonencouraging. They tend to apply standards to their own performance that are quite excessive and unrealistic. For example, a 13-year-old girl worried excessively about her school performance and believed that if she wanted to go to college, she had to be challenged so she could realistically assess the impact of any one test grade on her entire college application. Of course, as we know, many college graduates have pursued careers successfully with school grades that were lower than 98%!

One way to help the anxious child begin to make more positive and realistic self-evaluations is to break the task into segments and help him reward himself for success on any one of the segments. For example, a child who wants to learn to sleep in the dark breaks the goal into three steps. First, he tries to sleep with only two lights on in the room, rather than the customary three and rewards himself for success on that task. Then he tries to sleep with only one dim light on and eventually with only a small night light. Each step becomes a goal in itself and is rewarded as such.

Using "Superhero" Characters

In past years it might have been Superman; more recently, Batman, Spiderman, or even a Teenage Mutant Ninja Turtle can serve as a superhero. Consider a child's response to the question "How would Superman handle this situation?" Oh, there might be a magical solution of flight or avoidance, but generally speaking children see their heroes as having solutions to the tough problems that they face.

We engage our youthful clients in the identification of superhero figures who can serve as models for managing those situations that are disturbing. Consider the following illustration of a television character as a superhero model.

Client: It doesn't seem possible, but he makes basic things funny by laughing at himself.

Therapist: If you can laugh about something, you are well on your way to handling it.

Client: I don't think there's any other way to think about it for me.

Therapist: Do you have a hero or is there someone who handles things differently than you, that you like how they think about things?

Client: Yea, like Eddie Murphy or Michael J. Fox—they seem like they don't care what anybody thinks. They are just themselves. I don't think they are like that really, but maybe acting is the way they get out their anxiety.

Therapist: But you might like to feel like that sometimes—like you don't care what everybody thinks. Maybe right now you can't figure out how you might think differently, but how would one of them think about a social situation?

Client: He would think everything is a joke. He'd make something funny out of something that's not.

Seeing how an identified hero figure manages in difficult situations can help spark additional ideas for coping strategies for the child client. A 10-year-old boy who was afraid to walk home from school for nine months following a confrontation with an older child who pushed him off his bike, used this method as one of his coping strategies. He decided that he could take deep breaths when he was walking, think "nothing will happen to me" or "I can handle this," or go into a store or to someone's doorstep. He also brought "X-man" (a superhero figure) along with him on the walk and imagined that X-man would be right behind if he needed him.

Building a "Coping" Template

Cognitive-behavioral theorists have promoted the notion that individuals perceive and make sense of the world through their cognitive structures—also referred to as schema. Such a template has an influence on what is perceived and how it is processed and understood. Anxious children see the world through a template laced with threat and questions. Our treatment builds on educational experiences and therapist-coached reconceptualizations of problems to build a new "coping" template. That is, the treatment goal is for the child to develop a new cognitive structure, or a modified existing structure, through which he or she can now look at formerly anxiety-provoking situations. The child's acquisition and use of a coping template is a major goal of the treatment—a goal that requires combining many skills taught to the child and the therapist's use of several treatment strategies.

STRATEGIES FOR INTERVENTION

We have described a variety of skills typically referred to as "coping skills"—methods to cope with situations and events that would otherwise produce distress. Relaxation, imagery, problem solving, etc. are all ways that children and adolescents can cope with anxiety provocation. The question remains, how best to provide anxious youth with these skills? What treatment strategies are most appropriate for the transmission of the coping skills to those children who need them most? In the next section, we describe several strategies that facilitate client acquisition of the coping skills. For instance, we describe features of the therapeutic relationship that foster coping, as well as strategies such as coping modeling, behavioral rehearsal (role plays), behavioral experiments, and exposure. These intervention strategies are used to maximize the effective communication of the coping skills described earlier.

Therapeutic Relationship

As described in chapter 2, the therapist's posture when providing a cognitive-behavioral intervention is one of collaboration. The therapist does not have all the answers, or even most answers, but rather has some ideas that can be tried and some ways to evaluate these ideas. For example, of the many coping skills that were identified and described earlier in this chapter, some will be more (and less) potent for different clients. Part of the therapist's task is to individualize and to help the client determine which coping approaches are most useful for him or her. The therapist dispenses rewards and arranges times that are "fun."

The therapeutic relationship is essential to the success of treatment with an anxious child. Some anxious children worry about pleasing the therapist just as they worry about pleasing others. For example, some children put painstaking effort into preparing anything that is asked of them, like writing in their journals or drawing a cartoon character. The therapeutic relationship is essential in helping these children risk being imperfect or producing what is, in the child's perception, flawed work—without criticism or hovering.

Some children see their anxieties as weaknesses or flaws and are reluctant to reveal themselves to the therapist. They tend to reassure the therapist there is nothing wrong and that they can take care of the problem by themselves. One child with overanxious disorder and social phobia assured the therapist that the problem was just in his attitude and that he could take care of it on his own by simply changing his attitude. He stressed that the therapist did not need to concern herself with his difficulties because he was in control. The therapeutic relationship is essential here in helping the child to take the chance and allow another person to see how much difficulty he is really experiencing.

Coping Modeling

The observational learning paradigm (e.g., Bandura, 1969; 1986) has had a profound impact on psychology and psychotherapy. The consistent finding that behavior can be acquired, facilitated, reduced, or eliminated through the process of observing others' behavior, and the effects of their behavior, has direct treatment implications. Indeed, modeling is central to social cognitive theories of human behavior (Bandura, 1986). When perceived as a reasonable individual—respected, liked, and possibly even admired (and occasionally associated with positive reward)—the therapist can be a powerful model for nondistorted thinking, careful reasoning, and nonanxious behavior.

Several different types of modeling have been utilized, which include symbolic, live, and participant modeling. Symbolic modeling consists of the child observing either a child or adult model approaching the feared situation or object via video recording. The advantage of this tactic is that the therapist has control of the model's behavior and the stressful situation or object. Also, symbolic modeling allows for repeated presentations of the approach sequence (Ross, 1981). In contrast, live modeling involves the child watching a "live" model reacting to either a feared situation or object. While the child does not participate in the anxiety-provoking stimuli during live modeling, participant modeling requires the child to "copy" a model by approaching what is feared (Strauss, 1987). Participant modeling has frequently been found to be the most effective modeling approach (Ollendick, 1979) and our program makes most consistent use of participant modeling.

Ross, Ross, and Evans (1971) successfully used modeling procedures in the treatment of a six-year-old boy who feared interaction with his peers. Generalized imitation, participant modeling, and social reinforcement were the main treatment procedures utilized in this study. Directly following treatment and upon follow-up, the child was able to interact positively with his peers and to display few avoidance behaviors. Modeling procedures have been shown to have considerable clinical utility in the treatment of anxious and fearful children (e.g., Lewis, 1974; Melamed & Siegel, 1975).

The therapist can also serve as a coping model not by behaving in an error-free (adjusted, nondistorted) manner, but by exhibiting misbehavior, lack of attention, and cognitive misperception while also displaying strategies to correct these difficulties. The therapist might display some of the child's own difficulties but would add a strategy for self-catching and self-correcting the difficulties. For example, to serve as a coping model for anxious children or adolescents, the therapist would become anxious, identify the feelings of anxiety, and demonstrate alternative ways to cope in anxiety-provoking situations. With depressed children, the therapist would model ways to self-disclose personal feelings and to check on the accuracy and validity of one's personal interpretations of the world. The modeled cognitive-processing style would provide the client with an alternative perception and reaction to an anxiety-provoking situation.

A shared experience with the child, often outside the therapy office, can provide an occasion for modeling and a forum for discussing interpersonal interactions, expectancies, and outcomes. Catherine shared a walk with her therapist and interacted with passersby; a simple "hello" and an exchange of glances took place. Catherine later reported that she could tell, "The people didn't like me—they looked at me funny." The therapist replied that he couldn't tell whether the people liked him or not. They looked tired, they were older people, and who knows what they were thinking? After discussion, Catherine concurred that she really couldn't tell whether they liked her or not, and that maybe she had been harsh with herself.

Coping modeling is an important component of child and adolescent therapy, but it should not be provided in an identical manner for all clients. Clinical decisions about the optimal manner of demonstration are dictated by the nature of the client's difficulties. Modeling is a valuable opportunity for children and adolescents to observe and learn; the therapist should plan demonstrations that are focused on the child's specific cognitive and behavioral needs. Modeling can also serve as a first step toward role playing, where the child or adolescent, along with the therapist, acts out alternative solutions to the actual situations that are difficult for the client.

Modeling involves demonstrating a controlled reaction in a fear-producing situation and showing the child an appropriate response to use in the fearful situation. As a result, fear may be reduced and appropriate skills acquired. In addition to the demonstration, if needed, the child can be instructed to imitate the model. Regular feedback and reinforcement is

provided for performance that matches that of the model. Therefore, operant principles are used to maintain the desired behaviors (Ollendick &
Francis, 1988).

Rehearsal—Role Plays

Practice is an important strategy in enhancing coping skills. Without it,
we are left with a treatment that lacks the enactive performance-based
features that are integral to therapeutic gain.

Role plays let both the therapist and the client experience how it feels
to utilize each of the alternative solutions generated for a specific problem.
Role plays provide opportunities for the therapist to guide the experience
and to reinforce progress; this guided and reinforced practice is important
in the remediation of cognitive, behavioral, and emotional difficulties.
When introducing this strategy, the therapist may wish to take the lead
in role playing a situation, with the child or adolescent following in a
tag-along procedure (see Ollendick, 1986). While role playing, the therapist elicits information about whether the client's feelings or thoughts are
similar to or different from those of the therapist as the situation evolves.
Then the child can attempt to role play a situation independently, with
support and encouragement from the therapist. Role playing can start with
minimally stressful situations and, as the child masters the skills, move on
to progressively more stressful situations. The therapist can begin with
imaginal scenes and then move to real-life sessions that can be arranged
in the office, home, school, or community.

We have found that children can work with imaginal role plays, but
developmental factors influence the use of this strategy. With younger
children, who need guidance to "get into" the role play, the therapist
should evoke the imaginal scene as concretely and with as much detail as
possible. For instance, the therapist might say, "You are sitting in the
middle of your classroom with the other kids seated around you and the
teacher directly in front of you. It is reading class. The teacher has just
asked your friend Mary to answer a question out loud. Your teacher looks
in her book at the next problem, then looks up and calls on you for the
next problem." A slow pace, along with concrete details, helps younger
children become involved in imaginal role plays.

Role plays can often be developed for use with more than one subject.
The decision to use such role plays should be guided by the nature of the
specific psychological difficulties. For example, an intervention using cognitive therapy for anxiety would involve the testing of personal assumptions. In a group format, caution would be needed to prevent the therapist's rational analysis of a situation from being overtaken by the
anxiety-provoking views expressed by the members of a homogeneously

anxious group. Group activities can be especially appropriate for dealing with clients' misperceptions of the judgments of others. An example is an adaptation of the type of skit described in the perspective-taking training literature (Chandler, 1973; Little & Kendall, 1979): A skit involving a criminal, juror, and judge can be enacted and discussed, with individual feelings and perceptions considered. Then, with the roles changed, the skit can be replayed, and clients can experience how an event unfolds from another's perspective.

Role plays are helpful in teaching relaxation skills. We often ask the child to teach the relaxation steps to the therapist once they have learned it in session and practiced it at home. This role play provides the therapist with another opportunity to serve as a coping model—demonstrating mild difficulty and then successful mastery of the relaxation procedure.

A few examples of role plays in action will help illustrate their value. One example of a particularly effective role play involved a 13-year-old girl who was separation anxious and worried excessively about her mother's health. The goal of the role play was to help her overcome the anxiety of talking directly with her mother about her concerns. Talking directly to her mom was not something she believed she could do. Initially, the therapist played the part of the child so as to model appropriate strategies for coping with this situation. Then the therapist and child switched roles so the child was able to practice her coping strategies.

Another example involved a 12-year-old girl who was severely anxious about finding her way to her classrooms at school. The first time through, the child played the little girl so she could identify what questions to ask and what to do; the therapist was the principal standing in the hallway. The second time through, the child played the principal and the therapist was the little girl. The therapist emphasized the anxiety more than the child had during the first role play. This gave the child the chance to help someone else cope with the anxiety, thereby reinforcing her skills and confidence in her ability to cope with anxiety-provoking situations.

Exposure

Exposure is often used in treating anxiety disorders: exposing the subject to the fear-evoking experience, either imaginally or *in vivo* (Hatzenbuehler & Shroeder, 1978; King, Hamilton, & Ollendick, 1988). According to Marks' (1975) description of procedures for treating anxiety, "an important mechanism shared by all of these methods is exposure of the frightened subject to a frightening situation until he acclimatizes." In our terms, exposure is important because it allows the subject to experience anxiety, with cognitive and behavioral coping skills available, until the distress abates.

Three variants of exposure have been described: implosion, flooding, and response prevention. Implosive therapy is an imaginal procedure used to create high levels of anxiety (Stampfl & Levis, 1967). In implosion, the therapist and subject attempt to create feared images that are dramatic and exaggerated. As this imaginal exposure is prolonged, it is expected that extinction of the fear would occur. There is only limited research to support this approach, and its overall effectiveness has been questioned (e.g., Rimm & Masters, 1979)—especially with children.

Flooding, unlike implosion, involves exposing the client to the actual (not imaginal) anxiety-provoking stimuli. Some treatment research has shown that flooding is helpful in the treatment of the more complex anxiety disorders, such as agoraphobia and obsessive-compulsive disorders (Kleinknecht, 1985). Lastly, response prevention, used mainly with obsessive-compulsive disorders, involves the literal prevention of the client from engaging in compulsive rituals while in the presence of the stimuli that are linked to these behaviors. According to Rachman and Hodgson (1980), the anxiety generated from being exposed to the ritual-inducing stimuli subsides as well as the urge to perform the ritual.

Recent clinical research with adult clients by Foa, Steketee, and Grayson (1985) demonstrated the efficacy of both imaginal and *in vivo* exposure. They found that exposure treatment was moderately effective in ameliorating obsessive-compulsive symptoms. Indeed, exposure continues to be viewed as an active ingredient in successful treatments of anxiety disorders (Wilson, 1984; 1990).

Arranging for exposure treatment requires active involvement by the therapist to bring the client into the situation that has been the source of emotional discomfort. The case of a snake phobic being exposed to a snake, though the basic nature of exposure is evident, is not typical. Often, our exposure experiences with children and adolescents are more complicated. For example, a nine-year-old boy who was afraid to interact with adults in public places was unable to order food in a restaurant or go into a drugstore to buy a candy bar. The *in vivo* exposure sessions started with the lowest level anxiety by having the child ask a simple question of an adult in our clinic who was prepared for the interaction. Then the child had to ask an adult in the clinic, who was not expecting to speak with him, for directions to another location in the building. Next, the child had to approach a group of adults and ask one of them to help him find a room. Later, the therapist and child ventured into public settings and went to a bookstore; the therapist accompanied the child while he bought a pencil. This gradual process continued until the child was eventually able to enter the bookstore on his own, ask for directions, check on prices, and make his purchase while the therapist waited outside—out of view.

Detrimental concern about speaking to a group led to the following exposure exercise for a 13-year-old girl with overanxious disorder. In the initial *in vivo* session, the child read a poem to the therapist, and then to a group of adults in our clinic. She then wrote her own speech and presented it to the therapist who listened uncritically the first time through and asked questions about the topic after the second read through. The next step involved presenting the speech to a group of supportive listeners, followed by a presentation to a group who were more critical but asked questions. The final step was to present her speech to a group of her peers. At each step, she and the therapist thought through the experience; she identified her fears, examined her self-talk, developed strategies for coping with those fears, and assessed how effectively she had coped with them.

Effective treatment of anxiety disorders in children and adolescents requires exposure to the once-feared situation. To the extent possible, *in vivo* exposure, where the situation is as real as possible, is preferred. In our treatment program, described in detail in the next chapter, the exposure experiences begin with mildly distressing situations and build to more intense anxiety provocation, but they are not undertaken until the client has first had a chance to better understand the cognitive, behavioral, and physiological signals of anxiety and the several coping skills that can be employed to manage them.

Chapter 5

Integrated Cognitive-Behavioral Treatment Program for Anxiety Disorders

Experience is the child of thought, and thought is the child of action. We cannot learn men from books.

—Benjamin Disraeli

Our treatment program for anxiety disorders combines the treatment components described earlier, including relaxation, cognitive strategies, problem solving, and imaginal and *in vivo* exposure. The overall approach is cognitive-behavioral, integrating the demonstrated effectiveness of the behavioral approaches, with an added emphasis on the cognitive information-processing factors associated with each individual's anxieties. The training program is divided into two segments; the first eight sessions comprise the training segment and the second eight the practice segment. In this latter segment, the children begin to use the skills acquired in the first eight sessions in the specific situations that provoke anxiety for them. A workbook, the *Coping Cat Workbook* (Kendall, 1990), contains exercises coordinated with the cognitive-behavioral treatment program.

A RESTATEMENT OF THE GOALS OF TREATMENT

There are three basic goals of this treatment approach. Children and adolescents with anxiety disorders have a generally cautious and careful style of approaching and thinking about the world. Many of the parents report—especially in cases where their children have an overanxious disorder (OAD) diagnosis—that their children have demonstrated this style

74

since they were very young or for as long as the parents can remember. Many of the children corroborate this description of their behavior. Other parents report a change in behavior following a specific incident in the child's life (e.g., change to junior high school, bad social experience, or divorce), but we see these event-caused disturbances less frequently. Given the more typical long-standing behavior pattern, it is not expected that the child will completely change over the course of treatment. When the child leaves the program free of his former diagnosis, it is a special accomplishment (and it does happen). Often, the child demonstrates meaningful improvement in the *management* of his anxiety—not a cure. We suspect that these children will always be somewhat inhibited and worrying. Nevertheless, our goal is for the child to recognize anxiety, to learn some skills to cope with anxiety, and to reduce the debilitating aspects of the anxiety. Anxiety will be experienced, but it will not be disturbing.

A second goal for treatment is to help the child reduce the level of personal distress. The third primary goal is to improve the child's performance on developmental tasks and to create a sense of mastery of challenging and difficult experiences. These last two goals often go hand in hand, in that reduction of distress often leads to improved performance on challenging tasks. Likewise, improved performance leads to less distress. The specific causal connection is difficult to document.

For example, a 10-year-old boy who completed our treatment was interviewed at one year follow-up. His father was attempting to describe the change he had noted in his child. The evening following the interview, his son was planning to tryout for the all-star soccer team in his community. The father stated that in the past, it would have been difficult for his son to even agree to attend the tryouts for a regular team, let alone an all-star team. The son was nervous about the tryouts but did not hesitate to attend. He did report to his father that he was not sure if he wanted to be on the team if his two friends were not also selected, because then he would not know anybody on the team. However, he decided to tryout anyway and later make a decision about whether he wanted to play on the team. The child still showed some of the concerns that he presented with prior to treatment, but the concerns were no longer so disturbing as to inhibit his involvement or enjoyment of activities.

SESSION DESCRIPTIONS

Throughout our treatment, the various strategies outlined in chapter 4 are employed to introduce the important concepts and skills. The concepts and skills are introduced in a sequential order from the most basic to the more difficult. The therapist functions as a coping model as new skills are introduced and demonstrates the skill in each new situation.

Within each session and throughout the training program, the level of anxiety is gradually increased, beginning with nonstressful situations and gradually incorporating higher levels of anxiety. "Show That I Can" (STIC) tasks are assigned as tasks to be completed outside the therapy session to help reinforce what has been addressed during the session.

The First Eight Sessions

Training sessions 1 through 8 focus on four basic skill areas: (a) an awareness of bodily reactions to feelings and those physical symptoms specific to anxiety, (b) recognition and evaluation of "self talk," or what a child thinks to himself when he is anxious, (c) problem-solving skills, including modifying anxious self-talk and developing plans for coping, and (d) self-evaluation and reward.

Session 1. The first session is primarily dedicated to building rapport and making the child feel comfortable with the therapist. It is important that the therapist acknowledge, listen to, and respond to the child's concerns. One of the overarching goals of treatment is to help make the child into a reporter of and expert on his own experience, so that she can take steps to begin taking charge and coping with her anxiety. It is especially important to proceed slowly with anxious children because the therapy situation alone is one that provokes anxiety, and the therapist often becomes another person that the child feels she has to please. Feeling that they are in charge of at least some aspects of the therapy seems to help anxious children gain a sense of control and can help to relieve, to some extent, anxieties about being in therapy. We encourage the development of a therapeutic relationship.

Planning an enjoyable activity to do together during the first session has positive effects. Many anxious children are very serious and can be reluctant to engage in playful activities. A light-hearted interaction style is part of developing rapport, and for many children, it continues to be an important part of the treatment process. The therapist can underscore the plan of making the sessions not only a place where the child can learn new skills, but also a place for therapist and child to have fun together.

Occasionally, an anxious child readily admits that he is overwhelmed by worry and eagerly accepts the offer of help from the therapist. More often, we find that it takes a number of sessions before the children begin to trust and to discuss their problems with the therapist. Other times, children, and often adolescents, are angry and deny anxiety. We continue to marvel at the difference between the children's report of their anxiety in the initial interview with our project diagnostician—where they tend to report a good deal of distress—and their denial of any problems in the first session with the therapist. Some children, especially teenagers, feel that they are "forced" to be in treatment by their parents; so, they deny any difficulty and say that they see no reason for treatment, or—if they acknowledge that there are problems—they claim they do not want help. When extreme resistance or anger is noted, the child can be given several days to think about being part of treatment and to talk it over with his parents and/or the therapist.

As suggested in our treatment manual (Kendall, Kane, Howard, & Siqueland, 1989), the therapist and child talk during Session 1 about the reasons for the initial referral. The therapist's position is that she does not want to force the child to change or insist on participation if there are no problems. Instead, the therapist offers herself as someone who might be able to help the child with some things that don't seem to go as well as the child would like. The following is a transcript of the first few minutes of the first session with a child who was somewhat resistant to treatment.

Therapist: So now that I've heard your Dad's side of this whole thing, what are your goals? What do you want to be? No, that's not the right question. What can I do for you? What can I help you with?

Client: Well I didn't want to come here in the first place.

Therapist: You don't want to be here?

Client: No.

Therapist: Nothing? Just stay out of your way.

Client: I told my dad, I told him it's, I mean, I don't think anybody can change me. I mean you could get the best watchamacallit in the world to come and try and help me, but that's not going to help.

Therapist: Yea.

Client: And the only person that can help me is myself.

Therapist: Oh really.

Client: But I'm not exactly up on this.

Therapist: What did you say?

Client: I'm not exactly up on this stuff.

Therapist: So you're not convinced that this is really going to do much for you. Well, I understand that. That makes sense. What are the things that you can help yourself with.

Client: My attitude.

Therapist: Your attitude. What's wrong with your attitude?

Client: I just don't like, I might, well I mean, nothing is going really wrong.

Therapist: Right.

Client: Cause sometimes I just don't feel like doing something.

Therapist: Right.

Client: I mean, everything's really fine at school and everything, but, I don't know why I'm here.

Therapist: You're not sure why you're here, but it seems maybe kind of scary to be here?

Client: No, not scary. It's just that I don't see the point for me being here.

Therapist: Yea.

Later . . .

Client: I don't care what you say about me. I mean I don't care if you make me stay here for five years, but it's not going to start to change my perspective on things.

Therapist: Mm mm. Yea.

Client: Sorry to be rough on you, but I don't think that this is going to help me.

Therapist: Mm mm. Yea. Well, I can see why, I mean it makes sense that you would wonder. You don't know me.

Client: I don't care if I know somebody like my mom or something, it doesn't make an effect on me whether I know them or not.

Therapist: Yea. Mm mm. Well, other than your attitude, are there things that trouble you? Are there times in your life where you feel like things aren't going the way you want them to go?

Client: Sometimes.

Therapist: What kinds of times?

Client: I don't know, just any old time it could happen to me.

Therapist: Yea.

Client: I mean it could happen to me when I get home from school. Or if I'm eating dinner. Late at night or on the weekend. All kinds of different times.

Therapist: Yea.

Client: Not constantly, not rarely, any time.

Therapist: Now what happens when it happens?

Client: I just get frustrated.

Therapist: Yea.

Client: I just do anything to feel better, I mean, I might wreck my room or might you know go through my closet. I might go to sleep. Anything.

The therapist's collaborative, nonconfrontative posture in the initial sessions helps the child to adapt to the therapeutic situation. Acceptance breeds cooperation.

The first STIC task introduces the child to the idea of using a diary format by asking her to write down an example of a time during the week when she was feeling good. The child is asked to describe what she was doing and how she knew that she was feeling good. The idea of reinforcement is also introduced with the STIC task: a reward for completing a specified number of STIC tasks (usually four) is discussed with the child. The child and therapist work together to develop a reward menu consisting of both material and social rewards, and the therapist draws from this menu as the child earns rewards.

Compliance with STIC tasks is encouraged by the reward system. Children receive two points or stickers for successful completion of each task. When the child accumulates eight points or stickers, he or she receives a small reward, such as markers or a book, following both the 4th and 8th session. The timing of rewards is negotiable; teenagers sometimes want to work for a somewhat larger reward at a later session. There are also rewards following the 12th and 16th sessions, but these rewards are more social than material, involving extra fun time with the therapist. Anxious children are often unable to think of their own rewards. Therapists have to remember to be uncritical and to provide rewards for less than perfect performance.

Sessions 2 and 3. The goal of the second and the third sessions is to introduce the concept of physical reactions to feelings and help the child identify his own anxiety-specific physical symptoms. The therapist and child begin by discussing how different facial expressions and postures are related to different feelings. All concepts are first introduced in the abstract or by referring to other people, rather than focusing on the child's own experience. The child is shown pictures or drawings from magazines, books, or educational materials and is asked to identify emotions associated with different facial expressions and body postures. The therapist then moves on to discussing how the child knows what different friends or family members are feeling, based on their facial expressions and body postures. In this way, the therapist can begin with people who are familiar to the child without having to focus immediately on the child's own specific concerns.

The concept of role playing is introduced at this point, and the therapist and child role play various emotions and their expression. The child is then invited to participate with the therapist in role plays, using a tag-along procedure described by Ollendick (1983). The therapist role plays a situation, with the child following along with him. The therapist describes what he is feeling or thinking and asks the child if she is experiencing the same thing or something different. Finally, the child is encouraged to role play scenes alone, practicing the newly acquired skills by herself. All or some of these variations in role plays are used, depending on the child's skill level and understanding of the concept being introduced.

Sometimes with very anxious children, the therapist may notice a great deal of distress in the child even when the therapist is only role playing her own experience with anxiety (often seen in our children with concerns about separation). These children tend to have difficulty differentiating their own emotional experience from the experiences of others around them, especially their parents. In these cases, the therapist proceeds more slowly toward independent role plays, until the child begins to develop the skill of noting and describing her own emotional experience. For this type of child, the tag-along procedure may be especially effective in beginning to make these discriminations. With adolescents, the tag-along procedure may not be necessary.

In Session 3, the child is asked about his own physical reactions to emotions. While children often recognize the particular physical symptoms they experience, they do not make the association that these symptoms are likely related to increasing levels of anxiety. Often anxious children appear to have difficulty distinguishing between different feelings, especially fear, sadness, and anger. Younger children often have difficulty distinguishing between sadness and fear. Still other children report becoming very sad about being unable to cope with their anxiety and occasionally cry in anxiety-provoking situations. The following is a transcript from part of a session with a 12-year-old, overanxious boy.

Therapist: You said you sometimes get confused about when you're sad and when you're angry. How do you carry yourself when you're angry or what is your body like?

Client: I get agitated, but the sadness and anger go hand in hand.

Therapist: Does one come first?

Client: The sadness I guess.

Therapist: Do you get mad about being sad.

Client: Sort of. Well when things haven't been going my way, sometimes the anger. Sometimes when I'm so angry, I start crying, like if things have been going badly all day.

Therapist: Can you tell when you're in the sad part or the angry part from the way your body feels?

Client: Not really, but when I'm sad I just sit around and listen and when I'm angry I start moving around.

Therapist: So when you're angry you're active and when you're sad you're kind of passive. Does your body get tense when you're angry?

Client: Sometimes I get tense and sometimes I get a headache.

After having ascertained what somatic responses the child recognizes and what feelings he or she associates these responses with, the therapist can then model recognition of anxious symptoms. In the present case, the therapist began by disclosing her own bodily reactions to anxiety and then asked the child about his experiences and sensations.

Therapist: How about when you get nervous or worried? When I have to give a talk and I get nervous, my face gets really red and hot, I talk really fast, I start to get sweaty, and my heart starts pounding. Sometimes my stomach starts to hurt and makes noises.

Client: Yeah, my hands start sweating sometimes, I start sweating all over sometimes, and sometimes a lump gets in my throat like THUMP, right there.

Therapist: You mean you can't swallow. I get that sometimes. So you get sweaty, and you get a lump in your throat. Does your heart start pounding?

Client: Sometimes, and I get a queasy stomach. If I get really nervous, sometimes I feel like I get dizzy.

Therapist: Any other things you can think of?

Client: My voice starts quavering or cracks.

Therapist: Mine does too, it gets weak sometimes. So those are all signs for you that you are nervous or worried. Once you know what those signs are, you can begin to figure out what to do about them.

This child was bright, articulate, and able to label his own reactions, but younger or lower-functioning children may have more difficulty with this skill. The therapist can make up stories about an imaginary group of kids or a basketball team in a stressful situation and have the child (with the therapist's help) talk about various physical symptoms the imaginary characters could be experiencing. The therapist can then ask if these reactions are similar to the child's experience. Here's an example of an 11-year-old boy who has more trouble describing his experience.

Therapist: Well, what about how you feel?

Client: I try to just block it out.

Therapist: Do your hands get shaky then?

Client: Sometimes they are.

Therapist: How about if you have to go up and talk in front of a bunch of people?

Client: That gets me worried.

Therapist: Really. What happens then?

Client: Well, I had to do that this morning.

Therapist: You did? What happened?

Client: We had to give a presentation.

Therapist: What was the presentation on?

Client: I think it was like a talk show, and it was good because all I had to do was read from my paper.

Therapist: But you did have to talk in front of people.

Client: Yea.

Therapist: Were you sort of worried about doing that?

Client: I was kind of shaky.

Therapist: Were your hands shaky or did your legs feel shaky?

Client: Not really.

The STIC tasks for Sessions 2 and 3 focus on writing down a pleasant and an anxious experience, as well as paying particular attention to physical symptoms. As treatment progresses, the children generally become more and more successful at completing the homework tasks. The information the STIC tasks can provide for the therapist is valuable to therapy progress. The therapist can often expand on what the child has written, because these are actual examples of experiences that are specific to the child and may bring up concerns that may not arise during the session. The beginning task for each session is to review the week's STIC task. The therapist can often spend up to 15 minutes going over the task to review past concepts and introduce the concepts to be presented in the current session. If the child has not complied with the STIC task, the child is often asked to do the task during the session, to think back over the week and talk about anxiety-provoking experiences with the therapist's probing.

Session 4. Once the children have begun to identify their own physical symptoms of anxiety, they are taught in Session 4 to use these physical reactions as cues to begin relaxation. The children are taught both a deep-breathing exercise and a modified progressive muscle-relaxation technique. The therapist focuses on the three to four muscle groups identified as causing the most problems for that particular child. The therapist can gently point out muscle tightness she noticed in sessions of which the child was not aware.

Only a very few anxious children are uncomfortable or have difficulty with the relaxation procedure; most children report that it is quite helpful, especially the deep-breathing exercises. Some of the adolescents, however, become nervous when the therapist is beginning the relaxation procedure. The therapist acknowledges the discomfort, labels it for the adolescent, and assures the client that it might seem strange at first but that relaxation will get easier with practice. The following is a transcript of an adolescent who initially experienced embarrassment and discomfort when relaxation training was introduced.

Therapist: I'm going to do this [relaxation] with you. We find that if kids work on relaxation and practice it, they can use it in different situations. It often makes things better. Okay, push that chair all the way back. The first and most important thing is to find a comfortable and quiet place to relax. I'm going to do this at the same time, because I like this and it makes me feel relaxed. Find a place where you can be alone and nobody will bother you like away from your brother. Usually you close your eyes and you can do that if you feel comfortable. For now, you need to keep them open so you can see what I'm doing. Usually you begin with deep breaths, really filling up your abdomen. When your band teacher told you to take deep breaths [prior to a recital], did he suggest anything else?

Client: No, he just said take a few deep breaths and you are going to be fine.

Therapist: So let's start with that. Breathe in and breathe out. Breathe in and breathe out, repeat.

Client: (starts to laugh uncomfortably) I was just thinking what if you fall asleep on me.

Therapist: (laughing) I usually don't get *that* relaxed. You just kick me if I fall asleep. Does this seem kind of strange or corny?

Client: Yeah.

Therapist: It probably will feel like that at first. It will seem easier after we go through it. When we talked about this before, you said when you get nervous you get sweaty and your heart starts to beat faster. Is there a particular part of your body that hurts or gets tense that lets you know you are nervous?

Client: My knees, there is something with my knees. They start bobbing up and down. It's really weird. I don't think many other people have this.

We tend to use a regular reclining chair for adolescents and a beanbag chair with younger children. When possible, we also use a dimmer switch to turn down the lights. The children may or may not want to close their eyes with the therapist there. If the child is comfortable enough with the therapist, the therapist can approach the child and feel her muscles to help demonstrate the difference between tight and relaxed. This interaction can be helpful in explaining the goal of relaxation; but a few children may feel uneasy, so the therapist should use her knowledge about the relationship with the child before proceeding.

The therapist then models and discusses with the child times when using relaxation will be helpful. Sometimes the relaxation is introduced, but the child does not use it. To overcome this, the therapist can suggest that one can always take a few deep breaths and relax some muscles in any academic or social situation without appearing very conspicuous to others or "looking weird," as the anxious child might fear. It is important to differentiate for the child between the relaxation-training exercise itself and the goal of the exercise. The exercise is used to teach the child how relaxed muscles feel as compared to tense muscles. The child is encouraged to practice, so eventually she is able to make her muscles feel relaxed without using the actual exercise. Once she can achieve relaxation without first tensing, she will be able to relax inconspicuously in any environment.

The therapist models relaxation for the child and encourages him to give it a try. For the younger child, a script that puts the exercises in a story-like scenario (for example, Koeppen, 1974) encourages participation. For the older child, a script by Ollendick and Cerny (1981) is recommended (see Appendix).

An audiotape of the therapist going through the relaxation procedure is given to the child to allow him to practice at home. In addition, the child can demonstrate the procedure for his parents who might like to try it and/or help the child find a time and a place to practice at home. Introducing and explaining the relaxation procedure to the parents of the younger child will help the child remember the steps and remember to practice. The adolescents may prefer that the therapist not discuss this with his parents and feel more comfortable about practicing the relaxation alone, without parental involvement. The STIC task for this session is to practice relaxation daily and to note any positive experiences or difficulties encountered with the relaxation procedure.

Session 5. During the fifth session, the second key concept of the program is introduced: self-talk—what children say to themselves when they are anxious. Self-talk includes the child's expectations and attributions about herself, others, and situations. The child may experience these cognitions as actual internal dialogue, but she may also have the experience of images or pictures of expected events without any accompanying dialogue. For the anxious child, these expectations and attributions seem to focus around catastrophic appraisals of future events, negative self-evaluation, perfectionistic standards for performance, heightened self-focused attention or concern about what others are thinking about her, concerns about failure or not coping adequately, and sometimes accompanying feelings of worthlessness. The following is a transcript of a 12-year-old overanxious child talking about his thoughts before a music recital.

Therapist: What were you thinking to yourself before the concert?
Client: I was thinking I was going to make a mistake. If you make a mistake, it sticks with you and you feel stupid.
Therapist: Why does making a mistake make you feel stupid?
Client: Because you could have prevented it. You have a feeling of failure. I hate failure.
Therapist: What if you make mistakes sometimes like everybody else?
Client: That's the whole point, you are not like everybody else.
Therapist: Why can't you be like everybody else?
Client: Some people have more expected of them than others.
Therapist: Why do you have more expected of you?
Client: Because I'm supposed to be smart.
Therapist: So if you are smart, you are not allowed to make mistakes.
Client: No, and you drive yourself nuts, thinking of ways you could have done it better and you didn't do it, you drive yourself crazy and it's not easy.

Children are often not aware that they might be thinking things to themselves when they are nervous, and when first introduced it can be a difficult concept for younger children to understand. The concept can be introduced through the use of cartoons with empty thought bubbles. The therapist asks the child to generate various alternatives of what the character might be thinking in the depicted situation (see Figure 3.1). The child's responses to these cartoons inform the therapist about the child's thought processes and the rigidity or flexibility of the child's thinking. For example, a 13-year-old female with strong obsessive-compulsive tendencies saw a picture of a boy mowing a lawn with an empty thought bubble and suggested that the boy was thinking, "Did I go straight? I wonder if I missed a part back there."

Often when the children do provide the therapist with illustrations of their anxiety-provoking cognitions, they will nevertheless have difficulty recognizing that someone could think differently in that kind of situation. If the child can generate alternative ways to view the situation, we consider it a sign of likely treatment success. The therapist helps the child by modeling various coping statements that a child could use in an anxiety-provoking situation. Some children will reply that simple statements, such as "I'll do the best I can," have been tried and were not so helpful. Do not be quick to accept this out of hand! Instead, question the child further about his thoughts, and trace the ideas back to address the child's more fundamental world view. As is often the case with anxious people, a simple mistake can lead to thoughts and feelings of stupidity or craziness or rejection, and this self-talk needs to be identified and changed.

The therapist also checks with the child about whether he believes what he is saying, because the child may be able to think of alternatives but not see or feel that they are valid. The anxious child will typically need to be encouraged to generate thoughts that are nondistressing and relevant to the particular situation, and will need assistance in seeing their true merits.

At first, the cartoons (with blank thought bubbles) can portray fairly simple, nonthreatening scenes in which the character's thoughts are likely to be fairly obvious. The therapist then introduces situations that are more ambiguous or could provoke anxiety. The therapist helps the child generate various thoughts for the character, both thoughts that might provoke anxiety as well as ones that would help the person feel less anxious. The exercise illustrates to the child that the way he or she thinks about things also affects what the child might feel or do in that situation. The following are a nine-year-old's responses to a variety of cartoons depicting possible anxiety-producing situations.

Cartoon 1:   One boy sitting down playing trumpet and looking at another
      kid on stage playing trumpet.
Therapist: What could be in that boy's thought bubble?
Client: "I'll never play as good as him."
Therapist: And how would that boy feel if he were thinking that?
Client: Nervous and bad.
Therapist: What's another possibility of what he could be thinking?
Client: "I think I play good."
Therapist: That's a good one. Or he could think, that other boy has
      been playing a long time, maybe I can play like that if I keep on
      trying.
Cartoon 2:   Kid sitting in classroom with teacher at blackboard which
      reads "Math Test Tomorrow."
Therapist: What could he be thinking? What's in his thought bubble?
Client: "I'll never pass that math test."
Therapist: What's another kind of thought?
Client: "I could probably do it—I have tonight to study."
Therapist: What will happen if he's thinking, "I'll never pass," when
      he goes to study. Would he be able to study?
Client: He'd probably be all worried.
Therapist: What if he thought, "I'll do okay, I have tonight to study?"
Client: He'd probably start to study.
Therapist: Would he be able to ask for help if he needed to?
Client: I think so.

As in most of the sessions, the therapist moves on to the modeling, tag-a-long and role-play sequence with the child to introduce various situations and alternative thoughts for these situations. The therapist notices any distortions in thinking and considers with the child the likelihood that what the child is fearing will happen. The therapist has the child begin to ask: How likely is it that that will happen? Has that happened before? What if what I fear really happens? Finally, the therapist helps the child begin replacing fear-related thoughts with coping thoughts. The STIC task for this session asks the child to record two times during the week that she felt anxious, paying particular attention to her thoughts in these situations.

Session 6. The third concept or skill is problem solving, introduced during Session 6. The session begins with a more extensive review of the previous week's STIC task. On a blackboard or write-on, wipe-off board, the therapist uses a modified "triple-column" assessment by labeling three columns as "Situation," "Feelings," and "Thoughts." The incident described in the child's STIC task is then written in the situation column, the somatic symptoms under the feelings heading, and the self-talk under the thoughts heading. An example of the triple column is provided in Table 5.1 and is derived from the following discussion of a child's STIC task.

Client: My anxious experience (referring to the STIC task) was when I had to do an oral report. I was so nervous. My palms were sweating, and I was very shaky. My friends were nervous, but when I told them I was nervous they just started to laugh. Now I don't get it why they laughed at me. They just laughed, you know? They said, "You know Lynne, I'm really nervous about this." "Yeah, me too," and they laughed. I don't understand why.

Therapist: What were you thinking about? What was your thought about what . . .

Client: I was thinking, "Why are they laughing? What's so funny about me being nervous? I didn't laugh about them."

Therapist: Did you think that they were being mean?

Client: Yeah I did.

Therapist: That they don't like you? Do you know what else you were thinking?

Client: I was thinking that they were being mean because they were just like laughing at me, I thought they were laughing at me because they (imitating laugh). I thought why? You know. Why were they laughing at me.

Therapist: Let's take the last thing that you said and just try to think this through.

Client: OK.

Therapist: Now you're in a situation such as giving an oral report.

Client: Mm mm.

Therapist: And the feelings you had were that your palms were sweating and that you were shaking. You were shaking right?

Client: Mm mm.

Therapist: OK. Now, when I was saying, what were the thoughts that were happening? You were giving an oral report and your friends were laughing. That was the situation. Your friends were laughing, but you said they were nervous too.

Client: Mm mm.

Therapist: Now, if that were to happen, let's sort of role play this together. So, how many friends were there?

Client: Um, there was two or three I think.

Therapist: So, let's play it out. I'll be three people.

Client: OK.

Therapist: And you be you. So you're the director too because you know what happened. Let's play it out. What happened?

Client: Well, first you were nervous and you were telling me all about it every single time. Lunch time, play time, and um, right before the report. And um, I said, "Well I'm really nervous too." They laughed and giggled.

Therapist: All three people did?

Client: Yeah.

Therapist: Or just one?

Client: First Debbie did and then I told, um, Christina and she didn't laugh, but then she was going to laugh at me because Debbie was laughing at me. I didn't know why she was laughing at me.

Therapist: So, let's just act this out. I'll be Debbie and you be you. OK? So first I told you . . .

Client: Mm mm.

Therapist: "Lynn, I'm nervous about having to give this oral report today."

Client: "Yeah, me too."

Therapist: "Really? Wow!" (Out of role) Was it like that?

Client: Mm mm. And then she started laughing.

Therapist: And how did she laugh?

Client: She like snickered, you know what I mean.

Therapist: Like this? (imitating a laugh)

Client: Yeah.

Therapist: You know we may never figure out exactly why she was laughing. She could have been embarrassed and when you told her you were nervous, maybe she gave a nervous laugh. Maybe she was thinking Lynn always does so well and even she is nervous or something like that. But let's get at what you were thinking when she was laughing. If that were me what I might be thinking is, "I thought she was my friend. She must not like me or think I'm really silly." What were you thinking to yourself?

Client: I thought that she was my friend, but then I thought maybe she is not a true friend to me.

Therapist: That's what we were talking about. If you see somebody laughing at you, a negative thought in your thought bubble might be "She must not like me." What could be a positive thought? What can you do if you think somebody is laughing at you because they don't like you? What could be another way to think about it?

Client: Maybe she is just laughing because she is surprised.

Therapist: Good, yeah. Or she could have been thinking about something else that was funny. Or she caught someone's eye across the room, and she was laughing because they were laughing. Could it be something like that? So, there are different ways you can look at it.

The therapist and child begin to problem solve by generating various alternative solutions to cope with the difficult situation. Many times the anxious child's only coping response is to withdraw from the provocative situation, and he does not believe there is anything he can do to make the situation less frightening. It seems as if anxious children are unable to use whatever problem-solving skills they may have once they enter a stressful situation. Using problem solving in frightening situations is introduced by first talking about nonthreatening situations. For example, the therapist might begin by saying: "You've lost your shoes in the house. What are some ways you could go about trying to find them?" The therapist provides other examples and situations, helping to generate alternatives, evaluate the possibilities, and make a decision about what is the preferred solution. After experience with the problem-solving step, a fourth column labeled "Attitudes and Actions" is added. The child indicates what actions would be useful in that situation.

At this point in the program, the strategies that have been introduced in earlier sessions are presented as steps in the problem-solving process (both relaxation and changing anxiety-producing thoughts into coping thoughts). When in an anxiety-provoking context, the child can take some deep breaths to calm himself down and can begin to relax those parts of his body that might become tense. The child is reminded to recognize his thoughts by asking what he is expecting to happen or what he fears will happen.

Other coping strategies are more specific to individual problems. Often possible solutions take the form of enlisting friends or family members for

Table 5.1. *An Example of a Child's Entries into the "Triple-Column" Procedure*

Situation	Feelings	Thoughts	Actions
Example 1 (from transcript)			
Before giving an oral report when I said I was nervous my friends laughed.	nervous palms sweating shaking	"Why are they laughing at me?" "Why are they being mean?" "Don't they like me?"	Think maybe my friend was embarrassed too so she laughed. Think maybe she is laughing because she's surprised. Think maybe she thought of something funny or she caught someone's eye across the room.
Example 2			
A kid comes over to say "Hi" . . . a kid I don't know.	upset stomachache heart pounding sweating	"I don't know what to say." "I look dumb." "He's not going to like me." "If I say something stupid, he'll never talk to me again."	Let him talk first and I can just listen. Take some deep breaths and relax. Think how do I know he won't like me, I've never met him. Think nobody says the perfect thing every time. I'll ask him what he did this weekend.

support or advice; thinking about or watching how others cope with situations; or rehearsing and practicing various skills in academic, performance, or social situations. In addition to challenging the assumptions and expectations that something horrible is going to happen, it is also helpful to discuss with the child what might be done if his worst possible fear came true. For example, "Yes people might not laugh if you drop your tray in the lunchroom, but then again they might laugh, and everyone has to learn to cope with some very embarrassing situations." Encourage the child to remember similar experiences peers may have had and to learn how to begin to walk away and to laugh along with others when in embarrassing situations.

The child generates and evaluates the different possibilities on her own to decide which solution feels best for her. Older and/or brighter children can readily engage in this task, whereas younger or lower-functioning children may have to be taught this skill by example from specific situations.

Especially with younger children and sometimes with adolescents, it is helpful to have the client choose a cartoon character or hero whom they admire or feel can cope with difficult situations. The therapist encourages the child to think about how that character might handle anxiety-provoking situations. As a problem-solving strategy the child can pretend to be that character or take that character along with him into scary situations for support or a little extra help. Recall the 10-year-old boy who was afraid to walk home from school for 9 months following a confrontation with an older child who pushed him off his bike; he used this as one of his major coping strategies. He decided that he could take deep breaths when he was walking, think "nothing will happen to me" or "I can handle this," or go into a store or to someone's doorstep if he was afraid. His hero was X-man, who came with him on the walk, and/or he imagined X-man walking behind him if he needed assistance.

Older children and adolescents can also identify imaginary or real people whom they admire as good copers and can use them as models. At times, if the client cannot generate coping thoughts or is unwilling to consider other possibilities for himself, he can think about how the hero might think differently. Recall the illustrative transcript provided in chapter 4 (see p. 65–66).

The STIC task for this session involves writing down two anxious experiences using the triple-column procedure. Following this session, the therapist begins developing a hierarchy of anxiety-provoking situations to be used in upcoming sessions.

Session 7. The fourth concept concerns self-evaluation and reward. Anxious children often have difficulty evaluating themselves fairly, tending instead to set extremely high standards for success and being satisfied with nothing less than perfection. However, it is not clear that these children are aware of this process. The therapist introduces the possibility of evaluating situations based on "partial success," and helps the child think about things she liked about the way she handled the situation and what she might like to do differently next time. The key concept here is for the child to see that how people evaluate their performance has a direct impact on how they feel afterward. A positive self-evaluation, or even a partial positive evaluation, leaves one feeling competent and willing to tackle the next situation.

Rewards are effective: they build self-confidence. Anxious children need to reward themselves for accomplishments that they are proud of—including partial success. This idea can be foreign to an anxious child, as is evident in the following transcript (12-year-old, male).

Therapist: How about, in situations for you, when you do something wrong. Will it go away? Know what I mean? What happens to you after that when you do something . . .
Client: Partly wrong.
Therapist: Yeah. Are you gonna figure out which things you liked about how you did?
Client: Well, if I like something, I like it, if I don't, I don't. It's either, it's, it's total success or total failure.
Therapist: Oh is it?
Client: Because, um, what would it be if it wasn't?
Therapist: Partial success.
Client: That's disgusting.
Therapist: Yeah, why is that?
Client: Partial success. (sarcastically) You don't have very high standards do you young lady?
Therapist: I have uh, what I would call realistic standards for ordinary people.
Client: Are you saying that I'm unrealistic? Is that what you're saying?
Therapist: I think at times you can be about yourself. Wouldn't you say that?
Client: OK, at times.
Therapist: OK, you're giving it to me at times.
Client: I'll give, I'll give you that.

The therapist can help the child generate a list of possible self-rewards such as: spending more time in an activity the child likes (e.g., riding bikes or reading), giving yourself a pat on the back, telling yourself that you've done a good job, and spending time with family and friends. We find that anxious children rarely reward themselves for their accomplishments and rely on outside sources for this sense of achievement. It is important for the therapist to encourage and remind the child to reward himself. The therapist models this by allowing the child to pick a favorite activity for both child and therapist to do together following the session, when the child has met some predetermined, realistic goal. Allow time for these rewards, and follow through on plans to reward.

Session 8. The four steps taught in the earlier sessions are put together in the eighth session with the introduction of the acronym FEAR. Each letter begins a phrase that refers to one of the basic elements of the program:

F—Feeling frightened? (Recognizing physical symptoms of anxiety.)

E—Expecting bad things to happen? (Recognizing self-talk and what you are worried about happening.)

A—Actions and attitudes that will help. (Different behaviors and coping statements the child can use in the anxiety-provoking situation based on problem-solving.) For younger children "actions and ideas" can be substituted.

R—Results and rewards. (Self-evaluation and self-reward.)

The children can be encouraged to use this acronym to help them remember the steps. We also encourage children to generate their own acronym or method to remember them. One lower-functioning 12-year-old used the letters from his nickname to remember his more simplified version of the steps:

J—Be *joyful.*

A—Don't get *all excited*—use deep breaths to calm down when you notice physical symptoms, and stop to think of a plan.

Y—Say *Yes,* you can do it. Have confidence in yourself.

The following is a transcript of a 13-year-old male describing how, with the help of the "Fear Force," he used the four steps he learned to approach and talk with a girl he liked.

Therapist: So James, how did you get through the situation of talking to that girl?

Client: By using the Fear Force.

Therapist: Terrific, how did the Fear Force help?

Client: Well, Captain Nervous and Lieutenant Expect let me know I was anxious and expecting her to make a fool of me. So Attitude von Action came in to help me calm down by telling me to take a deep breath and to think before I speak. Even though I was nervous, it went okay and Sergeant Result and Rewards then said I should reward myself with some time listening to the radio.

Therapist: So the Fear Force helps you remember the plan for dealing with anxiety?

Client: Yeah, the Fear Force is just really my common sense which helps me get through times when I get nervous. I realize I can rely on what I think about the situation instead of what I should do all the time.

Therapist: Well, your common sense sounds pretty on the ball.

Client: Yeah, I think so.

During the session, the child makes a wallet-size card of the steps that he can take along and use in anxiety-provoking situations. Each child is encouraged to explain the four-step coping plan to his or her parents. This serves two purposes; it helps the children better comprehend and rehearse the coping plan, and it provides the parents with some understanding of the plan the children are using. With younger clients, we often ask the child to explain the steps to the parent in front of the therapist, so that the therapist can assist or answer questions. With adolescents, we suggest they talk to their parents about the steps, but allow the adolescent to discuss it independently unless he or she wants the therapist there.

The Second Eight Sessions: Sessions 9 to 16

The second half of our program employs imaginal and *in vivo* exposure to anxiety-provoking situations. The child begins to practice the skills learned earlier, but now he or she is in the actual stressful situations. These practice sessions begin with imaginal exposure to anxiety-provoking situations. For many children, imaginal exposure has less impact on anxiety than actual *in vivo* experiences. However, it does help the child begin to think through various coping strategies that might be used in these situations. The therapist begins with imaginal exposure and continues until the child's level of anxiety is reduced and the child is able to demonstrate use of the coping plan. At this point, the therapist and child move on to *in vivo* situations. The *in vivos* begin with the low anxiety-producing situations and gradually progress to the higher anxiety-producing situations.

In general, there are several features of the exposure experiences. The therapist presents the situation to be encountered, asks the child about aspects of the situation that are likely to be troubling, and asks the child to rate the level of anxiety using a 1 to 10 rating scale. The therapist models using the different coping approaches. The child is assisted in thinking through the coping steps and practicing use of the steps until calmer and ready to face stressful situations. Following the exposure, the therapist and child evaluate performance and think of an appropriate reward.

Many of our overanxious children have extreme difficulty with academic evaluation. The following is an example of a hierarchy devised for an academic evaluation *in vivo* experience. This particular child had a learning difficulty that had an impact on his performance of both perceptual and timed tasks. In this instance, the child had to cope with a "real" concern and difficulty, in contrast to learning to correct distortions in more "unrealistic" fears. The child had to accept the fact that this type of task is more difficult for him than for other children, but that he is likely to be asked to take timed tests in school. First, the child brought his math homework to session for the therapist to see the kind of math he was doing. The therapist and child informally worked on the math together, with the therapist paying attention to the child's anxiety around this task. The therapist then set up a more formal testing situation, focusing on the child's verbal abilities. Next, the therapist can move to a task that will be timed without telling the child to work quickly or otherwise emphasizing this fact. The therapist can heighten anxiety by talking about the timing of the task and how important it is to work quickly. Finally, the therapist and child devised various strategies to deal with this difficulty in school, such as alerting the teacher if he was struggling with an assignment.

Various *in vivo* experiences can be arranged in the office: setting up testing situations, having the child give a speech or read a poem in front of a small audience, using a video camera to tape the child, and/or having the child introduce themselves to other office personnel. Initial exposure experiences can be very simple, such as asking the child to draw something for the therapist. The simplest "task" can trigger some of the child's basic maladaptive assumptions—assumptions that will reappear in the more difficult situations. Two different sample transcripts illustrate this point.

Therapist: I want you to draw something for me.
Client: What should I draw? A butterfly? Or a cat?
Therapist: Well, which are you worse at drawing?
Client: The cat.
Therapist: How about a butterfly?
Client: Yeah.
Therapist: So butterfly, flower, dog, and person. You can draw any of those, but you also have to draw a cat. OK?
Client: Uh huh.
Therapist: OK. Now, get a piece of paper. Actually, why don't you put it on the blackboard. Now, one thing that I want you to do is if you start feeling just a little bit anxious drawing while I'm watching you, let me know. Oh, one thing I forgot to mention. You have to draw the cat with your eyes closed.
Client: I do? Seriously?
Therapist: Seriously.
Client: OK. Whoops.
Therapist: What can you say to yourself if it doesn't turn out how you want? It can't be perfect, but can you tell yourself something else?
Client: But I wonder what you'll think.
Therapist: Is it really that important?
Client: I don't know.
Therapist: Does it really matter what I think?
Client: I don't know.
Therapist: OK, well you might ask yourself that.

The following transcript involved a child 12 years of age with an overanxious disorder.

Therapist: What I'd really like to talk about now is what I'm going to ask you to do today. I know that actually getting out and doing things is the hard part. You still feeling like that's something you don't want to do?

Client: I don't know. It depends on what it is.

Therapist: OK, that's a good answer. You're good in your answers. Well, do you remember the, um, person that when you first came here, her name was Marti?

Client: Mm mm.

Therapist: Marti works with kids too, and she thinks it would be really helpful if she could learn something about the flight simulator that we've used. I told her, hope you don't mind, I thought you were pretty good at it. And she was wondering if you might be able to teach her something about it.

Client: OK.

Therapist: How does that sound?

Client: Like when?

Therapist: Today?

Client: Mm, I really don't know like a lot about it.

Therapist: OK.

Client: I'm mostly just like guessing.

Therapist: OK.

Client: I think I should read the book or something like that.

Therapist: OK. So it sounds like what you're saying to yourself is "I have to know a whole lot about this."

Client: Kind of, well yeah, I guess I am.

Therapist: OK. Let's say you don't have time to look at the book today.

Client: I'd just show her what I know.

Therapist: Very good. Just show her what you know. Well, what would that be?

Client: Uh, how to take off.

Therapist: Mm mm.

Client: How to take the flaps down.

Therapist: Uh huh.

Client: Mm, how to steer, how to show you different moves and how to change like the planet you're flying, like where you are.

Therapist: You know a lot. OK. That's a whole lot of stuff to show her. Do you even think you want to show her all that or . . .

Client: Probably I wouldn't.

Therapist: So, the thought that might be making things a bit worse was, "I'm going to have to show her a whole bunch, and I don't know everything about this." What you can do to cope with that thought is, "I'll just show her what I know." I'm just repeating back what you said to me. Would that help out or do you have it in your mind?

Client: Kind of have, yeah.

Often following the first successful experience, the child develops a new sense of competency and is more willing to engage in situations that provoke higher levels of anxiety. A large part of the treatment is to encourage risk taking, given the new set of skills the child has acquired. Later *in vivo* exposure experiences involve taking the child to a site outside the office such as a graveyard, the zoo, or a local shopping center. Many natural-occurring academic and social situations can be arranged in schools with the help of teachers and guidance personnel.

A child afraid of going into new places alone for fear of getting lost was taken to a shopping mall armed with his plan.

Therapist: How would you know you were starting to get nervous?
Client: My heart would start beating faster.
Therapist: What about your breathing? (therapist remembers about getting short of breath or asthma)
Client: I might start breathing faster.
Therapist: And what would you be thinking to yourself?
Client: I might get lost or I don't know where I am.
Therapist: And what are some things you could do if you start getting nervous?
Client: I could take deep breaths and say everything is going to be okay.
Therapist: That's good, but what if you were unsure where you were or got lost?
Client: I could ask somebody.
Therapist: Yes, you could ask somebody, but it would be a good idea to ask one of the guards or policeman. How are you feeling—do you think you are ready to give it a try?

The therapist and child then agreed on a number of trips within the mall with varying distances and degree of familiarity. The hierarchy involved going to a nearby store, going to a store on the second floor with the therapist, venturing to another floor alone, and locating a store that was unfamiliar to him. During one trip, the child had to ask the guard which way to go (so that he could feel comfortable approaching adults or authority figures if he needed to do that). Self-evaluation and reward was built into the experience: the child located a record store, went in and browsed until the therapist arrived, and picked out a tape as a reward.

The hierarchy may need to be revised throughout this process if the child does not report or show anxiety. One of the difficult features of *in vivo* exposure is for the therapist to *allow* the child to become anxious. Any natural tendency to reassure or comfort the child is held back, so the child can begin to develop independent skills for coping. Children may try to avoid the *in vivo* experience by engaging the therapist in talking excessively about the situation and all it's difficulties. The concerns are addressed, but the child is encouraged to approach the situation with these fears. The STIC tasks for the last eight sessions involve using the skills taught in the first eight sessions during out-of-session situations that arise during the week and recording any successes and/or difficulties using the steps.

Some of our best-laid plans have back fired and low-anxiety situations have been transformed into higher-anxiety situations; for example, when the elevator goes up four floors instead of one, or unexpected and unknown people turn up in the offices of colleagues while the child is in the middle of an exposure exercise. These are good times for the therapist to serve as a coping model, and these experiences remind both child and therapist that life does not always go as planned and one has to be flexible.

Other exposure experiences can be planned within the office but carried out with parental help as they occur naturally (e.g., going to a party or inviting a friend over to a child's house). Parental involvement allows the therapist greater flexibility in planning but this depends on the parents' abilities and motivation. More specific examples of how parents can be helpful are included in chapter 8. Such situations as family trips, separations, or sports-team tryouts are naturally occurring opportunities that can be used.

It is in sessions 9 through 16, then, that the children enter and face situations that were once too fearful. With the therapist as coach and collaborator, and the client prepared with the FEAR steps, the *in vivo* experiences lead the children to a new sense of competence and mastery.

"My Commercial." Our treatment provides a child or adolescent with the opportunity to create and produce a "commercial" about his or her experiences. The client is asked to put together a fun video, booklet, or audiotape to help tell other kids about how to manage anxiety. Examples include rap songs, mini-skits, and cartoons that are both informative and humorous. We give the children a copy of their product to take home and to show to friends and parents. The commercial provides an opportunity for success in a creative task and a demonstration of success in managing anxiety (see chapter 9 for an extended discussion and an example of this procedure, also called showing off).

Termination. Addressing the fact that therapy and the relationship with the therapist will end can be difficult for young clients. Children may begin to talk about more anxiety and physical symptoms during the final weeks of treatment. To help with termination, we tell the child at the end of each session (beginning at session 12) how many sessions are left. We encourage the child to talk about the end of therapy, and the therapist can share her feelings about the end of treatment, helping the child envision possible feelings he might have during the last weeks or after the end of therapy.

In the next-to-last session, the therapist recaps the progress the child has made and encourages the child to use the new skills in situations that might arise. The therapist provides ample support for the child in the belief that he is now ready to do well without the therapist. There can be discussion about possible upcoming difficult situations and how the child might handle these difficulties. The child and the child's parents are assured that they can call the clinic if problems arise. During the last session, the child receives the final reward for participation in the program. The rewards at this time are usually social, such as planning to spend time together at lunch, going out for an ice cream, or sharing some activity. The time is set aside for having fun, and the focus is kept on present and future accomplishments. The child is also given the completed and signed certificate of accomplishment (e.g., the back of the *Coping Cat Workbook*) as a concrete illustration of success.

Therapists can check in with their clients over the phone approximately a month or so after termination. For instance, one of the child's parents asked for a session when it was learned that their child would repeat a grade at school. The therapist and the child talked about this and role played answering peers' questions about why he was repeating a grade. In general, prior to the last session, the therapist discusses with the child's parents how to support their child in what they have learned and to encourage their child in using the steps and trying new tasks. Booster sessions and parent sessions are seen as further opportunities for problem solving and generalization of skills that the child will use in coping with the anxiety that accompanies new challenges and tasks.

Chapter 6
Clinical Case Illustrations and Research Results

Example is always more efficacious than precept.

—*Samuel Johnson*

It is not wise to buy a home without seeing it first, and it would be foolish to judge a house simply by looking at a map of the roads. To get to know a neighborhood—the people and the feeling—it is essential for a potential neighbor to take a walk through the neighborhood, visit some local stores, and get to see the community in action. Reading a book about an approach to psychotherapy is, unfortunately, somewhat like looking at a map and trying to judge a community. More is needed than a description of therapeutic strategies and procedures.

In an effort to improve the value of the written descriptions of therapy for anxiety disordered youth, we have (a) collected a set of four detailed clinical case illustrations and (b) conducted and reported preliminary data analyses. Our clinical illustrations portray our many cases: that is, we have selected cases with an eye toward representativeness. There are younger and older children, males and females, some where the outcomes were uniformly positive and some where there are lingering concerns. Our data analyses include comparisons of treated cases to wait list cases using assessments of change over time. It is hoped that this chapter proves useful reading in that it includes both clinically descriptive materials not contained in our earlier descriptions of treatment strategies and procedures and the results of research evaluating the effectiveness of the program.

CLINICAL CASE ILLUSTRATIONS

(The names and a few minor details of the cases have been changed in order to protect the anonymity ot the clients. Therapists are not identified by name. All clinical information is accurate.)

100

CASE #1
JAMES: 10-year-old white male
DIAGNOSES: Overanxious Disorder, Simple Phobia

Background Information

James presented as a slight boy who was small for his age. He and his younger sister lived with their mother and stepfather. There were two other teenage stepsiblings also living in the same household. James's natural father had died of a heart attack when James was five years old, and his mother remarried when he was eight. His stepfather was a fireman, and James reported that he was somewhat verbally abusive when he became angry; James felt that he could not predict or anticipate his father's behavior, and therefore felt quite worried around him. He was also frightened at times by his older stepsiblings' behavior.

Both James and his younger sister attended Catholic school where James was well liked and respected by both staff and peers. He was an exceptional student and very active in school activities, including lacrosse and choir.

Presenting Difficulties

Although teachers had identified a number of children they expected might be anxious, James was not one of them. Indeed, they were quite surprised to discover that he was extremely anxious. Interestingly, James was able to conceal his high levels of anxiety at school by working hard to please the adults and never drawing negative attention to himself. His teachers had always regarded his remarkable drive for perfection in his studies as simply a drive to excel and had not considered that it was extreme. In fact, James suffered with frequent nausea and occasional vomiting before school, and at least once a week he had to go home because of his stomach problems, usually before 9:00 A.M. It seems that because James was so likeable and socially adept, the teachers missed the warning signs of distressing levels of anxiety. Apparently he simply didn't fit their stereotype for a troubled child. Instead they considered him a hardworking child who was somewhat sickly and suffered from asthma.

However, James's anxiety disorder was no surprise to his mother. She was clearly concerned about him, particularly because he worried all the time about performing perfectly and became extremely upset with himself for the tiniest mistake. In addition, she found it troubling that James suffered frequent stomachaches and headaches that she believed were related to events at school, such as tests, sports events, or choir concerts. She was also concerned because he could not sleep in the dark and would not sleep unless his sister was also in the room. She was very willing for

James to participate in the treatment program, hoping for help with his difficulties.

James's initial diagnosis, based on both parent and child report on the Anxiety Disorders Interview Schedule (ADIS), was overanxious disorder and simple phobia. His trait anxiety T-score on the State-Trait Anxiety Inventory for Children (STAIC) was 68, his state T-score was 48. His mother's report on the Child Behavior Problem Checklist (CBCL) indicated very high levels of internalizing behaviors (total internalizing T-score of 78), including significant elevations on scales for physical complaints, depression, anxiety, withdrawal, and obsessive-compulsive features. The specific behaviors targeted for treatment included going home due to stress-related nausea or vomiting, being unable to give an oral presentation without excessive anxiety, and being unable to sleep alone in the dark.

Summary of Treatment

James's main concerns centered around situations in which he might be evaluated, such as getting a grade or performing in front of others. In addition, he had significant worries about being safe and fears that he might be harmed in any number of situations.

James was always eager to begin sessions. Due to transportation constraints, he was seen in the school library during his lunch hour rather than in the clinic. He seemed to enjoy the attention from the therapist and rapport was easily established. James was also willing to discuss his fears and worries with the therapist, though he had so effectively hidden them from his teachers. It was clear that he had good social skills and was an enjoyable child. It was also clear that James had many nervous mannerisms, including great difficulty relaxing and slowing down. For example, he almost always had finished his lunch before the therapist could get her coat off and sit down. He was not impulsive and could concentrate adequately, but he tended to work quickly and intensely.

The first eight sessions of the treatment proceeded quite smoothly. James learned the four basic concepts quickly and was able to recite the four-step coping plan without difficulty. In Sessions 2 and 3, the ways in which emotions are expressed in physical reactions were discussed. It seemed that James had not recognized the connection between his physical symptoms and anxiety-provoking experiences. Once this connection was elaborated for him, he began to recognize it for himself, particularly in terms of becoming sick in school. In addition, it was in these sessions that James revealed how his stepfather and stepsiblings expressed their emotions, especially anger, and how frightening these situations were to him. It was clear that this concern would be an issue that would require attention in therapy.

In general, James seemed to benefit from many of the specific strategies used during the therapy. He was conscientious about completing his "Show That I Can" (STIC) tasks and frequently gave useful examples of anxiety-provoking experiences that could be employed to make the concept being discussed that day more relevant to his experience. He seemed to really enjoy the role playing experiences and was willing to throw himself into the imagined situation. James's willingness to become involved and experience a certain degree of anxiety inherent in such situations made role playing a very effective intervention. Coping modeling was used less often with James, partially because he was such an enthusiastic role player. He was also enthusiastic about the relaxation techniques introduced in Session 4, and found deep breathing to be most useful, because he could do it quickly without other children being aware of it.

James grasped the concepts presented in Sessions 5 through 8 and was able to recall personal experiences relevant to the concepts presented. After introducing the concept of self-talk, it became clear that James tended to catastrophize—a bump on the knee left him wondering whether he had broken a bone and worrying if he would end up in the hospital.

James was able to develop adequate problem-solving strategies, although he had difficulty generating more than two or three possible solutions. In terms of reward, James had no idea that he was constantly evaluating his own performance and finding it lacking. The notion of self-evaluation was difficult for James to grasp, and he resisted developing a reward menu for himself. In order to encourage self-reward, the therapist provided James with opportunities to reward himself during sessions. Initially the therapist helped him reward himself for success in situations that were not specifically a planned part of the therapy, like playing a game of checkers with him as a reward for doing well on his report card. This helped him understand the importance of evaluating and rewarding himself for good performance, and this concept was then extended to coping effectively with anxiety-provoking situations.

By the end of the eighth session, he was able to recite the four-step coping plan without difficulty and was able to apply it in imagined, role-played situations. However, beginning with Session 9 and the *in vivo* experiences, James began to complain often of somatic symptoms. Interestingly, he still seemed eager and enthusiastic about treatment. Because the role-playing experiences had been so useful to James, the imaginal experiences did not heighten his anxiety. Accordingly, the majority of experiential sessions were actual *in vivo* situations.

The first *in vivo* exposure (low-level anxiety) included James's cleaning the chalkboard and floors in the classroom; he worried that the chalk dust and floor cleaners would harm him. When presented with the tasks, James was initially reluctant and displayed numerous nervous mannerisms. In the process of talking through the four-step coping plan, it became clear that James had catastrophized the consequences of exposure to chalk dust and floor cleaners. Clearly, although there is a minimal risk associated with floor cleaners, he had grossly exaggerated both the consequences and likelihood of any difficulty. James was able to develop a plan for handling this task safely, to complete the task, and to report feeling a great sense of accomplishment following it. Another low-level *in vivo* experience involved singing in front of the therapist. He was initially very reluctant to sing, fearing that if he made a mistake, he would be embarrassed and the therapist would be displeased. Once he identified these fears, James was able to plan for the possibility of making a mistake and was able to complete the task.

Medium-level *in vivo* exposures involved exposure to the dark in a sequence of increasingly darkened rooms. This experience was somewhat difficult to arrange in a school building, but the principal was very helpful in making various closets and cubbyholes available to the therapist. Before each *in vivo* experience, James used the four-step coping plan, although the plan did not change much for each experience. A second medium-level experience involved going to the cemetery to visit his father's grave. This task was somewhat less difficult for James than he had expected, perhaps because in discussing his expectations and coping plan, he was able to express to the therapist other emotions related to his father's death.

James's mother was enlisted to help with the final *in vivo* experiences as these situations included difficulties in the home. James reported great anxiety about sleeping in the dark and sleeping alone. His mother was taught the FEAR steps and was included in the planning process as James and the therapist prepared for him to sleep with only a night light. He practiced this in imaginal situations with the therapist while his mother participated, so that James and his mother would be able to refer to the practice during the actual experience that evening. James was able to fall asleep using only the night light and maintained that behavior during the follow-up period.

Another challenging *in vivo* experience involved James talking to his mother about his feelings toward his stepfather. This task was very difficult for James. The therapist and James role played this situation several times prior to approaching his mother. Eventually, James's mother was invited into the session and he discussed his feelings with her. He was very surprised to learn that his mother had already suspected that he was frightened by his stepfather and was very willing to help him problem solve around this issue.

James concluded therapy by writing a rap song and taping it for his commercial. At posttreatment, James reported a significant decrease in anxiety with a T-score of 42 on the STAIC trait version. He was able to sleep in the dark and did not continue to go home during the school day. In addition, he was trying to teach an anxious cousin the four-step coping plan. His mother also reported improvement on his target behaviors, and the total internalizing T-score on the parent CBCL was 71 with subclinical levels of symptoms on most internalizing scales. In addition, James showed substantial reductions in his levels of depression and somatic complaints, although these CBCL scales were still within the clinical range. At follow-up, his mother reported that James had maintained treatment gains on target behaviors. The parent CBCL report was essentially unchanged from posttreatment with a T-score of 73, although there was some increase in anxious behaviors.

CASE #2
THERESA: 12-year-old girl
DIAGNOSES: Overanxious Disorder, Separation Anxiety Disorder

Background Information

Theresa presented as a tall, attractive girl who was very concerned about her appearance. She was always friendly and polite but exhibited nervous mannerisms such as twisting her hair or wringing her hands. She lived in an intact nuclear family: her mother was an intensive care nurse and her father worked as a salesman. Theresa was the oldest of four siblings. She reported normal sibling squabbling with her sisters and being particularly fond of her brother. Theresa's mother reported that she and her daughter had a conflicted relationship. At times, Theresa would openly show her anger toward her mother, while at other times, Theresa had great difficulty being separated from her mother.

Both parents had high expectations of their own performances, although they did not openly communicate equally high expectations for Theresa's performance. Theresa did quite well academically, usually making A's in an accelerated program. She found the occasional B+ difficult to cope with and worried about not making the honor roll. It seemed that Theresa was not openly manifesting her anxiety within the classroom, based on her teacher's surprise at discovering she was receiving treatment for anxiety disorders. While Theresa was overly concerned about what others thought of her, she did appear to have a fairly normal social life with a group of girl friends. She was particularly close to one girl, whom she had known since she was a toddler.

Presenting Difficulties

Theresa's mother contacted the clinic because she was concerned about her daughter's extreme anxiety regarding school. Over the previous few weeks, Theresa had started to cry and protest going to school in the mornings. Despite her daughter's protests, Theresa's mother insisted she go to school, and Theresa managed to comply.

Theresa was also experiencing a great deal of anxiety in relation to her studies—she was constantly plagued by fears of failing. She pushed herself very hard to study, often staying up late at night. At the same time, Theresa resented studying so hard and worrying all the time about school. She complained of "being overworked" and although only in the sixth grade, was already concerned about working hard in high school and college. Indeed, her anxiety about school was so great that she would sometimes experience a vague, overwhelming feeling occasionally accompanied by somatic complaints, such as shaking, headaches, and chills. While it is unclear if these were true panic attacks, the intensity of the somatic responses, accompanied by Theresa's inability to clearly describe what specific situations led up to the feelings, gave them the flavor of panic attacks. However, she had no accompanying thoughts of going crazy or dying.

Theresa had bouts of insomnia associated with her concerns over school. The problem with insomnia threatened to generalize when she began avoiding sleepovers because she feared not being able to sleep and imagined that others would see her struggling to fall asleep.

Theresa was extremely self-conscious and perfectionistic. She worried that others might think she was incompetent and incapable. In fact, her concern about grades stemmed from a fear of being teased should she fail, according to her own standards. In addition, she was very anxious to please others. She felt particularly anxious when faced with choices, fearing that if she made the wrong choice she would hurt others' feelings. For example, she described one occasion when both her brother and a neighbor had asked her to play with them. She so feared being perceived as mean by one or the other that she was unable to make a choice. She ran back and forth between them until becoming so anxious and overwhelmed by the situation that she had to lie down in her room. Fortunately, Theresa was motivated to try to change the patterns that were causing her such great distress.

Theresa's initial primary diagnosis, based on both parent and child report, was overanxious disorder. In addition, Theresa's report included a limited number of depressive as well as obsessive-compulsive features. Her mother's report included symptoms of school phobia, separation anxiety, and a few depressive features. Theresa's self-report scores indicated high levels of anxiety (STAIC Trait T-score = 65; Revised Children's Manifest Anxiety Scale [RCMAS] T-score = 58). Her mother's report on the CBCL also indicated high levels of anxiety with a T-score of 72. The specific target behaviors selected for treatment had to do with going to school, taking a test, and having to choose particular friends to spend time with. As treatment was initiated during the summer, no information was available from the teacher prior to the beginning of treatment.

Summary of Treatment

The major focus of therapy for Theresa was on her "need to be perfect" and her attempts to please everyone in order to avoid their disapproval or anger. These issues became evident during the first sessions of treatment.

It was fairly easy to establish a superficial rapport with Theresa because it was so important to her that the therapist like and approve of her. However, it soon became clear that it would be more difficult to establish a relationship with Theresa in which she could trust the therapist enough to reveal her imperfections, her worries, and her secrets. Thus, while she quickly picked up on the concepts that were being presented, she had difficulty discussing her own experiences with reference to these concepts. Overcoming Theresa's desire to please and appear perfect involved the therapist's coping modeling of her own imperfections and finding humor in her own mistakes. The use of humor was gradually extended to include Theresa's imperfections as well via the use of gentle teasing. The therapist also directly challenged Theresa's expectation of perfection and created ambiguous situations in the sessions in which the right way to complete the task was not apparent. The therapist was then very accepting of Theresa's efforts and performance.

Because Theresa had strong somatic responses bordering on panic symptoms, she was well aware of her somatic reactions to anxiety. However, Theresa's ability to accurately recognize the association between the onset of anxiety and somatic symptoms fluctuated. While she could label feelings such as stomachaches or headaches related to lower levels of anxiety, high levels of anxiety seemed to leave her feeling overwhelmed and confused. These feelings were presented to Theresa as a somatic cue similar to a headache or stomachache.

Theresa's difficulties with perfectionism became evident in her concerns with the homework (or STIC) task. For instance, she would often write several pages about an incident, providing a very careful description, although asked to write only a brief paragraph. Initially, she was nervous about presenting the material to the therapist and would ask the therapist to read the material. With encouragement, she progressed to reading it orally herself and was eventually able to simply recount the material verbally. Thus, Theresa was encouraged to let go of the initial control she wanted over how the STIC tasks were presented in therapy and risk doing a "less than perfect" job in presenting the material to the therapist.

While Theresa's extreme physiological reactions to anxiety suggested that relaxation training might be especially beneficial, she initially experienced some problems learning these skills. She tended to rush into the exercises and try do them with such vigor that she would make herself *more* tense. In essence, she was experiencing relaxation-induced anxiety. For example, she reported that in one situation she started to get very frightened and began to tense and relax her hands. She did this to the point of actually digging her fingernails into the palms of her hands. To help counteract this, Theresa was instructed to start slowly, taking deep breaths only until she could think a bit more calmly. In addition, she was reminded that the tense-release exercise pattern was only for practice in non-stressful situations and was done primarily to help her learn how a relaxed muscle feels. Under stressful circumstances, she was taught to focus on realizing which muscles were tense at the time and to concentrate on relaxing them.

The concept of self-talk was difficult for the therapist to address with Theresa. She was very bright and to some extent aware of her cognitions in anxiety-provoking situations. She was able to mount arguments to the therapist's attempts to modify her cognitions in those situations and was unwilling to accept counterarguments. Finally, the therapist began asking her to take someone else's viewpoint on the situation and to describe their cognitions. For instance, Theresa was convinced that if she did not get all As on her report card she would be teased. No amount of discussion altered her conviction. Eventually she was asked to consider what she would think of a friend if they did not always get As. She responded that it would be fine. The therapist then discussed the differences between her response to this situation and her perceptions of how others would respond to the same situation.

In essence, the therapist was helping Theresa to shift her focus away from what she thought others were thinking and onto what others were doing. She was often asked to explain how she would know if somebody was angry with her or thought she was stupid. She was asked to identify the behaviors indicative of such responses. Theresa's extreme fear of looking "stupid" and being laughed at in dance class provided a good example. Theresa was encouraged to watch the other dancers and see if they too made any mistakes. She was to notice if others were laughing at the person, whispering behind the person's back, or if they were concentrating so hard on their own work that they really didn't notice others' mistakes. Theresa discovered that everybody made mistakes and nobody seemed to notice, much less laugh.

Another method used to challenge Theresa's catastrophic perceptions of situations was to model her behavior in an extreme form, so that she could see the humor in the situation. For example, the therapist, with a very straight face, commented that Theresa's tendency to twist her hair would probably make her go bald. Taken off guard by the matter of fact way this statement was delivered, Theresa burst out laughing, as she recognized how ridiculous the statement was. Theresa learned to take some teasing and to be able to see the humor in situations, and this in turn helped her to overcome her catastrophic expectations.

Problem solving was very difficult for Theresa to master: having relied heavily on her mother to help her cope with difficult situations, she consequently never developed the skills or confidence to attack problems. Even in the later stages of therapy, Theresa would claim that she did not know what she could do in a situation in order to cope. The reasons for this difficulty were not exactly clear, because as an exceptionally bright child she potentially had the resources for coping. In the beginning, the therapist generated possibilities to help Theresa along. To help thwart Theresa's perfectionistic tendencies, the therapist would include some ludicrous possibilities as options. As therapy progressed, the therapist was less willing to generate the alternatives, and they would sometimes sit in silence until Theresa came up with some ideas. Interestingly, even as Theresa made progress in her skill as a problem solver, she had difficulty seeing that she was the one who was doing the work and coming up with the solutions. She tended to attribute the solutions to the therapist rather than see them as her own, and she consequently did not recognize herself as competent.

Her tendency to see herself as incompetent in the face of contrary evidence caused her to be very harsh in her self-evaluations and rewards. Though much of therapy helped Theresa overcome her perfectionistic standards, she found it difficult to completely change her pattern of harsh self-evaluation. She was able to begin becoming somewhat less self-critical in many areas but was unable to overcome her perfectionism in school work. Not surprisingly, Theresa also had a difficult time rewarding herself; however, as therapy progressed she was able to follow through with her rewards (e.g., watching 30 minutes of TV as a study break or having a special dessert). Positive self-evaluation was especially difficult for Theresa because she felt like she was "bragging," and she remained fairly dependent on external sources for approval.

Simply being in treatment for her anxiety problems was an *in vivo* experience for Theresa. As suggested by her experience with the STIC tasks discussed previously, she found the process of interacting with the therapist to be in itself anxiety provoking. Apparently, her overriding fear was that if she made a mistake, the therapist would become angry at her. She seemed to be in constant fear that if she did something in a less than perfect way, the therapist would see how stupid she was and would reject her.

Early *in vivo* experiences focused on the issue of perfectionism. One low-level *in vivo* experience involved asking Theresa to draw simple pictures with her eyes closed and then asking an unfamiliar person to help her hang these drawings on the wall. Though a relatively simple task, it allowed the therapist to address Theresa's fear of looking incompetent in front of others as well as her desire to feel in control of situations. Theresa initially divided the sheet of paper in half by drawing a line down the middle. On the side where she was to do drawings with her eyes open she wrote "Drawings I am good at," and on the side where she was to do drawings with her eyes closed she wrote "Drawings I am bad at." The therapist responded to this by telling Theresa she had to draw with her eyes closed on the side labeled good and with her eyes open on the side labeled bad. Although initially anxious about the task, Theresa was encouraged to use the FEAR steps to help herself. The therapist used coping modeling (i.e., drawing with her eyes closed) to help Theresa cope with her imperfect drawings. The drawings Theresa did with her eyes closed were fairly humorous, and via gentle teasing the therapist was able to help Theresa laugh at them. In this way, Theresa was helped to understand that teasing and laughter are not always malicious, and she could even see the humor in the situation herself.

The drawing task also afforded the therapist the opportunity to encourage Theresa to become more assertive about the way things were done and what she wanted. Thus, when Theresa asked what she should draw, the therapist helped her problem solve about how to figure out what to draw, rather than immediately giving Theresa a suggestion. Even small acts of assertion were difficult for Theresa. Another low-level *in vivo* experience involved choosing a candy bar from the vending machine to share during the session. The therapist explored Theresa's fears of making the wrong choice and, after talking through the problem, agreed to Theresa's request that if she did not like the kind Theresa chose, she would say so. In a more difficult *in vivo,* Theresa was encouraged to stick to her initial choice of the type of game she wanted to play, even though the two graduate-student confederates said they wanted to play different games.

A central anxiety-provoking conflict for Theresa consisted of the tension she felt between wanting to have fun and at the same time feeling "guilty" that she was not doing her schoolwork. Throughout the sessions, the therapist stressed talking about any fun things that Theresa had done during the week (e.g., family trips, going to the mall, and sleep overs with friends). The main message was that it was just as important to have fun as it was to work and achieve. This issue provided a good mid-level *in vivo* experience for her. She was asked to plan an activity for a weekend when she had lots of homework to do. She planned to go to a movie, and the FEAR steps were employed to explore her fears and help her cope with this situation. The important point was for Theresa to learn through practice that what she feared—failing—would not happen even if she allowed herself to have some fun.

Another mid-level *in vivo* task involved recording her own voice and playing it back. Having discovered that it was very difficult for Theresa to listen to her own voice on tape, the therapist asked her to record herself reading a portion of a story and play it back for the therapist. Coping involved thinking of strategies to use in making the recording, such as stopping the recorder and taking deep breaths if she became nervous and not letting on if she did make a mistake because the therapist would not know anyway. In addition, the therapist modeled her own reaction to hearing her voice taped, saying as Theresa had that she did not think it sounded like her, even though Theresa said that it did. Theresa was also encouraged to think of ways to gather information about whether or not she really sounded stupid, for example, looking for behavioral cues indicative of disapproval (laughter, raised eyebrows), and asking the therapist what she thought.

A high-level *in vivo* experience was developed out of this taping task when Theresa was asked to play the tape for three graduate-student confederates. This forced Theresa to introduce herself and explain her task. Because Theresa thought people might think she was "wierd" for doing this, she problem solved about how to present the explanation of her task. It was determined that she would say that her therapist was asking her to do it, which was in fact the situation, and she seemed to feel comfortable with this explanation. As in the previous taping task, ideas were generated about what to do in the course of taping and how to determine if others thought she was sounding silly. To encourage independence, the therapist left the room while the tape was played, and Theresa reported that this made the task harder for her. Again she was able to complete the task despite feeling somewhat anxious about it. The taping tasks provided Theresa with opportunities to take the focus off of herself and focus more on the responses of others. As noted, this was an important theme in her treatment, because Theresa was so self-focused and had great difficulty using other sources of information to help her maintain an accurate frame of reference about her experiences.

Posttreatment assessment results indicated that Theresa maintained the significant reductions in nearly all the symptoms she had reported at midpoint evaluation. She reported some increases in her ability to cope with going to school and taking a test. Her mother verbally reported vast improvement in her daughter but also noted a few continuing symptoms. The reasons for this incongruity in the mother's report were unclear. It is possible that the mother perceived improvement in her daughter's ability to handle her problems, though she believed that her daughter would always be an anxious person. When she referred to improvement in her daughter, it was improvement in her ability to cope, rather than a change in her personality.

Though some of Theresa's perfectionism remains and threatens to cause problems in the future, she did learn to question whether she really must be perfect. She was able to develop a more realistic assessment of when a "perfect" performance might be required and when something less would be quite acceptable. A big gain for Theresa was to take steps toward mixing work and pleasure so she did not feel trapped every time she had work to accomplish. Theresa may continue to have dependency problems when it comes to problem-solving situations, although it is hoped that her parents will continue to address these issues via their questioning of how she can use the FEAR steps in various situations. Theresa reported directly to the therapist that she felt she had gained confidence in herself. Also, she developed a capacity to laugh at herself if she made a mistake or looked foolish. This was particularly apparent in taping her commercial.

Theresa spent a lot of time on the taping, and even spontaneously played around with how to do various things in the situation she had created (such as pretending to go down a flight of stairs by sinking to her knees and becoming very melodramatic in her theatrical presentation of what she did when she became anxious). When she and the therapist watched the tape, there was a lot of laughter. She didn't seem to need to make this last piece of therapy perfect.

At the end of treatment, Theresa had difficulty separating from the therapist. She continued to have trouble recognizing that she was the one doing the work in the sessions, believing that it was the therapist who had the answers about how to cope. Several weeks after termination, the therapist received a phone call in which Theresa described severe bouts of insomnia accompanied by panic-like symptoms. Accompanying these anxiety symptoms were fears of failing school. The therapist worked to help Theresa use the FEAR steps in these situations. Additionally, a booster session was held to help Theresa recognize her own capacity to use the FEAR steps without the aid of the therapist. In a parent meeting, the parents were encouraged to continue to help Theresa in active problem solving. Also, a brief discussion of their own perfectionistic self-expectations may have slowed down the general pace of family life so that they could all enjoy themselves.

CASE #3

MIKE: 9-year-old boy

DIAGNOSES: Overanxious Disorder, Separation Anxiety, School Phobia, Avoidant Disorder, Attention Deficit Hyperactivity Disorder, and Oppositional Disorder

Background Information

Mike is a slightly built 9-year-old boy, with blond hair in a bowl cut. He reminds one of the Artful Dodger from *Oliver Twist.* Mike comes from a low income, white family with 8 children. His father worked as a sexton of a church located near their house. Mike's school was run by the same church, and his father also worked part-time in the school. The family did not own a car and traveled very infrequently. The family was very close and spent most of their time together. Older children helped care for the younger children. Mike was always described as sensitive and worried about everything.

A few months prior to treatment, Mike's mother was hospitalized for severe depression and was (again) placed on antidepressant medication. At the time of the depressive episode, she stated that she might leave the family and not come back. Soon after this incident, Mike began having difficulty going to school and became concerned about his mother being home alone with the young children during the day.

Presenting Difficulties

Mike's major presenting problems were his refusal to attend school and his increasingly fearful and agitated behavior when asked to enter his classroom. In addition, Mike was reluctant to venture out alone, to join activities, and expressed extreme discomfort in his interactions with peers. His family was especially concerned about Mike's quick temper, but they felt the anger was related to his nervousness. In addition, Mike had a number of specific fears, including doctors and elevators.

At the time of the intake interview, and in addition to the multiple disorders endorsed by both Mike and his parents, Mike showed scores in the clinical range on self-reports of anxiety and depression. At intake, his RCMAS T-score was 70, his STAIC-Trait T-score was 66, and Children's Depression Inventory (CDI) was 22 (above the cut-off score of 18 signaling significant depressive symptoms). In addition, the Teacher CBCL Internalizing T-score was 81; the Externalizing T-score was 53 (in the normal range). He had elevated CBCL scores on the subscales of anxiety, social withdrawal, and self-destructive behavior. Mike also received below average T-scores on teacher's report of social competence (CBCL scales of working hard, and happy). His parent CBCL showed below average scores on the competence areas of activities ($T = 31$) and social interaction ($T = 24$).

Regarding school difficulties, Mike's teachers and principal had been very patient with him, concerned over his level of distress, and had tried a number of strategies to get him back into the classroom. He began having difficulties getting off to school, and his mother was too overwhelmed to get him to school if her husband had already left for work. He would then spend the day at home, but his parents usually required that he stay in his room most of the day if he did not attend school. The school principal suggested that his father walk Mike to school. His father took him to the front door, saw that he got inside, and assumed Mike went on to his class.

Later in treatment, Mike revealed to the therapist that he would hide in the hallway between the double doors after his father left and remain there until he was discovered. When faced with going into the classroom, Mike was often unable to do so and would throw tantrums or cry when his principal tried to encourage him to enter the room. When he was unable to go to class and could not be calmed down, he spent the day doing his work in the principal's office. If forced to enter the classroom, he would lash out or scream uncontrollably. On at least one occasion, he ran from his room and said that he wanted to kill himself.

Summary of Treatment

Mike's refusal to attend school worried everyone involved, and all agreed that this issue required immediate attention. Prior to and concurrent with beginning treatment, the therapist (in contact with school personnel) and Mike's father developed the following plan to increase Mike's school attendance. The teachers were to be prepared for Mike to act out and had agreed to work with the other children in the classroom. They would require him to be in the classroom even if he was upset. Mike's father was to bring him to school, take him to his classroom, and see that he actually went inside. A daily "report card" for good attendance was drawn up and signed by his teacher each day for each period he was in the class. As a reward for good reports, Mike's family allowed him to stay up later than usual and to pick a television show he wanted to watch (quite a privilege in a family of 8 children).

As a transitional step, Mike was allowed to call his mother once a day to check on her. In the beginning, Mike made it to the classroom for several consecutive days. When he made it to the classroom, he was able to stay in the class for at least part of the day. During the first week of the plan, Mike would be allowed to spend the second half of the day in the principal's office, if he had entered the classroom. During the first few weeks of treatment, Mike only spent part of two days in the office.

Occasionally, Mike gave his mother a difficult time in the morning. In one instance, he insisted that he would not go to school without clean and pressed clothes. When the clothes were finally ready late in the morning, his mother allowed him to stay home. At this time, it was decided that the father would not leave home before Mike, because his mother did not feel she could manage to get him to school if he struggled with her. At another time, Mike was legitimately sick for two days and had difficulty returning to school the first day after his illness. Mike continued to call his mother once a day from school to check on her until the middle of treatment. However, after 2 weeks, Mike was attending school regularly. The report card was used for a total of 3 weeks to help maintain gains.

The rest of the treatment followed in a manner consistent with chapters 4 and 5 (see also Kendall et al., 1989, treatment manual). Given that Mike was nine years old, some extra sessions were added by dividing some of the sessions that introduced the more difficult concepts, especially the cognitive techniques, into two sessions instead of one. Because he seemed easily frustrated and was impulsive, the sessions were kept short. His therapist used drawings to maintain his interest and to help him re-create experiences of the previous week that he couldn't write about. He had difficulty completing his homework at times, and his notebook had to be replaced after being lost somewhere in his house.

During the intake and early sessions, Mike was also quite depressed. During the intake interview, he spoke quietly and at times laid down on the couch. At the same time, he answered the diagnostician's questions and was excited about being in the program. Mike formed an especially close relationship with his therapist and looked forward to sessions. Following the initial sessions, Mike's depression began to lift, and he became actively involved in sessions.

With the lifting of the depression and the shortened sessions, the first eight sessions proceeded quite smoothly. However, the family was often in a confused state. Around the fourth session, Mike missed a number of sessions because of communication problems in the family regarding appointment times. Mike would become extremely concerned if he was going to be late or miss a session, and he insisted that a member of his family call the clinic. The therapist noted that even though Mike used the deep breathing from the relaxation program regularly, he never fully learned the progressive muscle relaxation. His tape was lost a number of times, and access to the one tape recorder in the family was difficult to obtain.

The therapist opted to begin *in vivo* experiences around his more specific fears. For instance, Mike was unable to ride in elevators. In a low-level *in vivo*, Mike was to ride up one floor in the elevator. Sometimes, *in vivo* experiences do not go as planned, and by some fluke of technology Mike was taken down two floors before going up three, where he was to find his therapist waiting. Even though Mike reported that he had been frightened in the elevator, he was pleasantly surprised by the fact that he had *survived* a three-floor ride. Following this adventure, Mike took the elevator for the one-floor ride and gradually worked up to four floors (the distance from the ground floor to the clinic). Mike and his father continued to practice taking the elevator on the way to sessions.

Another of Mike's concerns was going to the doctor's office. A visit for checkup and shots was scheduled during treatment. As part of a low-level exposure, the therapist pretended to be a physician and set up a mock visit. As the therapist began to probe about his concerns, it came out in the session that Mike was not afraid of the doctor or shots but was afraid of undressing. The therapist and Mike negotiated a plan for him to talk to the doctor about keeping his underwear on. At the beginning, Mike did not want to tell his parents about his concern or to enlist their assistance. After the session, he did decide to talk to his parents so that they could support him in talking to the doctor, and he proudly announced this fact to the therapist on his arrival at the following session.

A challenging high-level *in vivo* experience for Mike involved traveling by car. Much to the therapist's surprise, it was discovered that Mike had traveled by car so infrequently that he easily became car sick. During a ride, the therapist was unable to pull over to the side of the road because of traffic, and Mike became sick in the car. Nevertheless, Mike was proud of being able to ride in the car and so enjoyed playing with the steering wheel and blinkers prior to the trip, that even with the difficulty the trip was seen as a "partial success." In his SHOW OFF commercial (see pp. 174–178), Mike used a puppet and talked for over 10 minutes about cars, how they worked, and why a child shouldn't be scared of riding in one.

School personnel, Mike's parents, his therapist, and Mike himself were amazed by his progress. He was no longer depressed, his angry outbursts at home had decreased, and he seemed to be more confident about his abilities at school and in the home. At the end of treatment, Mike met criteria for only overanxious disorder and simple phobia (he still had some difficulty riding in cars), but both Mike and his father rated these difficulties as less distressing in contrast to the most extreme rating they had given these problems at intake. On the self-report measures, all of Mike's scores were in the normal range at outtake (i.e., CDI score = 4, RCMAS T-score = 39, STAIC state T-score = 30, and STAIC trait T-score = 31). On the Teacher CBCL, Mike showed average scores for competence in all areas and an Internalizing T-score of 62 and an Externalizing T-score of 45 with all subscales in the normal range. There is no doubt that Mike made significant progress; he appeared as a more confident and happy child at the end of treatment than during the intake interview.

This child had multiple problems, all of which could not be addressed in our 16-week treatment. For instance, Mike's anxiety around peer difficulties and performance anxiety in school situations were not completely addressed. Mike continued to go everywhere with his family, or at least with his two favorite brothers, and he had some difficulty falling asleep if his brothers were not in the room that they shared. At the end of treatment in the summer, Mike became worried about anticipated difficulties when school would begin again in the fall. The therapist helped Mike and his father anticipate possible difficulties. Since the father worked in Mike's school, it was arranged that Mike accompany his father to work the week before school in order to locate his classroom and to meet his new teacher. In the fall, Mike had no trouble beginning school.

CASE #4

DAVID: 13-year-old male

DIAGNOSES: Overanxious Disorder, Separation Anxiety Disorder

Background Information

David presented as a tall, heavyset adolescent living in an economically depressed, inner city area. He attended a large junior high school where a segment of the students were tough and "streetwise." There was a high crime rate in his neighborhood, and he had been mugged by gangs of juveniles twice prior to beginning treatment.

David was the youngest of seven children and the only child still living at home. He was substantially younger than his siblings who related to him more as parents than siblings. He had no contact with his father but was very close to his mother. He and his mother related to each other as peers, with David telling her his deepest secrets. His mother suffered from severe asthma and had a history of repeated hospitalizations.

Presenting Difficulties

David was referred for treatment because both his teacher and guidance counselor had noticed his struggle with high levels of anxiety. They had noticed that he worried a great deal in academic situations, such as taking a test, as well as in social settings, particularly in situations where girls were present. He experienced high levels of stomachaches and muscle tension in each of these situations.

In terms of his social difficulties, David was able to maintain superficial interactions with his peers. However, he was immature and often acted the class clown. It seemed that the other adolescents were laughing at his antics rather than joining in his joke. In addition, he tended to be picked on and bullied by the more aggressive students. He had few friends at school, and it was unclear how loyal or reliable these friends were for David. He had closer friends in the neighborhood but they were primarily younger boys. David seemed to feel a greater sense of control and safety with these younger friends. David had appropriate early adolescent interest in girls, but found interactions with girls very anxiety provoking and worrisome. He was quite concerned about how to approach girls and carry on a conversation. He indicated that he saw others being flirtatious with girls, but he was quite uncomfortable and worried about how to interact with them in a nice, friendly way.

Academically, David was identified as learning disabled and performed somewhat behind his peers. He was in the eighth grade, but functioned on the sixth and seventh grade level. His anxiety hampered his performance, particularly in testing situations. He had great difficulty concentrating because he was concerned that teachers or peers would look over his shoulder while he was working, that he would make mistakes and look incompetent.

David worried a great deal about being away from his mother, fearing that she would have a serious asthma attack and possibly die without anyone there to help her. This concern was not realistic, as she was perfectly able to make the necessary arrangements herself. Nevertheless, David was afraid to leave her alone and consequently would not participate in extracurricular activities. When he was away, he checked on her frequently by phone or would come home early to be with her. His mother's attempts to reassure him and encourage him to participate in more activities were unsuccessful. In addition, her hospitalizations were very stressful for David, although she regarded them as routine. He worried that his mother would not come home and tended to remain in very close contact with her while she was in the hospital.

David's mother reported that he had symptoms of overanxious disorder and separation anxiety. The results of David's structured interview concurred with his mother's description of overanxious disorder, along with symptoms of avoidant disorder and some features of separation anxiety (particularly around issues of his mother's health). His mother's report produced an elevated CBCL Internalizing scale score (T=64) with particularly high scores on the obsessive-compulsive scale and the immaturity scale. Teacher CBCL report indicated clinical levels of anxiety (T=73). The specific behaviors targeted for treatment included speaking in front of his peers, taking tests, and being away from his mother without constantly worrying about her health. Interestingly, David and his mother disagreed on how well he could cope with these situations. David claimed that he had only moderate difficulty coping, while his mother reported that he encountered significant levels of distress under such circumstances.

Summary of Treatment

David was seen for therapy in his school building in a private room made available by school staff expressly for this purpose. He was seen during one of his free periods during the day. This option was preferred because (a) his mother would find it difficult to bring him to the clinic and (b) many of David's concerns focused on his peers; being at the school provided the opportunity for *in vivo* experiences later in treatment.

David was eager to begin treatment, and rapport was easily established by recognizing that he and the therapist had shared interests. As David's therapist was male, certain interests and concerns were perhaps more easily discussed, including his feelings about girls. The therapist used humor and light conversation to begin the sessions and help David relax, and—because David was very cooperative—created a working alliance by involving David in the treatment process. The therapist presented himself as a consultant who could help David explore alternative ways of coping with his world, but also reminded David that he was the one who would actually make the decisions about what he needed and what was useful to him. David became an enthusiastic client, completed all homework assignments, and was eager to share his experiences with the therapist.

Relaxation training was especially useful for David. He enjoyed using imagery during the relaxation, choosing images of the beach, including imagining the sensations of swimming and lying on the sand with the warm sun beating on his body. He developed facility at becoming relaxed and used relaxation techniques to help control his anxiety in situations outside of the therapy context. Most notably he used the exercises at night before sleep because he tended to worry that his mother would have problems while he slept. David made a tape of his relaxation exercises and shared it with his mother. Interestingly, she also reported that the relaxation exercises were useful for controlling her own anxiety.

David was well aware of his somatic symptoms, including nausea and profuse sweating, but he was not especially focused on these symptoms. He was more concerned about his cognitions and spent much time worrying about his worrying. His age and level of cognitive development permitted a greater awareness of his own thoughts in general than would be true of a younger child. Nevertheless, he had some difficulty identifying his self-talk under stressful situations: with the therapist's assistance he was able to begin to identify his anxious thoughts with a minimum of difficulty, and he soon saw more general assumptions underlying his self-talk. For instance, David was particularly concerned about his mother's health and discovered that his anxious self-talk about her included fears that she could not take care of herself and would die if he was absent during an attack. He was eventually able to modify his self-talk to statements such as: "Mother can take care of herself. She has done so many times before and her attacks have never been fatal. The doctor says she is able to care for herself." Reframing his anxiety-provoking thoughts helped relieve some of David's discomfort at being away from his mother.

Although David was an adolescent and had developed some problem-solving skills, he had some initial difficulty generating solutions when his anxiety was elevated. Coping modeling and role play were very useful techniques for helping David learn to generate solutions under stressful circumstances. In particular, coping modeling was helpful in generating ideas about how to avoid becoming a scapegoat. The therapist behaved in ways that would encourage teasing or discourage it, and David made suggestions for both. Role play was very important in helping David generate alternative behaviors (e.g., behaviors that might discourage a mugger, such as walking with a purpose). Role play was also useful in helping him develop strategies for talking to girls in ways that were different from what he had seen other boys do, because he did not want to seem tough and flirtatious.

With a limited amount of practice, David was able to begin generating effective solutions to stressful situations. For example, David's anxiety about relating to girls made him an easy target for teasing by the opposite sex. After having been in treatment for some time and problem solving about this issue, David was approached by a girl claiming to think he was nice and feigning interest in him. Rather than get flustered as he had done previously, David labeled her behavior as false and told her that he was not going to be involved in her game. The girl was somewhat surprised, and stopped teasing him.

The low-level *in vivo* experiences for David focused on evaluations. The therapist actually administered an achievement test to David and watched over his shoulder to simulate the classroom situation David feared. The therapist explained the test by claiming to be interested in his academic performance in school. Initially David was somewhat concerned about this situation, but he and the therapist discussed the FEAR plan, and he was able to take the test with only minimal levels of worry.

The therapist was able to take advantage of a naturally occurring situation for the mid-level *in vivo* experience. David had decided that he wanted to invite a girl to go to the movies. David and the therapist first used imaginal experiences to work through the anxiety in a safe environment. David was then able to develop a very reasonable plan for approaching the girl, and he and the therapist decided on a time. The therapist then telephoned David following the experience to check on how well the plan had worked and how well he had been able to control his anxiety.

Another mid-level *in vivo* experience involved traveling alone on public transportation. David's mother brought him to the clinic for a session. This session involved using the four-step plan to prepare David to go home alone on public transportation. The most important aspect of this plan was problem solving as David had to anticipate and prepare for various difficulties he might encounter.

One high-level *in vivo* experience was for David to give a speech in front of his school's guidance counselors. This was very difficult for David to do and required careful preparation. David was involved in determining what steps he needed to take to prepare himself, as part of the problem-solving aspect of the coping plan. The plan he and the therapist devised included practicing the speech at home in front of the mirror and then in front of his mother. He then practiced it in front of the therapist in the regular therapy room and finally practiced in the actual room where the speech was to take place. In addition, he developed a coping plan that he would use if he made a mistake during the speech.

Another high-level *in vivo* experience involved going to the movies with the therapist one evening and leaving his mother alone during that time.

He prepared for this with a STIC assignment to play outside for brief periods after school without checking on his mother. The actual outing went well, with David reporting that he worried about his mother only infrequently while he was away.

Posttreatment assessment results from David, his mother, and his teacher indicated substantial improvement. The CBCL Internalizing scale scores from both parent (T-score = 52) and teacher (T-score = 49) indicated that his anxiety levels had decreased to well within normal limits. David's self-report scores were also within normal limits. Both David and his mother reported only mild levels of difficulty coping with each of the specific target behaviors and, overall, reported that David had made substantial progress. The therapist followed up David's treatment with phone calls made once a week for about a month. Both David and his mother indicated that treatment gains were maintained. Although the therapist offered to provide booster sessions at a later date if needed, there has been no further contact from the family.

RESEARCH RESULTS

The descriptive case illustrations provided earlier in this chapter offer an intimate look at a select set of representative cases. However, one must still ask about the overall effectiveness of the treatment for cases randomly assigned to treatment and control conditions. Therefore, in addition to the descriptive cases, a research evaluation of the effectiveness of our program was conducted and is described briefly here. Our research project was a randomized clinical trial, testing our cognitive-behavioral intervention for children receiving a diagnosis of an anxiety disorder. Anxiety-disordered children, based on a structured diagnostic interview, were assigned randomly to either a wait-list (8 weeks) or treatment (16 sessions) condition. Multiple-method assessments (e.g., parent and teacher reports, behavioral observations, self-report) at pre and posttreatment were employed: some 1-year follow-up assessments have occurred and the data are supportive (8 out of 8 cases *no* longer meet criteria for an anxiety disorder), but the number at the time of the writing was too small for statistical tests. Therapy was provided according to our manual and consistent with the procedures described in this book, and treatment integrity was examined and verified.

During just one year, well over 100 contacts were made to our clinic; a total of 82 cases completed the interview process, and 48 clients received an anxiety-disorder diagnosis. 27 cases have now completed the treatment program, and these cases include urban and suburban white and nonwhite youth. Uniformly, the accepted cases were seriously distressed regarding anxiety. Although homogeneous for anxiety disorders, the sample included heterogeneity around other serious difficulties (e.g., 14% comorbid for major depression; 10% comorbid for Attention-Deficit Hyperactive Disorder (ADHD); a child still sleeping with their parents at age 11; a child with severe worries about maternal health; a child who could not ride in a car). The clear majority of cases had anxiety problems that dated back several years. Certain cases were so distressing to parents that they commuted well over a hour to our Child and Adolescent Anxiety Disorders Clinic (CAADC). Indeed, none of the cases that are included in the analyses were suffering from a transient anxious emotional state nor were any identified as having only a simple phobia. There were 4 black males, 4 black females, 13 white males, and 6 white females: 86% received a primary diagnosis of overanxious disorder (OAD), 9% separation anxious, and 5% avoidant disorder. Cases were randomly assigned to either treatment or wait-list condition and to one of our therapists.

The dependent variables selected to assess treatment effects were analyzed using two-by-two mixed repeated-measures analyses of variance, with treatment and wait-list condition serving as the first factor and pre and postassessment serving as the second (repeated measures) factor. In some cases, alternate analyses were performed, and the rationale as well as results are reported separately in those cases.

Before reporting the major findings, it is first worthwhile to examine some preliminary comparisons. Comparisons between accepted cases who completed the treatment and those who did not complete treatment were performed (attrition was minimal). Nonsignificant differences in the gender, race, severity, and age of these subjects were found. Regarding treatment integrity, randomly selected portions of randomly selected tapes of therapy sessions were checked. The population of tapes included all sessions for all cases treated to date. Using a treatment integrity checklist, it was determined that strategies called for in specific sessions were indeed used in those sessions. Accordingly, because the application conformed to the treatment manual, the independent variable (treatment) was deemed to have integrity.

The major analyses were directed toward the examination of the effect of the treatment. Various two-by-two analyses (described earlier) were performed. The means and standard deviations of the various measures are presented in Table 6.1, and changes over time for the two conditions are presented in visual form in Figures 6.1, 6.2 & 6.3. Where significant main effects and significant interactions were found, only the interaction effects are interpreted.

Self-report Measures

For the self-report measures (see Figure 6.1), both the RCMAS and the STAIC-T evidenced similar results. For the RCMAS, the main effect for

Table 6.1. *Means and Standard Deviations of the Measures for the Treatment and Wait-List Conditions*

| | Treatment | | | | Wait-List | | | |
| | Time One | | Time Two | | Time One | | Time Two | |
Measures	M	(SD)	M	(SD)	M	(SD)	M	(SD)
Self-Report								
RCMAS	57.25	(10.89)	41.91	(11.16)	53.44	(7.40)	52.44	(9.07)
STAIC-T	55.25	(10.79)	33.17	(11.74)	54.30	(10.68)	48.90	(9.62)
CQ-C	3.38	(1.15)	5.62	(0.71)	3.90	(1.80)	4.26	(1.04)
CASSQ	47.25	(17.69)	33.42	(10.53)	41.00	(8.61)	39.64	(7.02)
CDI	13.07	(8.31)	4.43	(4.83)	8.82	(6.56)	8.55	(7.06)
FSSC-R	138.82	(22.85)	105.73	(21.84)	133.13	(12.21)	129.38	(14.81)
Parent Rating								
P-CBCL-INT	69.53	(6.40)	59.20	(10.28)	71.00	(5.79)	67.39	(8.16)
CQ-P	2.86	(0.93)	4.53	(1.04)	2.64	(1.01)	2.88	(1.11)
P-STAIC-T	53.00	(6.88)	35.86	(8.11)	51.75	(7.69)	47.75	(7.89)
Teacher Rating								
T-CBCL-INT	65.67	(10.27)	56.00	(7.91)	69.67	(7.53)	63.89	(14.04)

Note:
Self-Report
  RCMAS = Revised Children's Manifest Anxiety Scale
  STAIC-T = Stait-Trait Anxiety Inventory for Children—Trait
  CQ-C = Coping Questionnaire—Child
  CASSQ = Child Anxious Self-Statement Questionnaire
  CDI = Children's Depression Inventory
  FSSC-R = Fear Survey Schedule for Children—Revised
Parent Rating
  P-CBCL-INT = Parent—Child Behavior Checklist—Internalization
  CQ-P = Coping Questionnaire—Parent
  P-STAIC-T = Parent—Stait-Trait Anxiety Inventory for Children—Trait
Teacher Rating
  T-CBCL-INT = Teacher—Child Behavior Checklist—Internalization

condition was nonsignificant, while the trials effect and the Trial X Condition interaction were significant: $F(1,19) = 15.77$, $p < .001$; $F(1,19) = 12.15$, $p < .002$. For the STAIC-T, the main effect for condition was nonsignificant, whereas the trial effect and the Trial X Condition interaction were significant: $F(1,20) = 35.99$, $p < .001$; $F(1,20) = 13.26$, $p < .002$. As seen in Figure 6.1, decreases in self-reported anxiety over time were significant for the treated children over those in the wait-list condition.

Children reported their self-perceived ability to manage distressing situations on the Coping Questionnaire. Analyses of the Coping Questionnaire data (combined "coping" score for three personally relevant and severely distressing situations), showed a nonsignificant main effect for condition, a significant trials effect, and a significant Trials X Condition interaction: $F(1,24) = 20.66$, $p < .001$; $F(1,24) = 10.79$, $p < .003$. Treated

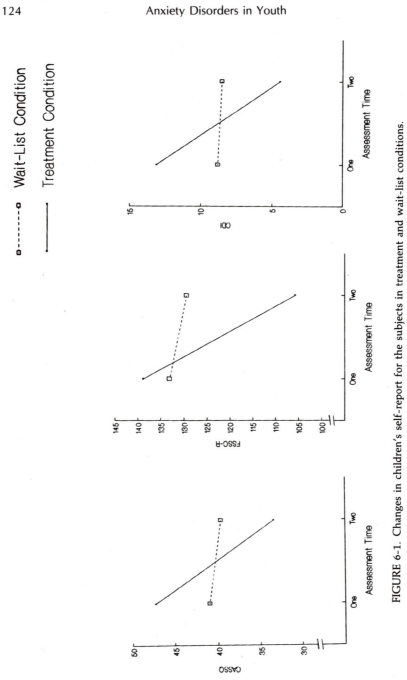

FIGURE 6-1. Changes in children's self-report for the subjects in treatment and wait-list conditions.

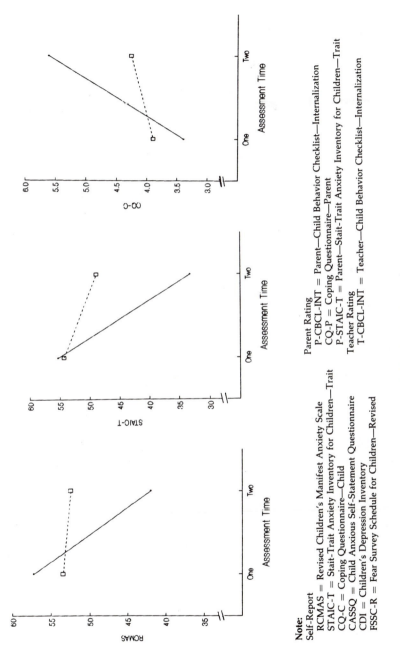

FIGURE 6-1. *(Continued)*

subjects' self-rated coping was found to be significantly higher, over time, than that of the wait-list subjects. When examining the Children's Anxious Self-Statement Questionnaire (CASSQ) and the Fear Survey Schedule for Children (FSSC-R), the significant interactions, $F (1,21) = 6.95, p <$ .02; $F (1,21) = 9.97, p < .005$, again reflected that the treated cases showed significant gains over time compared to the wait-list cases.

Although our treatment is directed primarily toward the remediation of maladaptive anxious affect, the high degree of overlap between anxiety and depression suggested that we assess and evaluate the effects of our treatment on self-reported depressive mood. Analyses of depression scores on the CDI produced a nonsignificant conditions effect, but the trial effect and the Trial X Condition interaction were significant: $F (1,23) = 15.03$, $p < .001$; $F (1,23) = 13.25, p < .001$. These data indicate that the wait-listed children's self-reported depression did not change meaningfully over time, whereas the treated children's scores showed significant reductions from pretreatment to posttreatment. Importantly, although our treatment focuses specifically on anxiety-related distress, there were significant gains made in the reduction of depressed mood. Uniformly, across several self-report measures, therapy was found to have significant beneficial effects.

Parent Reports

Several parent-report measures were examined and the results were consistent across the measures (see Figure 6-2). For the CBCL Internalization T scores, the condition main effect was nonsignificant, whereas the trial effect and the Trial X Condition interaction were significant: $F (1,26) = 28.63, p < .001$; $F(1,26) = 6.64, p < .02$. For the P-STAIC-T, while the condition effect was nonsignificant, the trials effect and the Trials X Condition interaction were significant: $F(1,13) = 18.88, p < .001$; $F(1,13) = 7.30$, $p < .02$. As shown in Figure 6.2, the children in the treatment condition, but not in the wait-list condition, showed a significant decrease over time on Internalization problems and parents report of trait anxiety. For the Coping Questionnaire as completed by the parent(s), there was a significant interaction, $F (1,21) = 5.82, p < .006$, similar to that found with child self-reported coping, which again indicated that treated subjects, relative to wait-list, were rated as showing significantly greater coping abilities at the end of the therapy.

Teacher Reports

Teacher reports were examined somewhat differently from the other measures. Because children who qualify for an anxiety-disorder diagnosis (e.g., OAD) based on structured diagnostic interviews with parents and child do not necessarily have observable anxiety problems in school, some

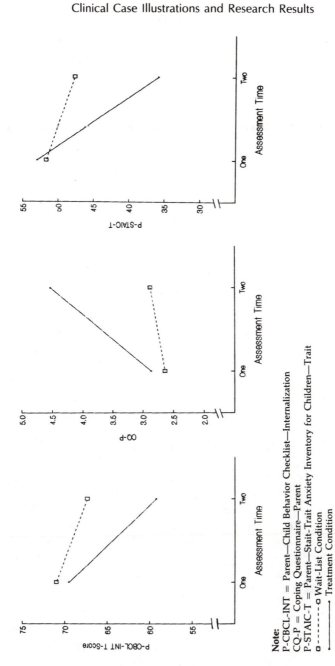

Note:
P-CBCL-INT = Parent—Child Behavior Checklist—Internalization
CQ-P = Coping Questionnaire—Parent
P-STAIC-T = Parent—Stait-Trait Anxiety Inventory for Children—Trait
□ - - - - - □ Wait-List Condition
━━━━━ Treatment Condition

FIGURE 6.2. Changes in parents' ratings for the children in the treatment and wait-list conditions.

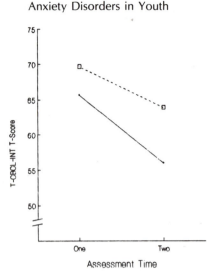

Note:
T-CBCL-INT = Teacher—Child Behavior Checklist—Internalization
□ - - - - - - □ Wait-List Condition
•————————• Treatment Condition

FIGURE 6.3. Changes in teachers' ratings for the children in the treatment and wait-list conditions.

teacher-ratings data did not indicate the existence of problems in the classroom at the initiation of treatment. Therefore, in addition to an analysis of all subjects data, the teacher-ratings data were also examined for select subjects with initial anxiety-related classroom difficulties. The results of analyses of the teacher's CBCL Internalization T scores for all cases indicated a significant main effect for trials, $F (1,19) = 8.98, p < .007$ (see Figure 6-3). Teacher's ratings suggested positive improvements for subjects in both conditions. When the subjects with identified classroom anxiety problems were examined separately, subjects in the treatment group showed greater gains than those in the wait-list, although the number of subjects per group was too few to consider the test meaningful.

Structured Interview Diagnoses

Diagnoses based on structured interviews were completed pre and posttreatment and were examined for evidence of any treatment-produced effects. Because the clear majority of cases were diagnosed OAD, the percentage of those cases with an OAD diagnosis at pretreatment was compared to that at posttreatment. Using the parents' diagnostic interview data, 60% of the treated cases had *no* diagnosis at posttreatment, while only 7% of the wait-list cases showed such change. Using the child's diagnostic interview data, a full 80% of the treated cases *did not* receive a diagnosis at posttreatment, whereas only 40% of the wait-list cases changed from OAD to nonOAD status. At one-year follow-up, fully 100% of the treated cases (8 of 8) did not qualify for an anxiety disorder diagnosis.

CLINICAL SIGNIFICANCE

It has been argued that convincing demonstrations of therapeutic efficacy must provide evidence, whenever possible, that once troubled and disordered clients are now, after treatment, not distinguishable from a meaningful and representative nondisturbed reference group. Normative comparisons (Kendall & Grove, 1988), so defined, provide one methodology for documenting such changes. The present examination of clinically significant change used the normative comparison methodology.

We examined the percentage of cases, in the treatment versus wait-list condition, who went from being among a deviant group (initial scores above 1.5 standard deviations from the mean) to being within a nondeviant group (subsequent scores within a normative boundary). When the STAIC-Trait Anxiety scale and, separately, the RCMAS were examined, the results indicated that 100% of deviant cases at pretreatment were returned to within nondeviant limits at posttreatment.

Our clinic remains active in the provision of services for anxiety-disordered youth and, appropriately, continues to assess and evaluate the outcomes of our program. We are following our completed cases and examining long-term maintenance of gains. Another randomized clinical trial is currently underway and the results, once the treatment outcome study is completed, will be reported in the journals. As we learn more about the treatment, the clients we are serving, and the strengths and weaknesses of various additional therapeutic strategies, we can update and revise the program for maximal intervention efficacy.

Chapter 7

Dealing With Potential Difficulties

First say to yourself what you would be; and then do what you have to do.

—*Epictetus*

We endorse the provision of structured, manualized, interventions for specifically identified problems but recognize the need for individualization of the program for specific client needs—we want to maximize gains while operationalizing our treatment (see also Dobson & Shaw, 1988). As a result, therapists not only learn the strategies of a specified intervention program, but also make the necessary adjustments for the program to be a "good fit" for each child. It is difficult to imagine children whose problems are so circumscribed that they fit only the basic *Diagnostic and Statistical Manual of Mental Disorders-Third Edition-Revised* (DSM-III-R) criteria for a diagnosis of Overanxious Disorder, Separation Anxiety Disorder, or Avoidant Disorder of childhood or adolescence. Rather, many children who meet one set of diagnostic criteria often present with a variety of other symptoms as well. Among these are depression, panic attacks, hyperactivity, and obsessive-compulsive patterns.

In addition to these problems of comorbidity, children may show behavior that, while more directly connected with one of the primary anxiety disorders, is extreme and could potentially interfere with treatment and therefore demands special attention. Such anxiety-related behaviors include denial of anxiety, overcompliance and noncompliance, and hypercriticality. Further, therapists need to be sensitive to the impact of stressors, low income, and general problems in the home environment of the child.

In determining how to best address these potential difficulties, the therapist can benefit from focusing on the goals of the therapy as well as reconsidering the techniques of the treatment program. With such knowledge, the therapist can sensitively modify cognitive and/or behavioral components of treatment to best help the particular child. In many cases, working with difficulties will entail extra parental support. Parents can often help in breaking the environmental patterns that may be contributing to the maintenance of difficulties. For instance, parents may encourage a highly perfectionistic child to reduce personal standards by rewarding less-than-perfect behavior.

In the section that follows we will consider the potential difficulties linked with comorbidity (depression, hyperactivity, obsessive-compulsive patterns, panic), denial of anxiety, and matters of compliance.

COMORBIDITY

Depression

The overlap between anxiety and depression is becoming increasingly recognized (Kendall & Watson, 1989). Kendall and Watson (1989) list a number of symptoms that anxiety and depression share: irritability, agitation and restlessness, concentration difficulties, insomnia, and fatigue. Given the overlap in symptomatology, it is not surprising that a number of studies have revealed a high correlation between self-report measures of anxiety and depression (see Gotlib & Cane, 1989 and Brady & Kendall, 1991, for a review). However, while there is strong indication for the comorbidity of depression and anxiety in both children and adults (Finch, Fryer, Saylor, Carek, & McIntosh, 1990; Saylor, Finch, Spirito, & Bennett, 1984), the degree to which they overlap remains in dispute.

Given this overlap it is to be expected that a number of children seeking treatment for anxiety problems may also be experiencing some depressive symptoms. It is the recognition of the possibility for debilitating depression that prompts us to use the Children's Depression Inventory (Kovacs, 1981) in our battery of diagnostic tests; thus, we can be alert to depression from the start of treatment. In the course of considering in what ways the present treatment program can be modified to address depression, it is worthwhile to briefly consider some of the similarities and differences, particularly at the emotional and cognitive levels, that have been posited between depression and anxiety.

Regarding differences at the emotional level, fear has been posited as a central component of anxiety, while sadness has been considered central to depression (Izard, 1971, as cited in Kendall & Watson, 1989). In addition, anxiety and depression have been differentiated along dimensions of the global constructs, negative and positive affect (Watson & Clark, 1984). Anxiety has been characterized as a pure state of negative affect (e.g., fear, nervousness, guilt, anger, contempt), regardless of the presence or absence of positive affect. On the other hand, depression has been characterized by high negative affect and low positive affect (e.g., not excited, enthusiastic, or joyful; see Kendall & Watson, 1989). These findings suggest that while an anxious (but not depressed) child may experience a number of negatively valanced emotions, he or she may still have a relatively strong capacity for enjoyment. On the other hand, a child who is both anxious and depressed may carry the double burden of experiencing a number of negative emotions with less hope of any relief offered by intermittent enjoyment. Under such a burden, the anxious and depressed child may lose motivation; in fact, diminished performance in school work is indicative of childhood depression (Matson, 1989).

The presence of depression has implications for the treatment of anxiety. First, because a cognitive-behavioral program involves a number of assignments that are to be done outside of the session, therapists may face a situation in which the dysphoric child's low motivation interferes with finishing these tasks. If the child is feeling hopeless, he may not see the value of completing these at-home assignments. Thus, the therapist moves the client along, offering the hope that he or she believes the child will feel less sad and that completing the assigned tasks is one important step for feeling better. To sustain an atmosphere of hopefulness, the therapist is particularly encouraging about any attempts that are made to complete the tasks. If possible, parents may provide an important resource, encouraging the child throughout the week to complete the assignments. It is important that parents avoid being overbearing and inadvertently critical of their children's work. It is the case that some parents of children with anxiety problems have been overly critical and judgmental, and this is also the case for parents of dysphoric and depressed children. Helping parents to become supportive and encouraging, without "hovering over their children" facilitates treatment progress.

Within each individual session, the therapist will want to emphasize "fun" activities; anxious children who are also depressed may have developed the habit of assuming they aren't going to have fun, so why try. For example, by engaging in various games (e.g., computer games or traditional board games) the child may be surprised that he is capable of engaging in a pleasurable activity.

Recognizing that he is capable of enjoying activities is then tied to the child's implementing the fourth and final step in our FEAR acronym—Reward. With an increasing capacity for pleasure, the child will more readily think of ways of rewarding himself. Helping the dysphoric child discover means of self-reward is an important intervention in itself.

Working with an anxious child who is also somewhat depressed may entail addressing certain ongoing cognitive activities less likely to be found in a purely anxious child. Anxious children who are also depressed have cognitions typically associated with anxiety as well as typically depressogenic cognition; the more depressed cognition includes a greater emphasis on personal degradation and a greater preoccupation with the past (Beck, Brown, Steer, Eidelson, & Risking, 1987). Because depressogenic attributions often involve focusing on past behavior as well as self-degradation for performance in past situations, depressive cognition can be addressed at the "E" (expectations), "A" (actions and attitudes), or "R" (results and rewards) stage of the FEAR plan. In evaluating their performance in anxious situations, depressed children would be expected to make more internal attributions about negative outcomes than anxious children who are not depressed (see also Kendall, Stark, & Adam, 1990). By exploring these expectations and attributions for performance, therapists can help children become more aware of these patterns and help them start to replace their dysfunctional distorted thinking with more realistic conclusions.

Conducting personal experiments, as used in treating depressed youth (see Stark, 1990; Hollon & Beck, 1979), was modeled after the collaborative empiricism of Beck's cognitive therapy for depression (Beck, Rush, Shaw, & Emery, 1979; Hollon & Beck, 1979). In these "tests," clients are asked to describe situations and report their attributional conclusions. A shared experience with the therapist allows both the child client and therapist to have some first hand experience that can then be discussed. As the client details the reasons for certain attributions, the therapist can help the child think of ways to test such notions. For example, if the client and therapist have a shared interaction with another youth and the client thinks that the other child did not like him, the therapist would be able to ask, "What made you think that?" and, possibly, "Is there any other way to explain it?" After related discussions, and perhaps even further testing of such notions in which the child asks the other person if he liked or disliked him, the therapist and child work together to develop attributional patterns that are more consistent with the data and less biased by the depressed client's views about himself. To facilitate a lasting cognitive change in the anxious and depressed child, the therapist can reward the child, tying the new casual attributions that have been generated into the "R" stage of the FEAR program.

Hypercriticality

When working with an anxious child who is hypercritical, the therapist can encourage and reward less-than-perfect performance on many at-home and in-session tasks. These highly perfectionistic children fear doing anything that appears "sloppy." For instance, one little girl became upset when she accidently got a pencil mark on a piece of paper on which she was about to draw. She immediately wanted to get a fresh sheet. The therapist asked her to use the original sheet and to use the FEAR steps to cope with appearing sloppy. The therapist may want to explore what the child fears will happen if he does something less than perfect, particularly in reference to how they thinks others will perceive them. Hypercriticality can be addressed at the results and reward stage of the FEAR steps. These children find it very diffi.ult to realistically assess their performance, re-garding anything less than perfect as failure. One of the aims of our program is to help children realize that they do not have to perform perfectly in order to feel they have succeeded, and this point should receive special emphasis when working with a hypercritical child.

Hyperactivity

Although anxious children may exhibit signs of motor agitation (e.g., hair twisting, stuttering, wanting to leave an anxious situation; Barrios & Hartmann, 1988), hyperactive children are characterized by more impul-sivity and globally overactive behavior. In addition to impulsive motor behavior, hyperactive children show extreme impulsiveness (acting with-out thinking) in situations that require careful thinking (Kendall & Bras-well, 1985). In treating an anxious child who may also exhibit some signs of overactivity, the therapist modifies both cognitive and behavioral as-pects of the current treatment program. At the behavioral level, the ther-apist may want to create a more structured approach to teaching some of the skills that are introduced during the first eight sessions. Children with difficulties staying focused on task benefit from structured environ-ments.

Also, anxious-overactive children find it difficult to learn to relax. For instance, because it may be anxiety provoking for these children to do muscle relaxation (see Heide & Borkovec, 1983; 1984, for a discussion of relaxation-induced anxiety), the skills might be introduced more gradu-ally, with structure, and in terms of a game in which the child is told that he is learning to be a rag doll. The therapist can move around the room with the child telling him when to make various parts of his body like a rag doll (i.e., relaxed) and when to make them like a robot (i.e., tensed).

In this manner the therapist can participate as a coping model who also learns that it is safe to become relaxed. It may also be helpful to oversee some of the "Show That I Can" (STIC) tasks—have the child draw pictures of anxiety-provoking situations in sessions or right after the sessions before he or she goes home, thus modeling and providing structure. This effort would be intended to prepare the child for the more concentration-demanding task of writing about anxiety-producing situations in his or her journal.

Other aspects of the current treatment program lend themselves to working with children whose anxiety problems include some hyperactive patterns. Cognitive-behavioral programs for hyperactive children have used modeling of self-instruction to help impulsive and hyperactive children "stop and think" (Kendall, 1989) and cope in various situations. A portion of our program also involves the therapist's planning and modeling coping procedures. Repeated exposure to anxiety-related situations and "stopping to think" about how to cope with them helps the child reduce impulsivity and cope with anxiety. Overactive children have low levels of frustration tolerance and benefit from learning how to deal with failure without becoming excessively frustrated. We have often found it useful to model coping with making mistakes while working with anxious children who tend to see any error as indicative of personal failure. For instance, the therapist may intentionally fumble with audio equipment (when taping a session) and model a coping style of self-talk. In addition to modeling how to cope with the anxiety of possibly feeling foolish, the therapist working with an anxious child with some signs of hyperactivity might add coping with the frustration of making a mistake. This additional element of potential frustration in the face of making a mistake is added at the "E" of FEAR as one of several cognitive facets in the situation that may be anxiety or frustration producing.

Obsessive-Compulsive Patterns

Obsessional ruminations and compulsive ritualistic behaviors have routinely been seen as reflecting distressing levels of anxiety. Former versions of diagnostic nomenclature placed obsessive-compulsive patterns within the "neurotic" category; however, as advances have been made and diagnostic systems have moved more toward descriptive disorders, neurotic problems are now identified as anxiety disorders.

Although somewhat rare, there are cases of children whose anxiety disorders include certain obsessive-compulsive features, and working with an anxious child who has obsessive-compulsive patterns can be particularly challenging. Among the anxiety disorders, patients suffering from obsessive-compulsive disorder report the highest levels of anxiety and fear as well as depression (Turner & Beidel, 1988). Though obsessive-compulsive disorder is not listed in the DSM-III-R as a childhood anxiety disorder, it has been suggested that the tendency toward obsessive thought patterns and compulsive behavior seen at an early age later develops into full-blown obsessive-compulsive disorder (Turner & Beidel, 1988). Even rarer are cases of children who actually receive a diagnosis of obsessive-compulsive disorder with an age onset as young as three (Rapoport, 1986).

Because it is often thought that obsessions and/or compulsions are anxiety-reducing for the sufferer, the child with such patterns may be highly resistant to changing them. The child may be quite rigid, hypervigilant, and even hostile about protecting this anxiety-reducing behavior because of a vague, overwhelming fear of some disaster or harm befalling him or her. Often individuals with obsessive-compulsive disorder do not trust their feelings and perceptions about situations, and there is a strong tendency to avoid experiencing emotions if they are going to feel bad or out of control. Unlike treatment for cases of comorbidity with depression and hyperactivity, the preferred way of treating obsessive-compulsive disorder may not mesh as easily with the program described herein. For example, the general emphasis in treatment for obsessive-compulsive disorder has been on exposing the individual to the anxiety-provoking situation without allowing the obsessive-compulsive pattern to take place. The individual is exposed to his or her anxiety at high levels. There is no attempt to help the client learn to cope with and reduce the anxiety. In fact, according to Turner and Beidel (1988), any attempts at anxiety reduction, particularly through cognitive activity, can be seen as interfering with the ultimate treatment goals for an obsessive compulsive client. But, the difficulty in treating a child with obsessive-compulsive patterns should not preclude efforts to address these patterns within the broader framework of treating the primary problem of overanxious disorder, separation anxiety, and/or avoidant disorder. The FEAR strategy can be applied to anxious situations that do not necessarily entail the obsessive-compulsive behavior, while at the same time using more circumscribed exposure experiences (with response prevention) to address the obsessive-compulsive difficulties.

The severity of obsessive and compulsive patterns varies greatly among the children. One distinction to keep in mind when deciding how to address such patterns is whether or not the pattern seems to represent a budding obsessive-compulsive disorder or is rather a less severe by-product of the perfectionism characteristic of another anxiety disorder. To illustrate these possibilities consider two examples of anxiety-disordered children who have been treated in our clinic. In the case of a girl we'll call Maggie, the therapist noticed that she was very perfectionistic. Overly concerned with making any type of error, she had difficulty completing the self-report forms in a timely fashion because she needed to check each page several times to make sure she had answered every question and to query about any item for which she was not absolutely sure that the answer she gave was precise. In a second case, a client we will call Sara demonstrated a more extreme obsessive-compulsive behavior pattern that truly interfered with her life. She was preoccupied with not being interrupted and, therefore, spoke very rapidly, fearing that any break in her speech would result in an interruption.

Because Maggie's behavior appeared to be directly related to her overall perfectionism, rather than being a compulsion to check her answers, the problem was addressed within the framework of our program for overanxious youth. The therapist chose to set up an exposure experience requiring the child to complete a detailed task within certain time limits that would preclude excessive checking. In presenting the task, the therapist helped the child work through the FEAR steps, so that she could cope with the anxiety that would arise in the face of possibly making an error that she did not have time to correct. Such experience, especially when repeated in various forms, helps the child to learn to be less perfectionistic, a common problem in overanxious disorder.

For Sara, a more behavioral intervention, with less concern about use of the FEAR steps, seemed appropriate. Thus, the therapist asked Sara to engage in a conversation with someone who was instructed to interrupt her. It was anticipated that initially the child's anxiety would mount, but repeated experience with the situation would lead to extinction of the anxiety and a concurrent reduction in the compulsion to speak very rapidly. While our efforts did produce modest improvements, Sara was not kept on our protocol and did not complete the treatment program.

Because children with obsessive patterns are already extremely caught up in their own cognitive activity, any attempt at a cognitive exploration of the problem may backfire—leading to an escalation of their tendency to do too much thinking. A child whose overriding problem is obsessional thinking may not be appropriate for a "heady" and thoughtful cognitive-behavioral program. However, for a child whose primary problem is generalized anxiety disorder with mild obsessive and/or compulsive features, the goal would be to reduce obsessive or compulsive patterns, so that the anxiety related to the overanxious disorder can be fully addressed.

Panic Attacks

The child who experiences panic-like symptoms shows extreme concern for physiological responses associated with anxiety. Like obsessive-compulsive disorder, the DSM-III-R does not list panic attacks among childhood disorders; yet, there are a few children with a primary diagnosis of another anxiety disorder who have reported panic-like symptoms, such as a racing heart, shaking, chattering teeth, and dizziness. Additionally, ill-defined feelings of being overwhelmed have also been reported. Nelles and Barlow (1988) have suggested that while children may manifest the physiological signs of panic, sometimes receiving a diagnosis of hyperventilation syndrome, it is debatable whether prior to adolescence children are cognitively capable of making the internal attributions for their symptoms necessary for the cognitions characterizing panic attacks, as for example, "I'm losing control" or "I'm going to die" (p. 369). Nelles and Barlow note that the incidence of diagnosed panic disorder in children is extremely low.

Despite the low incidence of childhood panic attacks, it is worthwhile to consider how our program might be used to address these symptoms, even if they do not constitute a full panic attack. Because the panic-like symptoms can themselves be anxiety provoking, it is appropriate to address them within the FEAR plan, so that the child can learn to cope with such distressing physiological arousal.

Such an approach entails helping the child identify what the initial physiological cues are that may spark the fear of experiencing intense physiological arousal. Having learned what responses typically foreshadow this arousal, a child can proceed to cope via the first of the FEAR steps-"Feeling frightened?" For instance, a child reports that a suddenly racing heartbeat is his typical response before the general escalation of other physiological responses, and he or she learns to use this response as a cue to ask him or herself if he or she is feeling frightened. However, in the case of panic-like symptoms, the question would be used to identify whether the child was feeling frightened about the heartbeat because it signaled the possibility of panic-like symptoms, or for fear of some external circumstance. The child would then use the recently acquired skills to "calm down"; while taking deep breaths often works to initially calm anxiety, they may in the case of nascent panic-like symptoms exacerbate hyperventilation which has been associated with the onset of panic (Ley, 1987). Thus, the child might want to focus on relaxing tensed muscles.

Should the child's level of cognitive development permit, he or she might be encouraged to use the next step—"Expecting bad things to happen?" The child would be encouraged to focus on panic-related cognitions: Is he expecting to lose control, or is he fearing that he might be overwhelmed by the physiological symptoms and actually die? The goal of the first steps would be to nip in the bud the mounting physiological symptoms and the distorted thinking about these symptoms before a full-blown panic-like experience ensues. Because the escalation of physiological symptoms may be extremely rapid and intense, making the child aware of distorted thinking may be especially difficult; the therapist will have to prepare to be particularly persistent in probing about this information.

At the Actions and Attitudes step of the FEAR plan, the child should be encouraged to think of various ways of coping other than merely escaping from the arousing situation, because such action readily reinforces avoidance behavior. Coping may involve the use of relaxation not only to nip the anxiety in the bud, but also to lower anxiety if it has begun to escalate (see Barlow & Cerny, 1988, for a cognitive-behavioral treatment of panic in adults). Coping may also include coping self-talk: "I know how to breath; my body knows what to do."

DENIAL OF ANXIETY, REALISTIC FEARS, AND OVER AND NONCOMPLIANCE

Denial of Anxiety

Anxious children may exhibit a number of behaviors that can interfere with treatment. Often, these behaviors are related to their presenting problems. Among the most common is the initial denial of anxiety. For instance, consider the following: One of the instruments used to assess anxiety in children is a self-report questionnaire that asks the client how frequently she has difficulty making up her mind. The child is seated at a table and is reading and rereading the item. The alternatives are read and reread, and the therapist is approached with a question about the item. Even after the therapist has provided clarification, the child continues to labor over the item and "shows" genuine difficulty making up her mind. Eventually, after much consternation, the child reports that she does not have difficulty making up her mind. Thus, the questionnaire data (self-report) seems in contradiction to the observed actions. While it is only speculation, it seems that the child wants to present in a favorable manner (fake good) and has misinterpreted her own difficulties in making decisions in order to avoid reporting anxiety (see Kendall & Chansky, 1991).

More generally, it is not unusual for a child to be relatively willing to report some anxious feelings during a diagnostic intake interview, only to report during an initial therapy session that he or she has no real problems with anxiety. More than likely, such denial represents the child's attempt to appear competent in the eyes of the therapist. It can be very helpful at such times for the therapist to disclose her own feelings of anxiety in certain situations. Such an approach normalizes the experience and can relieve the anxious child of the need to appear perfect and competent. Sometimes, children actually exhibit several signs of anxiety (e.g., extreme hair twisting, nervous giggling, nervous motor activity); yet, when questioned whether they are feeling anxious, they report no anxious feelings. This situation can be dealt with in several ways. The therapist may draw attention to the behavior and question: "I notice you're twisting your hair. I twist my hair when I'm nervous, do you?" It may be helpful again for the therapist to self-disclose as a coping model—showing how it can be easy to say you aren't anxious when really you are. This modeling can include statements about how it is difficult to get help coping with anxious feelings if people don't let anybody know how they are feeling.

Realistic Fears

Therapists need to be sensitive to the reality basis of a child's distress. Children from low socioeconomic (SES) groups have been found to have more fears about specific events or things (Angelino, Dollins, & Mech, 1956)—perhaps resulting from the reality that their environments contain more threatening events. Such first-hand experiences with very threatening situations—situations that children in other circumstances would simply never have to face—can result in detrimental anxiety. For example, one of our adolescent clients had a fear of being stabbed; as it turned out, she had actually been stabbed and had seen others being stabbed during various gang-related fights. Stressful and threatening environments contributing to the child's anxiety are not limited to children from low SES groups. Children from various backgrounds may live in chaotic homes where there is little hope of receiving parental support, because the parents themselves are under great stress (e.g., from work, marital problems, being a single parent, or illness).

At a pragmatic level, a disorganized home environment may create difficulties for treatment effectiveness in terms of lost relaxation tapes, notebooks, or other session-related materials. Likewise, the child may have trouble completing schoolwork, which in turn may contribute to his or her anxiety about school performance. On an emotional level, parents who are under stress may at times be somewhat unpredictable. Thus, for example, one 12-year-old boy suffered a great deal of anxiety about being hurt by bigger children. In relatively ambiguous situations, such as being bumped in the hall at school during the crowded rush to classes, he would perceive the other children as trying to harm him. The origins of these fears became clearer when, during the parent session, the mother reported that the father (who was currently working two jobs) was presently very moody and unpredictable in his behavior toward the child—at times lashing out and hitting him for only minor transgressions. Similarly, if a parent is him or herself experiencing extreme anxiety and presenting the world as a threatening place to the child, the child's fears may be grounded in the fear-filled "reality" that is presented by the parent. While these situations often call for the parent getting some type of support or even professional help, the focus is on helping the child learn to recognize realistic fears and stressful circumstances and to identify strategies to cope with them. An integral part of this involves helping the child learn to distinguish between what are reality-based fears and what fears result from misinterpretation or overgeneralization of situations which are similar to fearful situations that the child actually faces (e.g., the threat of an unpredictable father versus being bumped in the school hall).

Over- and Noncompliance

Anxious children are concerned about pleasing others, and in some instances, they become overcompliant. Indeed, one of the reasons that anxious children often go without treatment is because—unlike children with more externalizing symptoms (e.g., conduct disorder),—anxious children's symptoms often result in compliance with others. The signs of overcompliance may include completing all at-home assignments perfectly, as well as dutifully fulfilling any in-session requirements. There is a sense that the child is just going through the motions, afraid to question any assignments or express when he or she does not understand. The child may become anxious if he believes he has not done something exactly as it was supposed to have been done. One way to address this is for the therapist to encourage "noncompliance." For instance, an overly compliant child can be told that he must choose to not complete one of the STIC tasks (home assignments). This deviation from doing what is expected may be very anxiety provoking. Yet, such a situation provides an opportunity for helping the overly compliant child learn to cope with anxiety when he misconstrues that something was done "wrong."

Though anxious children are often very eager to please, occasionally children are reluctant to comply with the various activities involved in cognitive-behavioral treatment. Noncompliance can range from an out-right failure to complete the STIC tasks to passivity within the sessions. In trying to handle noncompliance, the therapist may want to ask what the behavior represents—what is the catastrophe that the child has thought of? For instance, a child may report that he or she is bored in the sessions and simply doesn't believe that there is very much to work on. However, such behavior may reflect a real fear of discussing very upsetting thoughts and feelings. A very intelligent 13-year-old girl, for example, felt ashamed that she was terrified whenever one of her parents was 15 minutes late after work. She had great difficulty opening up and telling the therapist that she imagined her parent to be dead.

Great patience and a willingness to try different approaches are needed in dealing with the noncompliant anxious child. Acknowledging that the child doesn't seem interested in what is being discussed and following with probes about the reasons for this disinterest can be helpful. Asking the child how things might be better for him or her in the sessions, or an open recognition of some of the child's nonanxious emotions, such as anger or depression, are other possibilities. Extra efforts at rapport building may be required, such as finding a favorite activity (e.g., computer games) and using it during part of the session, while at the same time accomplishing the session's tasks. The goal is to strike a balance between making the noncompliant child aware that you empathize with the difficulty of dis-cussing problems (and even their feelings that nothing is going to help), while at the same time projecting confidence that if they are willing to participate more thoroughly they really will be able to help themselves in difficult and painful situations.

CLOSING COMMENTS

While our program allows for the flexibility to deal with children who have a variety of problems, the primary focus is on helping them learn how to manage and cope with distressing anxiety. Thus, in assessing whether or not a child's problems are amenable to treatment within a cognitive-behavioral program, one must consider how much the child's general functioning will be helped if he or she learns to cope more suc-cessfully with anxiety and how far treatment must deviate from the basic treatment strategies. In making such decisions, it may be helpful to conceptualize potential difficulties in treatment as lying along a con-tinuum ranging from symptoms of anxiety to the presence of other dis-orders. Some problems, such as hypercriticality or overcompliance, are most likely the products of the child's fundamental anxiety. Other prob-lems, such as comorbidity with depression, obsessive-compulsive patterns, or hyperactivity involve a more complex situation that may include functional difficulties outside the realm of anxiety. The degree to which our program will prove useful for children displaying symptoms of other disorders will vary with the individual child and the skill of the therapist. Hopefully, our suggestions will help determine how best to approach potential difficulties in treatment and help facilitate flexible applications of a structured intervention.

Chapter 8
Working With the Family

Nobody who has not been in the interior of a family can say what the difficulties of any individual of that family may be.

—*Jane Austen*

Our cognitive-behavioral model of psychopathology rests on consideration of the social and interpersonal contexts and contingencies in the child's world; they are inextricably linked (Kendall, 1985; 1991). The child's expectations and attributions are responses to the external social milieu, and reciprocally the child's thoughts and actions are responded to by those in their context. The family is the child's first social context and plays an enormous role in shaping the child's expectations, attitudes, and understanding of the world. While the mutual influence of child and family is ineluctable and pervasive, finding the best pathway into this network when problems arise is not always so obvious.

Thus far we have considered interventions that focus primarily on the individual child. In this chapter we discuss several ways in which the family unit is involved in the assessment and treatment of childhood anxiety disorders—both in a more distal role of supportive consultants in the child's treatment and the more proximal role of participants in the treatment itself. We first look at family factors contributing to childhood anxiety, including genetic components, parenting styles, and patterns of family interaction. Finally, we discuss a proposed cognitive-behavioral model of anxiety disorders based on a systemic view of the mutual processes of attribution, expectation, and action within a family. We also discuss potential components of a family cognitive-behavioral treatment for child and adolescent anxiety disorders.

FAMILY FACTORS CONTRIBUTING TO THE DISORDER

Family factors in the etiology of childhood anxiety disorders have been described from several perspectives. Early studies addressed parent psychopathology, attributing causality primarily to the parents. For example, some writers have hypothesized that mother-child overinvolvement resulted from the mother's own separation anxiety (Eisenberg, 1958 a&b; Prince, 1968). More recent investigations have estimated concordance rates between parent and child anxiety (as well as other disorders) suggesting a familial and possibly genetic component (Cloninger, Martin, Clayton, & Guze, 1981; Crowe, Noyes, Pauls, & Slymen, 1983; Harris, Noyes, Crowe, & Chaudery, 1983). In addition to these studies, another line of research has focused on the impact of stressful life events on anxiety disorders, particularly those which change the family constellation. For example, maternal separation, parental divorce, and the death of a parent can each be stressful life events that could contribute to child maladjustment. In this section, we consider the impact of stressful family events, general parenting styles, and parents' cognitive functioning on childhood anxiety disorders.

Predispositions

To what extent do children who display anxiety-disordered patterns of thought and behavior carry a predisposition toward such a disorder? Do the anxiety disorders tend to run in families, such that genetic predispositions can be contributing to the observed disorders? In this section, we review research indicating that while some anxiety disorders appear to have a partial genetic basis (i.e., panic attack) other anxiety disorders (e.g., generalized anxiety disorder) do not reveal such a distinct genetic pattern, although the incidence of anxiety disorders, as well as other disorders, is often higher in the relatives of anxious probands in comparison to control groups. In reviewing the literature, we first examine the relationship between various anxiety disorders (e.g., panic disorder, agoraphobia, generalized anxiety disorder, and simple and social phobias) and patterns of problems found among relatives of the diagnosed individuals. Studies of children of anxious parents as well as parents of anxious children are among those that will be discussed, as will be studies revealing varying patterns of disorders among male and female relatives of anxious probands. Findings from studies on the relationship between anxiety and depression in individuals and families are also presented. Finally, we also briefly consider possible parent-child patterns of interaction and other environmental factors that may relate to the anxiety disorders of childhood.

Patterns of Problems Among the Relatives of Anxiety Disorder Probands. Research findings suggest a general increase in anxiety disorders and other types of pathology among the relatives of individuals with anxiety disorders (Carey & Gottesman, 1981), including increased depression, various anxiety disorders, and alcoholism (Munjack, Howard, & Moss, 1981; Noyes, Clancy, Crowe, Hoenk, & Slymen, 1978; Solyom, Becky, Solyom, & Hugel, 1974). Thus, therapists working with anxious children are best prepared to treat, to refer other family members, or to at least to be sensitive to the impact that other members of the anxious child's family may have on his or her functioning.

A number of studies have examined rates of anxiety in the relatives of anxiety disorder probands. Some studies have compared rates of pathology in relatives of individuals suffering from panic attacks with rates among relatives of individuals suffering from other disorders or normal controls (Cloninger et al., 1981; Crowe et al., 1983; Crowe, Pauls, Slymen, & Noyes, 1980; Harris et al., 1983). Overall, evidence for a familial pattern in panic attacks exists, with rates of this disorder appearing significantly more frequently in the relatives of panic-attack probands. There is some indication of increased rates of alcoholism among the male relatives of panic-attack probands and that female relatives are more susceptible to panic attacks than males (Crewe et al., 1980). Evidence for a genetic component in panic disorder emerged in Torgesen's (1983) comparison of concordance rates of anxiety disorders in monozygotic and dyzotic twin pairs. However, no clear familial pattern for generalized anxiety disorder has appeared (Crowe et al., 1983; Torgesen, 1983). The presence of panic attacks may also increase the general risk for anxiety among relatives of anxious probands. Cloninger et al. (1981) suggested that increased rates of anxiety neurosis among female relatives of anxious female probands was largely accounted for by the relatives of individuals suffering from agoraphobia with severe panic attacks. While male relatives of anxiety probands were not at an increased risk for anxiety, they showed a somewhat elevated rate of alcoholism (though the authors note that appropriate population estimates for alcoholism had not yet been determined for this study).

Other studies have examined rates of pathology in the relatives of individuals with a broad range of anxiety disorders. Comparisons have been made between relatives of anxious probands and those of normal controls as well as relatives of individuals suffering from various types of anxiety disorders (e.g., agoraphobia and simple phobias). Studies comparing relatives of anxiety probands with those of normal controls (e.g., Solyom et al., 1974; Noyes et al., 1978) show significantly higher rates of pathology (e.g., alcoholism, depression, and anxiety neurosis) among the relatives of anxious probands. Munjack et al. (1981) found higher rates of affective illness in the relatives of agoraphobic patients in comparison to relatives of simple and social phobics; relatives of agoraphobic patients also had higher rates of alcoholism in comparison to relatives of simple and miscellaneous phobics but not in comparison to the relatives of social phobics.

Family Patterns in Anxiety and Depression. The relationships between depression and anxiety and different familial patterns of pathology have also received attention (Leckman, Weissman, Merikangas, Pauls, & Prusoff 1983; Livingston, Nugent, Rader, & Smith, 1985; Weissman, Leckman, Merikangas, Gammon, & Prusoff, 1984). Livingston et al. (1985) reported that for both depressed and anxious children, relatives were at an increased risk for alcoholism and depression, but other disorders were less frequent. A combination of depression and anxiety has been shown to relate to increased risks for both disorders in children as well as other relatives of probands (Leckman et al., 1983; Weissman et al., 1984).

Rates of pathology among the children of depressed and anxious parents have also been compared (Turner, Beidel, & Costello, 1987; Sylvester, Hyde, & Reichler, 1987). Turner et al. (1987) found that children of anxious parents were over two times as likely to have a *Diagnostic and Statistical Manual of Mental Disorders-Third Edition* (DSM-III) diagnosis than were children of dysthymic parents. Likewise, children of anxious parents were twice as likely to have an anxiety disorder. In comparison to children of nondisturbed parents, the children of anxious parents were nine times as likely to receive a DSM III diagnosis and seven times as likely to have an anxiety disorder. Sylvester et al. (1987) found that children of depressed and panic-disordered parents showed higher rates of depression and anxiety and poorer rates of adjustment than did children of controls.

Children of Anxious Parents and Parents of Anxious Children. Comparing the impact of differing types of anxiety disorders among parents on their children, Silverman, Cerny, and Nelles (1988) found the highest rate of clinical diagnosis and/or Child Behavior Problem Checklist (CBCL) score in the clinical range for children of agoraphobics (81%) followed by children of mixed phobics (75%), children of generalized anxiety patients (29%), and children of panic disorder patients (0%). Thus children of agoraphobics were rated by both clinicians (via diagnosis) and their parents (via the CBCL) as having the highest level of diagnosable problems as well as more discrete behavior problems.

Finally, rates of pathology in parents of children with varying anxiety disorders have been compared (Berg, Butler, & Pritchard, 1974; Last, Hersen, Kazdin, Francis, & Grubb, 1987). Last et al. (1987) found that a majority of mothers (83%) of a combined group of children diagnosed with overanxious disorder (OAD), separation anxiety disorder (SAD), or both, had a lifetime history of one or more anxiety disorders, with generalized anxiety disorder being the most common. Mothers of children with both OAD and SAD had the highest lifetime history of anxiety disorders (with almost every mother in this group having a history of at least one anxiety disorder), though they were not significantly higher than mothers of children with only one of the anxiety disorders. 41 percent of the mothers of children receiving diagnoses of both OAD and SAD revealed a history of simple phobia.

In the Last et al. (1987) study, mothers of a control group of children diagnosed as conduct disorder, attention deficit disorder, or oppositional disorder revealed a significantly lower lifetime rate of anxiety disorders. In comparison to the group of control mothers, the current rate of anxiety disorders was significantly higher among the mothers of the combined group of anxious children, with more than half of the mothers from these three groups presenting with an anxiety disorder at the time that their children received a diagnosis. While the lifetime rates for affective disorders were higher among the mothers of the anxious children, in comparison to the control group mothers (at least one half of the mothers in each of the three anxiety groups had a history of an affective disorder) the difference was not significant. The most common affective disorder for all groups was major depression. No significant differences between current levels of affective disorders emerged between the mothers of anxious and control-group children.

While the results of these studies indicate increased risk of pathology among the relatives of anxiety probands, they provide only clues to the mechanisms of transmission for the various disorders. Factors involved in the etiology of anxiety disorder appear to include genetic elements, more notably for panic disorder. However, the variety of disorders that can emerge also indicates that environmental factors, such as patterns of familial modeling or communication, play a key role in the development of anxiety disorders. Understanding what environmental, social-learning, and cognitive factors contribute most to the genesis of specific anxiety disorders in children would be particularly helpful for psychopathologists and therapists alike. We now turn to a consideration of possible family environmental factors that may contribute to the development of anxiety disorders in children.

Stressful Family Events

Stressful life events, especially parental separation, divorce, death, or marital conflict, impact on the family unit. Yet the relationship between these events and anxiety disorders in children remains somewhat unclear. Early attempts to understand child anxiety suggested a causal relationship between children's early separation from the mother and anxiety (Bowlby, 1961). More recent studies have found a high rate of death or illness in the parents of school-phobic children (Waldron, Shrier, Stone, & Tobin 1975), and retrospective studies have found a significant increase in stressful life events, including maternal separation in adults with agoraphobia (Faravelli, Webb, Ambonetti, Fonnesu, & Sessarego, 1985).

Critics of separation theories have pointed out that separation is not consistently found in the history of separation anxiety disorders, and Gittelman (1986) cites Hersov's (1960) systematic study of separation in school-phobic children, wherein he found that these children had significantly *less* separation in their histories than did controls. Others propose that the impact of a separation cannot be determined apart from its cause, as the cause may have consequences of its own, independent of the separation. For example, Gittelman (1986) argued that in many studies, the separation often is due to health conditions requiring the child's hospitalization. Concerns about illness may incur psychological distress for both parent and child, independent of a separation; likewise, caring for a sick child requires greater closeness and contact. Factors such as these need to be considered separately in the child's history.

A related issue is the child's concerns about the health of a parent. As noted, in our clinic we see a number of children whose parents report illness or chronic medical conditions, and the children's fears for their parents' health are an ongoing source of stress. Relatedly, there is often some caution about health in general in the family, and this may lead to an "overprotective" or "enmeshed" configuration as both parent and child organize their lives around keeping in touch.

Marital Conflict. Some evidence links school phobia to marital discontent and concomitant dependence of the mother on the child to compensate for an unsatisfactory spousal relationship (Eisenberg, 1958 a&b; Waldron et al., 1975). Overall, however, empirical evidence does not exist for the association between marital conflict per se and internalizing disorders, such as anxiety, among clinical samples of children (for a review see Emery & O'Leary, 1982). However, one nonclinic sample found marital conflict to be related to aggressive behavior in boys and to a lesser extent, anxious withdrawn behavior in girls (Block, Block, & Morrison, 1981). There is some evidence that a combination of marital conflict and opposite-sex dominance may relate to internalizing disorders in both sexes (Gassner & Murray, 1969; Hetherington, Stouwie, & Ridberg, 1971; Schwarz & Getter, 1980). Gassner and Murray (1969) compared a clinical sample of male and female children with internalizing disorders with normals. Children in the clinical sample were more often from families with high marital conflict and opposite-sex dominance (as measured on the revealed differences task). Hetherington et al. (1971) replicated this finding for males in a clinical sample comparing internalizing, socialized-aggressive, and conduct-disorder delinquents.

Having discussed the impact of stressful events on the child and family, we now explore the contribution of parenting factors on childhood anxiety.

Parenting Styles

We use "parenting style" to refer to the general organizing manner in which a parent conceptualizes and conveys the tasks of parenting. Thus, parenting style is an important consideration in the assessment and treatment of distressed youth. There are many different ways that parenting styles can impact on children. The first is through modeling: the child responds to events as he has seen the parent respond in the same situations. A child whose parent panics about social obligations will observe and may later tend to be afraid to go to parties or play with peers. Second, the translation of style into a pattern of decision-making impacts on the child. Additionally, the individual child's response to the parent's style may be salient: one child in a family may be easily threatened by a parent's authoritarian style. Lastly, the style dictates the overall tenor of the home environment. As an example, a child who lives in a very controlled, restricted, and rigid home environment may feel constantly subject to criticism or he or she may find it necessary to be on guard all the time, afraid to make a mistake.

Modeling. Modeling, imitation, and observational learning are terms that describe procedures to *change* maladaptive behaviors; in our discussion, we focus on ways in which behaviors are *learned* through observation (Bandura, 1986). A parent who is agoraphobic attempts to justify or conceal his or her avoidant behavior so as not to lose status with the child. While this is confusing for the child, it may also elicit worry about the parent. The limitations of the parent in turn limit the child's activities, as the parent may be unable to provide transportation or even negotiate plans over the phone with other parents (Silverman, et al., 1988). Either via modeling (i.e., watching the parent's dysfunctional behavior) or from sheer restriction of activity due to pragmatic constraints (i.e., parent is afraid to leave the house so is unable to take the child to activities), the child is more likely to remain at home. In fact, in extreme cases the parent may reinforce the child for staying home as he or she gives parent access to a "safe person" (Silverman, et al., 1988). Agoraphobia illustrates how parenting style, in this case the avoidance behavior of the parent, organizes the household and dictates the behavior of the family.

Although modeling is a pervasive way in which behaviors and attitudes are learned, some argue that this method may be particularly salient to the learning of emotional reactions to events, and see this as explaining the higher concordance between maternal and child anxiety in younger children (Winer, 1982 cited in Barrios & Hartmann, 1988). Barrios and Hartmann (1988) discuss the concept of social-referencing theory (Klinnert, Campos, Sorce, Emde, & Svegda, 1983) wherein children look to others for cues to respond to an "ambiguous situation or a situation that exceeds their ability to appraise its dangerousness," (p. 250) particularly when they are unfamiliar. Thus, young children may be more likely to seek out cues from mother or a significant other and use such cues to help determine how to respond to an event. If the mother's response is fearful or anxious, the child's will be as well. Silverman et al. (1988) have suggested that increased rates of avoidance among agoraphobic and mixed phobic parents, in comparison to panic disorder and generalized anxiety parents, may account for the generally higher rates of pathology in the children of the former two groups. This speculation appears to point to the role that modeling plays in the transmission of pathology from parent to child.

Specific Parenting Styles. Several parenting styles have been postulated to contribute to child maladjustment. Overprotectiveness, a style which includes excessive or maladaptive interference, restriction of activity and limit-setting that exceeds the actual needs of the child, has been associated with depression and anxiety disorders (Barker, 1976; Rutter, 1975 cited in McFarlane, 1987). More recent research suggests that overprotectiveness in combination with "irritable distress"—a style characterized by irritability, fighting, and emotional withdrawal is most disruptive to the child's emotional state (McFarlane, 1987; Parker, 1983).

In our clinic, we have seen variations on the overprotective constellation in the children with separation anxiety. In some families, there are very different rules for parental involvement inside the home versus outside of the home. For example, the parents of a 9-year-old girl displayed protectiveness and intervened frequently at school, calling teacher and principal meetings whenever they were unhappy with the school's actions. At home, these same parents were unable to set a bedtime for their daughter, who often stayed up until three in the morning watching television or playing computer games. When asked about setting a firm bedtime ritual with consequences for not cooperating, the parents were both fearful and incredulous that they did indeed have the authority to send their daughter to bed.

Another example from our clinic illustrates the impact on the child of an avoidant "style" parent. In this case, the therapist was trying to arrange a convenient appointment time with the mother of an overanxious adolescent. The mother's response to every option was fear, along with a listing of reasons why that time would be difficult. Finally, the therapist suggested an after-school appointment in which the therapist would pick the child up from school and return her home after the session, thus obviating conflicts with the mother's avoidance. The parent tried to avoid this suggestion by stating that the daughter had doctor and dentist appointments after school. It was only when the therapist pointed out that the daughter could miss the session on the few times (one or two) when she had a medical appointment that the mother realized she could "try" the plan. Not surprisingly, her daughter had a fear of new situations and/or changes in routine. She had gleaned from her mother's anxious and avoidant approach to life that new situations are threatening and full of problems rather than possibilities.

A child's emotional or physical state certainly has an impact on the parents. A child's initial avoidance could be a trigger for an overprotective parenting style in those prone to anxiety. While responsive parenting is necessary and adaptive, excessiveness can lead to a dysfunctional amount of family involvement.

Parenting style colors all interactions with the child and thus is an important factor to consider. One contends with parenting style whether one intends to or not, and we propose that direct intervention is worthwhile. We propose helping parents extend or alter their style to be more adaptive. For instance, for the parents who were afraid to set a bedtime, the goal would be to assure them that setting limits (setting a firm bedtime) is a responsible, caring parenting behavior which is consistent with their (interest) style. Parenting style may be considered the manifestation of the parent's expectations and beliefs, and it is to a discussion of these issues that we now turn.

Cognitive Features of the Parents: Beliefs, Attributions, and Expectations

As we have already seen, a cognitive-behavioral treatment for the child focuses on the child's self-talk, guiding beliefs, specific expectations, and attributions about the cause of behavior. Cognitive-behavioral conceptualizations of anxious functioning propose that individuals constantly generate self-talk, expectations, and attributions in order to process and make sense of the world around them. Because we do not exist in a vacuum, it is equally important to consider attributions and expectations in an interpersonal context. For example, how do the beliefs and expectations others have for us impact on our behavior?

How Parent Expectations Influence Child Behavior. Beliefs here refer to global perceptions of the nature of a relationship, and are closely parallel to schemata (chapter 2). Attributions refer to inferences about causes active in a situation and are often based on beliefs. Expectancies are the predictions we hold, often derived from our beliefs and attributions about past behavior. A father's belief about his parenting role may be that discipline is necessary for his child to be successful. Although this belief may go unstated, the father's behavior may betray an underlying belief. The father might expect his child to be in the honors club or to get an outstanding report card; if this expectancy is not met, the father may attribute the cause of this failure to his child's not listening or being disrespectful and make his message stronger or become punitive—only adding pressure on the children and making success even less likely.

A thirteen-year-old girl had quit the swim team because of a panic episode during a race where she felt unable to breathe. After problem-solving sessions, the girl went to the university olympic-size pool, and after successfully completing the agreed *in-vivo* goal of one lap, she spontaneously offered to do another lap. When the therapist and child triumphantly returned to share the success with her parents, the parents said, "Oh that's fine, but why did you do breast stroke—that's too easy. Why didn't you do something challenging like freestyle?" The parents had great difficulty accepting the child's anxiety—it was inconsistent with their belief that the child was like any other child. This belief prevented them from appreciating the challenge of a pool-phobic child going to a large university pool and swimming among students and faculty!

As in the above example, parents' beliefs may help them to selectively attend to problems rather than progress, thus not supporting the accomplished gains. Therapists can model attentiveness to the child's needs and gains and praise for the child in the parent's presence, as well as offering reasonable expectations and attributions regarding child behavior. For instance, "Hey, one lap is progress. You can't expect immediate perfection. She made a great effort. I'm proud of her."

The topic of parent-child attributional processes has received scant theoretical or research attention. However, the role of attributions in shaping marital interactions has been studied (Bradbury & Fincham, 1990; Jacobson & Margolin, 1979; Schlesinger & Epstein, 1986), and these findings have implications for parent-child relations. In marital relations, distressed spouses tend to attribute positive behavior to chance or external causes and negative behaviors to stable, unchangeable aspects of a person (Baucom, Bell, & Duhe, 1982; Fincham & O'Leary, 1983; Holtzworth-Munroe & Jacobson, 1985). Also, regardless of any behavioral changes, these cognitive biases can impede change in therapy if not addressed. As Jacobson (1984) remarked: "It has long been recognized that treatment success depends upon change in cognitive and affective domains, and that behavior change is best thought of as a means to an end rather than an end in itself" (p. 287).

The overprotective mother of a shy, anxious, socially isolated adolescent was asked how she perceived her daughter. She responded that she saw her daughter as unable to be responsible for her behavior. In passing, the mother mentioned that the daughter wanted to run for class president, using this as an example of how her daughter was unrealistic and not responsible. The therapist addressed the mother's perspective and pointed out the significance of her timid daughter taking such a bold step as to put herself in the "public eye" and encouraged their support. The therapist might also have said, "You must be proud. Your daughter must get her determination and high hopes from you." Such a positive attribution to the mother, a single parent feeling stressed and hopeless about her own life, could have positive impact on both parties.

Attributional processes can perpetuate themselves in families. The work of Morton, Twentyman and Azar (1988) on families in which there is child abuse is illustrative. Morton et al. (1988) pointed out that, in general, abusive families are exposed to more stress in life (Justice & Justice, 1976) than other families and that abusive parents enter the scene with *biases* about their children. These biases, stemming from the high degree of stress, lead parents to perceive their children as difficult to control, hyperactive, or aggressive (Lynch, 1976). Some families "normalize" variations in behavior; others make internal, stable attributions about the child. The authors describe a four-stage process where child-parent cognitions and expectancies interplay and "set up" the potential for an abusive situation. Stage 1: the parent holds unrealistic expectations for the child; Stage 2: the child's actions do not coincide with these expectations; Stage 3: the parent misattributes the child's behavior as provocative and an attempt to anger the parent; Stage 4: the parent overreacts to the child's action and punishes him or her (p. 90). The self-perpetuating sequelae from such a pattern are numerous. For example, a child may soon try for negative attention because he or she feels this is all that is available. In addition, the parent may become frustrated from being so negative with the children, but attribute this to the child's behavior. Attributional processes can be like a runaway train down the wrong track, making it impossible to see progress or to give credit where credit is due. Helping parents to see that any given act may have many different frames is important to getting the attributional process back on the right track.

One can imagine parallel scenarios with anxious children and their parents. The mother of a separation anxious adolescent girl is very concerned about her daughter's ability to protect herself. The mother's belief about her role as parent is to protect her daughter, and her expectation for her daughter is that she will be taken advantage of because she is immature, gullible, and/or unable to be independent. Thus, her actions are to restrict her daughter's behavior. When the daughter shows an interest and engages in age-appropriate activities (e.g., requesting to go to a friend's house), her mother attributes this as rebellious and dangerous, thus countering by asserting parental authority to keep the adolescent at home. This parenting serves to make the daughter want to assert her needs further, and, in her frustration, she may do so in an immature manner, which only serves to confirm for the mother that her attributions and expectancies for her daughter were correct. Parental expectations play a large and important role in the development and maintenance of child behavior patterns, including those related to distressing anxiety.

Viability of a Diathesis-Stress Model in the Development of Anxiety

Clearly there exists a body of evidence (both research and anecdotal) that indicates the role of familial and parental influences in the development of childhood anxiety disorders. While the results of studies on the relatives of anxious probands provide strong and consistent evidence for familial predispositions to develop anxiety disorders, the heterogeneous quality of the type of disorders often existing among the relatives of anxious probands indicates that in general there is not a clear-cut genetic explanation for the transmission of anxiety disorders. Alternatively, family environmental factors—stressful events, modeling, parenting patterns, and cognitive features of parents—provide viable explanations for the transmission of various anxiety disorders from one generation to the next. Yet, these environmental factors may offer only a partial explanation for the development of anxiety disorders. Given the strong physiological component of anxiety (i.e., the rapid arousal of the autonomic nervous system), it is not unreasonable to consider a diathesis-stress model for the development of anxiety in which a genetic predisposition interacts with various environmental factors in the development of the disorder. Whether an anxiety disorder develops, and the specific form in which it manifests itself, may depend on the particular characteristics of the child's environment, both within and outside the family.

Future research on familial patterns of anxiety needs to examine the specific mechanisms of transmission of anxiety in families. At a broad level, this could involve examination of potentially stressful environmental factors, such as divorce or parental illness. More specifically, to gain insight into parental cognitive features and patterns of modeling, analyses could be carried out on the verbal statements, emotional responses, and actual behaviors of parents of anxious children in response to perceived stressors. Such observational approaches to research might be accompanied by investigating self-reported anxiety and related self-statements in parents and their children to provide a fine-grained analysis of the cognitive styles that may be passed on from parent to child. In the long run, it seems most reasonable to assume that no single factor, but rather a combination of factors, relates to the transmission of anxiety from parent to child.

Our discussion now turns to treatment, specifically how to address the important parental and familial factors which may be contributing to the anxiety in the child.

FAMILY TREATMENT

Parents as Consultants

We recognize the importance of parental involvement in helping the child to overcome his or her disproportionate anxiety. Our program's focus is primarily on helping the individual child learn to think and behave differently, but we also encourage parents to participate in a supportive role. Though our treatment program is not "family" therapy, parents are actively involved from the outset. By family therapy we mean those intervention strategies that treat family members as a group, often with a focus on the dynamics and interaction processes that family members display as they interact within the treatment context. Parents are involved in our program, but they are not themselves the target clients in the treatment protocol. Illustrations of how parents are involved include parental responses to inventories and the structured interview that is used to make a diagnosis. In addition, the child's therapist has meetings with the parent(s) (e.g., a full session after the child's third session), several in-person contacts (before and/or after sessions), as well as contacts over the phone, and parents may be actively involved in *in vivo* exposure experiences.

The meeting with parents at the time of the child's fourth session has several purposes. First, we provide additional information about the treatment and a description of where the child currently is in the program. Specifically, the parent is told not to expect an immediate reduction in the child's anxiety but to be encouraging as the child begins to apply the coping skills learned during the first eight sessions. Parents may be helpful in generating ideas about how they can help the child to reward him or herself for trying to cope with a difficult situation. This meeting also gives the parents a chance to discuss their concerns about the child and to provide further information about what they think may be particularly useful in helping the child.

Parent report, following the establishment of a relationship with the child, can provide an opportunity to follow-up on matters that were not previously clear. Information gathering from the parents can be particularly useful when the child has shown a tendency to withdraw in the face of discussing painful thoughts and feelings. We do not repeat all parent-reported information to the child, but the information is helpful in shaping the interaction between therapist and child, in understanding why a child seems to be having difficulty discussing problems in the session, and in the design of *in vivo* exposure experiences. Furthermore, these therapist-parent discussions often provide valuable information about the family's patterns of behavior surrounding the child. Understanding these family systems factors is useful in structuring role plays and *in vivo* experiences to address some of the elements of the family interaction patterns that relate to, and possibly maintain, the child's anxiety. For example, a 12-year-old may be reluctant to admit the extent of dependency she has on her mother, only mentioning to the therapist that she worries about something happening to the parent when she is late. Discussion of this with the parent may reveal that more severe dependency is manifest in a number of other ways—calling the parent in at night to spend an hour or two discussing worries, and over-reliance on that particular parent to the exclusion of other family members. This information helps us to create exposure experiences that build the child's independence. Even relatively small acts of independence and decision making without the parent are important steps toward a relaxed and autonomous adulthood.

Once the child has learned the components of the FEAR steps, it is helpful for the parent to understand these steps and, when appropriate, to aid the child in using them. Following the eighth session, as a STIC task, we have the child explain the FEAR steps to the parent. This task not only helps the child to understand the steps, but also enables the parent to facilitate the child's use of the FEAR plan in active problem solving. Though the FEAR steps are designed for the child to use, many parents of anxious children welcome the chance to help the child in using the FEAR steps, because it provides an alternative response to the unsuccessful strategies they have offered in the past.

Parents of anxious children may express guilt about their child's anxiety. Our effort to help them cope with these feelings involves a pragmatic statement and discussion to inform them that how the problem developed is not the current concern. We do not assign blame to the parents, family, or any other factors. Instead, we express the point of view that we want to work from the present toward teaching the child the most effective coping strategies that they can then use to manage any unwanted anxiety that may emerge. By enlisting the parent's help in information gathering and suggestions for problem solving, the emphasis is shifted from concentrating on the genesis of the problem and the assignment of blame to helping the child cope in the present and future. However, if the parent's own anxieties or other problems appear to be genuinely contributing to the child's anxiety, they are addressed. Such a discussion may involve observations and suggestions about how to change the "parent-child" situation, and even recommendations for the parent's own treatment.

More broadly, general environmental factors need to be assessed when working with families of anxious children. Has the child experienced any losses that may be contributing to his or her anxiety? Waldron et al. (1975) and Davidson (1961) found that a high rate of school-phobic children had experienced a death or illness in a parent or other relative. In fact, Waldron et al. suggested that certain types of school phobia represent the child's fear that something will happen to his parents if the child leaves. Our observations suggest that a number of mothers of anxiety-disordered children have some type of illness. Some of the children in treatment actually restrict their activities or frequently call home in order to check how the parent is feeling. Thus, the therapist may want to discuss fears that the child might have about the parent's well-being. This could involve helping the parent to realistically tell the child about any dangers and help the child learn that he is not solely responsible for the parent's health and well-being. Additionally, in large families with few resources, the parents may simply be too overwhelmed to help the child deal with his or her problems, despite a desire to do so. Sensitivity to the economic and other environmental stressors that the family as a whole may face is essential.

When working with the parent, the therapist needs to beware that joining with the parent should not jeopardize the relationship with the child. For older children, who may be making the first tentative steps toward independence, the therapeutic relationship may be especially valuable and important, because it is a place they can feel independent from the parent. To avoid arousing the child's suspicions that the therapist is repeating confidential material to the parent, the therapist checks to see if there are certain things the child does not want repeated; likewise, the therapist offers to answer any questions that the child may have about what the therapist and parent discussed. Ideally, by enlisting the knowledge and support of parents, without detrimental effects on the therapist-child relationship, we enable parents to play an active role in helping their children learn to cope with anxiety. Our emphasis is on helping the child to become an independent problem solver.

Systems Issues: The Interplay of Parent-Child Attribution and Behavior

The processes involving attributions, expectancies, and behavior operate continually in our interactions with others, and they can spiral into a chain reaction of negative or maladaptive interactions among family members (positive interactions can spiral too!). In all interpersonal contexts—including families—we are at once responding to the actions and statements of others, and in so doing we serve as stimuli for their reactions. Which came first, the undesirable behavior or the negative attributions? It is not possible to answer (Epstein, Schlesinger, & Dryden, 1988), nor is it necessary to address in our solution-based approach to treatment. As Epstein et al. (1988) noted, "Although it will be important in the development of preventive efforts to understand the causal links between family members' negative cognitions and behavioral interactions, the fact that these become intertwined components of family relationships suggests that therapeutic interventions aimed at both internal cognitive events and external behavioral exchanges will modify dysfunctional interactions" (p. 7). We concur.

Over the years, the role of the family in child disorders has led to the family's involvement in therapy and often the use of a systems model. Broadly defined, systems models (e.g., von Bertalanffy, 1968) posit that people are not independent organisms but operate within a network of activity. Changes in one part of the system will inevitably influence all other parts. Moreover, systems maintain themselves (e.g., status quo or homeostasis) by corrective feedback. That is, behavioral systems maintain the status quo and resist any attempts to change the system, even if toward positive change. As applied to a family, family members "get used to" keeping people "in the roles they are in." For example, as the anxious, perfectionistic child begins to feel more relaxed and confident, the parent might, unwittingly, convey critical expectations to return the child to his prior mode of functioning. Such an effect clearly illustrates the need for coordinating treatment efforts for parents and for children. A child's treatment gains toward greater independence and management of fears may be mislabeled as disobedience or may contribute to depression in a parent who might attribute the child's change to no longer being needed. However, if inaccurate parental responses are disputed, and the role of the parent is supported in a more constructive way, then we might safeguard the maintenance of the child's gains.

The systems approach reexamines child disorders while taking into account other family members, including the parents' marital relations and their interpersonal interactions. For example, an updated approach to "separation anxiety" would no longer see the problem as *mother's* psychopathology (e.g., Eisenberg, 1958 a&b), but could see how both child and parent issues may be involved. Although systems theory and cognitive-behavioral theory rarely cross reference, recent comparisons of the two (e.g., Leslie, 1988) suggest that sharing of techniques or borrowing of concepts might be mutually beneficial. It is not our purpose to critique or dispute the compatibility of the two approaches, but we do support a cognitive-behavioral model which takes into account a larger context of interaction and considers parents as well as children as potential participants in intervention, with the common goals of correcting maladaptive self-talk, clarifying expectations and correcting misattributions—all of which may be contributing to the disturbing and maladaptive anxiety in the child.

As we have seen, attributional processes play a powerful role in the child's progress: positive strides toward overcoming anxiety may be misattributed by the parent as something negative and undesirable, or as a chance occurrence not properly attributed to the child's effort. Such effects can snowball, triggering expectations or beliefs on the part of the parents at an even greater intensity. In other words, a child may be able to make greater progress with the support and guidance that can come from the context of a family.

Cognitive-Behavioral Family Treatment for Child Anxiety

Accepting the role that parental cooperation plays in the success of child-focused treatment, and given the hypothesized roles family members may play in the genesis and maintenance of anxiety disorders, we propose family-focused application of cognitive-behavioral treatment strategies for child anxiety disorders. While related treatment strategies have been implemented in other problem areas (see Epstein, et al., 1988), such as conduct disorder (DiGuiseppe, 1988), child abuse (Morton, et al., 1988), and addictions (Schlesinger, 1988), there are to date no published reports or descriptions of such an endeavor being used with child anxiety disorders.

The assumption of a cognitive behavioral model of family treatment is that the individuals' perceptions and cognitions influence the behavior of other members (e.g., Epstein, et al., 1988) and that the myriad of interpersonal exchanges, one's perception of and attribution about them, form a stable interaction pattern (cognitive structure) that may or may not be adaptive. While our cognitive-behavioral model for individuals encourages parental input and participation, the focus of the intervention is the child. The parents or other family members may change as an indirect result or as catalyzed from the changes they perceive in the child, but the parents or family members are not themselves "in therapy." A model of cognitive-behavioral family treatment for anxiety-disordered children may offer unique opportunities for change. We next sketch an overview of this important area, proposing several treatment goals and strategies for working simultaneously with the anxious children and their families.

A Working Model. Due to a lack of ample data, we cannot detail one type of "anxious family." Instead, our model begins with the child's difficulties, whether this be separation anxiety, social avoidance, or a generalized anxiety response and proposes that expectational and attributional exchanges between parents and children contribute to the maintenance of the anxiety. It is the goal of treatment to assess the particular maladaptive cognitive and behavioral patterns and to build individual competencies and/or improve family interactions to facilitate better coping with, or alleviation of, the child's anxiety.

Goals for Parental Involvement: From Consultants to Co-clients

The working relationship. Building a good working relationship with parents is an essential ingredient in any therapeutic endeavor. As already discussed, guilt is a common reaction in parents seeking help for a child; thus, from the outset the therapist must emphasis change—not blame—stating that the goal of treatment is helping their child better cope with fears and distress, and removing impediments to growth.

In addition to clarifying the purpose of the treatment, the therapist attends to the parent's attitude toward treatment. Typical responses to treatment range from overinvolvement to underinvolvement. Each parent's response to the treatment provides useful information to the clinician about what he or she will be conveying to the child. In the case of the underinvolved parent, the therapist will need to "get their attention"

(Margolin, 1987). For example, to the parents of a child who regularly slept nights in their bed for the past year, the therapist stated directly, "Your daughter will never reach her goal of being a veterinarian if she's still sleeping in her parent's bed," and "It may be hard now, but she will be very angry later on for your not getting her out of your bed." It is blunt, to the point, and gets parental attention. For the overinvolved parent, the therapist will need to be reassuring but firm in creating distance between the parent and child. For example, the parent should be assured that they will be consulted as needed and that they are free to contact the therapist with their concerns, but the time spent with the child alone need not be reexamined and/or discussed with the parent.

Assessment. Cognitive-behavioral treatments have from the outset sought to develop and include assessments that accurately tap cognitions and behavior (Kendall & Korgeski, 1979; Kendall & Hollon, 1981). As noted in chapter 3, family measures appropriate for cognitive-behavioral therapy are rare and need to be developed. One example of an appropriate measure is the Family Beliefs Inventory (Roehling & Robin, 1986). This measure assesses distorted beliefs such as perfectionism, unfairness, and approval, and has been associated with communication and conflict in adolescents and their parents. The findings of the researchers support the need to address irrational beliefs and other cognitive features in parent-child relationships.

Measures related directly to the assessment of cognitive factors in anxiety-disordered families are not yet available. However, observational strategies used with families offer some suggestions. The goal of the observations is to gather information, make inferences, and draw conclusions regarding the automatic thoughts, beliefs, expectancies, attributions, specific complaints, target behaviors to be changed, and some ideas concerning any misperceptions or misinterpretations of events that are characteristic of family members. One could observe the family "in action" in a discussion about the child's anxiety specifically or perhaps while interacting about a general or random topic. In either case, the interaction is informative in that it can help to reveal the characteristic patterns of familial interaction.

At times, separate parent and child meetings are appropriate, in order to assess information which parents and children may feel most comfortable revealing in the presence of the therapist alone. In our clinic, during our parent meetings parents will reveal that they struggled with similar fears (when they were younger) as those presently troubling their children. Such admissions are more likely in separate meetings and are useful for several reasons. First, they provide an opportunity for parents to join and confirm their willingness to help their child. Second, they give the therapist a more informed sense of what the child is observing in the home. Third, they provide an opportunity to clarify how the child's problem is similar to or different from the parent's. For example, both parents of a nine-year-old, who had been sleeping in her parents' bed for the past year, revealed that as youngsters they were afraid to sleep alone and either would sleep in their parents' room or on the floor outside their room. Here it was important not only to acknowledge the parents' identification with the child's difficulties, but also to clarify their role as *parents* and to point out the problems with their beliefs about their daughter's dependence and weaknesses. Overall, this approach to intervention builds on and expands beyond parents' role as consultants and allows greater depth in assessment and correction of parental beliefs and attributions which may be contributing to the child's difficulties.

Another example illustrates the crucial need to correct the parental misperceptions about what is or is not adaptive for the child. A 13-year-old girl with extreme separation anxiety and frequent panic attacks was suffering from nightly panics about not being able to breathe and possibly dying in her sleep. When discussing the seriousness of this problem with her parents, the father, a religious man, reported that it was enriching to think about death and existential issues, and that he thought about those issues often. In this case, the father was identifying with the girl's difficulties as a way of normalizing and diminishing a very serious problem. The therapist clarified that whereas the father was making a spiritual choice, his daughter was unwittingly controlled by fears of death and as a result was unable to function in her daily life. Furthermore, the therapist pointed out that age 13 is a time for socializing, for getting excited about parties and sports; not for lying in bed wondering every night if you're going to wake up the next day. Such clarifications are essential, as the parent will not "buy into" the treatment unless they agree that there is a problem. Once the problem was established, the parents were willing to cooperate with the treatment.

In addition to informal discussion and observational assessments, asking the family to complete behavioral logs outside of the session can add valuable data to the assessment process. For example, a parent who complains that his or her child does not have friends or never wants to participate in social activities can log, for a period of a week, specific aspects of their interaction around negotiating after school or weekend school activity, focusing both on the child's behavior as well as the parent's. To organize one's observations of family interaction, it may be helpful for the therapist to employ a two-by-two matrix (as shown in Table 8.1) and consider various combinations of child and parent cognition and behavior.

Table 8.1. *Mapping Out Cognitions and Behaviors of Children and Parents* *

	Level	
Person	Cognition	Behavior
Parent	"My daughter can't sleep alone" "I'm a terrible parent if I let my daughter cry"	Does not set a firm bedtime Brings daughter into parent's bed when she shows distress.
Child	"I can't sleep alone" "I'll be scared to death"	Cries endlessly Threatens that her stomach is coming apart

*This example pertains to nighttime routine for a separation anxious girl.

For example, a 10-year-old, separation anxious girl had slept in her parents' room for the past year. Her fears of sleeping in her own room revolved around danger—someone breaking into the house—as well as bodily concerns—her stomach is going to "come apart" from fear. The parents see their daughter as very young and helpless and feel that the only way to protect her from her fear is to allow her to stay in their room. Intervention in this case addressed the child's need for more independent skills to cope with her fears (e.g., talking with a stuffed animal about her worries, reading a book, listening to a relaxation tape). The parents were coached to support their daughter's independence by helping her problem solve about how to fall asleep in her room, rather than supporting her fear and allowing her to sleep in their room.

Once the various behavior and cognition combinations have been mapped out, the therapist (using a suggestion from the marital therapy literature [Margolin, 1987]) evaluates which "cells" are most dysfunctional and which are most likely to change. These data then guide the intervention. Mastery and competence are emphasized as crucial to maintenance— it may be important to first work on small changes that will reassure the family that change is possible and give them the confidence and motivation to tackle the more difficult and/or more emotionally charged problems.

Treatment Strategies. We have outlined the goals and assessment methods and now consider several treatment strategies to be implemented as meets the needs of the individual case. This section is illustrative, as space limitations preclude a more comprehensive discussion. Likewise, it is preliminary, as the efficacy of these broader system interventions is yet to be determined for the treatment of anxiety-disordered youth.

The process that takes place in therapy itself—asking questions; categorizing communication into attributions, expectancies, and behaviors; and providing an immediate reality check for each of these—serves as a model for the types of behaviors desired for the family in day-to-day living. For instance, the cognitive-behavioral family therapist teaches, by example, the importance of observation. Also, as previously suggested, the therapist encourages the spirit of *collaborative problem solving,* presenting treatment as a cooperative process in which family members can look at their behavior patterns, their expectations, and their attributions, examining and evaluating those that are adaptive and those that are not. Finally, therapy sessions can serve as a "laboratory": an opportunity for family members to test out new styles of communicating and new behaviors. The therapist can take these opportunities to check on expectancies, beliefs, and attributions via the *in-vivo* therapy experiences. The immediate feedback from the observations of the family members makes a family session an optimal laboratory for problem solving. In the next section we discuss specific cognitive and behavioral procedures which, used in the spirit of a cooperative team, can combine to remediate dysfunctional cognition and behavioral skill deficits. We will discuss cognitive and behavioral strategies separately, although in practice these strategies are used together.

Cognitive procedures. Cognitive interventions aim to change dysfunctional expectations, attributions, self-talk, and beliefs or attitudes into more constructive ones—such as a coping, problem-solving template. Within any particular family this may include changing: (1) parents' unhelpful expectations of their child (whether overestimation or underestimation of the child's abilities or fears), (2) the child's (and/or parent's) expectations about themselves, (3) the child's (and/or parent's) maladaptive beliefs, and (4) patterns of attributions about the causes of behavioral outcomes.

Cognitive-behavioral approaches emphasize a socratic/didactic therapeutic posture that involves the eliciting of cognition, testing of the validity of the thinking, and facilitating the use of less maladaptive thinking. Thus, a major aspect of treatment includes asking the child and parent what they are thinking about in a particular situation and then testing the validity of the thought by (1) questioning other "eyewitnesses" who may have a different cognitive assessment of the situation and (2) correcting or supplying factual information that may be lacking. For example, the mother of a 13-year-old girl with overanxious disorder had many concerns about her child's health as the girl had had cancer at age three. Anytime the daughter would mention any physical discomfort, however minor, the mother would restrict her daughter's activity to prevent any harm. The daughter enjoyed singing very much, but the mother decided this was dangerous to her health. Cognitive restructuring involved checking out the reality and extent of the girl's discomfort (which apparently was none!), as well as consulting with her doctor (who saw no reason why the girl could not sing). These interventions helped to challenge the mother's mistaken belief that she must protect her daughter's health. The mother was also reassured that there was no reason to restrict her daughter's activity. As a result, the daughter felt more self-confident and healthy. Moreover, the girl could now go to her mother when she was not feeling well, without worrying that as a result her mother would take away an enjoyable activity.

The following example illustrates how a parental belief can misguide the interpretation of behavior and lead to an unwanted self-fulfilling prophecy. The parents of a 10-year-old boy with avoidant disorder had concerns about their son's gender identity—the concern created a negative expectancy for everything the son did. The mother in this case was open about her concerns; the father, however, was unable to express them even to his wife and refused to engage in discussions about how to handle the problem. The father told the therapist that he would feel angry every time he saw his son playing with dolls. When asked about his automatic thoughts, the father replied that he thought to himself, "He can't be gay—I can't let him be gay." The therapist was able to help the father see the actions which followed these automatic thoughts—criticizing his son, storming out of the room, and overall sending a clear message of disapproval to his son. The father began to see why his son was afraid of him, a feeling which generalized to all of the son's activities. Indeed, because of the father's negative interactions with the boy, the son may identify less with the father and adapt fewer male attributes as a result. After challenging and correcting these expectations, the treatment turned to cooperative work between the parent and the child for the child's social avoidance.

The boy had avoided any new situation, particularly parties or events where he didn't know everyone; his fear, not surprisingly, was of being criticized or made to look foolish. The boy's self-talk concerned the idea that he was ugly and that people would hate him if they saw him. In addition to individual work with the father to correct his misguided expectations and attributions about his son, as well as work with the son to modify his negative attributions about himself, the first "family" step was to get the father and son to share an enjoyable activity. The therapist helped the father to explore his expectations for the kinds of activities he would prefer for his son. It was clear that the father's anger had prevented him from even considering playing sports (or spending any positive time) with his son. The family agreed that the father and son would take a special trip to the toy store and choose activities for them to play together. The father was able to express positive feelings toward his son, and in turn, the son felt more likeable and worthwhile. The task of helping the son with his social avoidance was well under way.

Another in-session strategy is that of monitoring parent-child interactions, especially those which, when unchecked, would strengthen a negative expectancy. For example, in working with a mother who is very critical of her son, the therapist commented that her son was yawning and looked tired and so suggested that an earlier appointment time would be set for next week. The mother replied, "Yeah, he's such a lazy bones." The mother took the yawn as confirmation for her belief that her son is unmotivated and unwilling to work on anything. The son then withdrew with a huff and the mother said, "See, he just won't work." The therapist then stopped the action and backtracked so that the mother could see how her expectations precluded any other possible interpretation of the yawn. Fortunately for the boy, she was able to see this and agreed that an earlier appointment time would be preferable. At the same time, the son could feel understood and supported: correcting the negative attributions of "lazy bones" prepares him to work next week.

Behavioral interventions. These can be used for a variety of different goals: changing an individual target behavior, practicing a behavior (rehearsal), and problem solving. Considering the distinction between distal and proximal roles, some interventions may focus on involving the family to help the child with problems outside of the home (distal), others may focus on helping negotiate attributional processes between family members (proximal). Below, we present an example of how the behavioral intervention of role playing would be used in each instance. In addition, other behavioral interventions are described.

ROLE PLAYING. Role-play activities were discussed in more detail in chapters 4 and 5 but are reconsidered here in light of the focus on family involvement in therapy. John, a 10-year-old boy, is uncomfortable asking questions in class for fear he will say the wrong thing or be tongue-tied. John has no difficulty speaking up for himself at home, and thus his family is surprised by his distressing discomfort with public speaking. The therapist enlists the family to create a mock classroom and to support John as he writes a short speech or reads a poem. The family is instructed to respond in an encouraging manner by being attentive, appreciative listeners.

As John gains confidence, family members might be asked to engage in "classroom-like" behavior (e.g., looking around the room, whispering to another person, writing notes). When John reacts anxiously to these behaviors, the therapist stops the action and helps John examine his expectations and attributions about such behavior. For instance, if John thinks that someone is whispering about how bored they are, the family can explain an alternative: that they were whispering about how confident he seemed. Actively engaging the family in the child's fears serves to both help the family better understand the child's concerns and help the child to feel supported. Also, the therapist can serve as coach to suggest what relaxation or coping skills the child might employ and when, thus modeling both for the child as well as for the parents how best to cope in a stressful situation.

In the next example we combine an in-session role play with an out-of-session "behavioral experiment." Behavioral experiments involve activities to test out the validity of one's beliefs and can be used in or out of session. Carol, a 13-year-old, separation anxious adolescent wanted to socialize more with her friends, but she also wanted to please her parents. Carol's parents had the expectancy that if they let their daughter go out with her friends to the mall, she would get lost or would spend all of her money and be stuck without a way to get home. Within a treatment session, the therapist had the family role play Carol asking her parents if she could go to the mall. The expectations and attributions behind the parents' concerns and restrictions were explored, and together the family came to an agreeable solution. Outside of the session, the family was asked to test out the solution and "analyze" the results of the experiment when Carol returned. The family documented the experiment and brought the results to the next session to discuss (and/or correct) attributions of success or failure, as well as make improvements in the plan for next time.

FAMILY BRAINSTORMING AND PROBLEM SOLVING. Problem solving refers to defining a problem or task and developing a plan of action which incorporates the specific difficulties involved and the generated strategies to cope with these difficulties. Oftentimes parents of anxious children report feeling impatient with their children as they struggle over what seem to be unimportant decisions or problems (e.g., deciding what to wear, whether or not to call a friend, which candy to choose from the candy machine). Part of this impatience results from the difficulty parents have in seeing the situation from the child's perspective. To enlist family members' help as well as to help them better understand both the state of anxiety and the perspective of youth, the anxious child describes his or her anxious feelings and self-talk in a particular situation, and, together, family members "brain storm" ideas, possible solutions, or coping strategies. For example, to help Joe, who has concerns about giving reports in front of his class, the first step is to help him to list his concerns. Next, the family brainstorms ideas to cope with his top concerns: stuttering, mispronouncing a word, being laughed at. The strategies include both cognitive ones: saying "I'm doing fine, keep going," as well as behavioral ones: practicing with family first or in front of a mirror and practicing the difficult-to-pronounce words several times.

EVALUATION AND REWARD. Just as evaluation of performance and the setting of reasonable goals were stressed in individual treatment (discussed in chapters 4 and 5), they are also highly important in the context of a family. Unless reasonable goals are set, partial successes may be misperceived and attributed as failures by other members of the family, thus undermining the effort of the individual and maintaining the status quo. Parents need to be reminded that the goal of treatment is to reinforce success and not to punish failure. Parents may require training in the differences between and ways to use reward, punishment, negative attention, and positive attention. In addition to teaching the family the concept of a continuum of success, the family should practice setting appropriate goals and generating ample rewards for the desired behaviors. The therapist can help the family in session to determine reasonable goals for a particular event to occur outside of session. In so doing, the therapist increases the likelihood that the *in-vivo* experience—whatever the outcome—will be seen in a positive, productive light.

FAMILY RELAXATION TECHNIQUES. Families can get "stuck" working on problems all the time, engaging in power struggles over whether the child will go to school that day or arguing why she is too nervous to take a test—to the point where the "fun" times are few and far between. Introducing a positive, concrete activity such as relaxation training, which the whole family can do, often relieves the helplessness the parents may feel about how to help their child, while also teaching a very valuable skill for them to practice. Teaching the family both the techniques of relaxation and the physical cues for when to employ them enables the family members to suggest or remind each other to use them when stressed or unsure of what to do.

CLOSING COMMENTS

Our discussion of predispositions and family environment factors in the etiology and maintenance of childhood anxiety provides a rationale for including the family in the treatment of child anxiety disorders. Of these factors, the impact of parental expectations and attributions—of themselves as parents and of their children's behavior—plays a critical role in maintaining a child's anxiety. The sampling of family treatment strategies we have suggested, as for example, role playing and evaluation and reward, are designed to address those cognitive and behavioral patterns which sustain and exacerbate the child's anxiety within the family context. While our present treatment focus is on the child, as we have suggested, intervention efforts can simultaneously address the coping skills of the child as well as the cognition and behavior of parents. Thus, parental involvement can facilitate and reinforce treatment gains rather than allowing the possibility of their impeding them. As discussed, the degree of parental involvement can range from parents as consultants to parents as clients within the context of family therapy.

Though the model for cognitive-behavioral family therapy, which has been used in marital therapy as well as for treating other family problems, appears to fit as an extension of our present program, research is needed to establish the efficacy of particular treatment strategies with the family as the target. In addition to investigating particular treatment strategies, research should also focus on when family involvement and even therapy, as opposed to a greater emphasis on the child alone, is indicated in treatment. While some children may benefit greatly from full-blown family treatment, other children may benefit most from treatment that is focused more exclusively on them, with family involvement remaining as purely supportive. Because there is no clear-cut picture of the "anxious family," a flexible approach in deciding how to best involve the family is warranted. However, the need to coordinate child treatment and parent participation, independent of the person targeted for treatment, cannot be emphasized enough.

Chapter 9
Maintaining Gains

First ponder, then dare

—*H. Von Moltke*

What are we to expect from our young clients as a result of treatment, and how can we put these expectations to use in providing optimal maintenance services? Recall the considerations raised in earlier chapters where the goals for treatment were discussed. In the course of the treatment, attempts are made to provide the child or adolescent with a generalized problem-solving approach—the FEAR plan—that can be used to better manage anxiety and anxiety-related problems. Each child is exposed to various cognitive and behavioral coping skills and has the opportunity to apply these anxiety management techniques in various anxiety-arousing situations. This teaching and application process (see Meichenbaum, 1986) has—by providing the child with coping skills and practice—sought to realign a maladaptive developmental trajectory to better prepare the child for the inevitable challenges to his or her later adjustment.

Does this mean that we should now expect our young clients to be able to master every new anxiety-producing situation encountered in a facile, carefree manner? The answer, quite simply, is no. It is the case that each child's response to a therapy program will be unique—some children will be more able than others to learn, apply, and generalize anxiety-management problem-solving skills. However, unbridled success and mastery for every child in all situations following the completion of therapy is not a realistic goal. The aim of our therapy is instead to provide coping strategies, or a "coping template," to which the child can refer as he or she is presented with anxiety-provoking situations. Better management of anxiety, not cure, is the fundamental goal of the program. Consequently, the termination of formal therapy does not begin symptom-free functioning—and neither does it signal the abrupt discontinuation of therapeutic activity and involvement. On the contrary, the end of therapy brings with it the therapeutic responsibility of assessing just how capable the child has become in applying the anxiety-management skills in real-life situations on his or her own. For example, mistakes will be made, parents may become overinvolved, new problems may need a fresh look, and certain parts of the problem-solving process may have to be reexamined. Thus, termination signals a time for the child to use the new skills in everyday situations and perhaps therapeutic contact at another level.

Given this framework, how can the therapist be beneficial in helping the child to consolidate the newly acquired arsenal of cognitive and behavioral skills after formal therapy is completed? The one guiding principle to posttreatment activity may be summed up in three words: practice, practice, practice! Direct intervention is but the first step of a process of adaptive change. Positive gains may diminish over time particularly during the first phases of a child's posttreatment "solo flight." To help ease the transition from formal treatment contact, several guidelines may be helpful in guiding children toward further consolidation of treatment-produced gains. The guidelines are logical extensions of the cognitive-behavioral treatment model and its related goals and expectations. Our discussion of how to best maintain gains includes consideration of effort attributions, relapse prevention, SHOWing off, and booster sessions.

EFFORT ATTRIBUTIONS

The management of anxiety through the learning and practicing of coping skills requires hard work and practice and, oftentimes, more than an occasional mistake. When treatment is completed, the hard work and practice in coping with anxiety will not somehow magically disappear to be replaced by carefree, nonanxious functioning. Children need to be reminded that the end of treatment does not mean the end of problems. Gains do not begin with the close of the final session of the treatment program. Instead, maintenance is a process that begins early in treatment. Consequently, the initial seeds for maintenance are sown during the skill-building phase of treatment and are cultivated throughout treatment and in its aftermath.

It is helpful to continually stress to the children—in various ways—the tangible benefits of hard work in helping them to cope with anxiety outside of the therapy setting. The therapist's coping modeling of the mistakes often made in attempting to recall steps of the FEAR plan, the difficulty sometimes encountered in generating alternatives and selecting solutions, and the necessity of going "back to the drawing board" if one solution does not work as well as expected are all examples of this early therapeutic emphasis. In addition, the therapist takes special care from early on to link the benefits of hard work in therapy sessions with their payoff outside in the "real world." In short, the therapist shapes and encourages "effort" attributions regarding the management of anxiety.

RELAPSE PREVENTION

Hard work will continue to be important in coping with anxiety once formal therapy is completed. Framing each new situation—in and out of therapy—as a fresh chance to practice the FEAR plan is essential in laying the groundwork for effective maintenance and generalization. For example, stressing follow-through on Show-That-I-Can (STIC) tasks can link treatment precepts with the child's daily activities. As termination approaches, the continued emphasis on the necessity of child-driven efforts, repeated application, and the mistakes that sometimes happen during the course of these efforts will have laid the foundation for relapse prevention.

As children accept the coping template associated with the FEAR plan, they experience not only the intended advances but also the occasional inevitable setback. However, in relapse prevention, mistakes and partial successes are constructively conceptualized as a vital part of the learning process itself—rather than, for example, as the confirmation of a worthless or untreatable child. The expectation that "things happen" opens the door for the paying of direct therapeutic attention to the inevitability of setbacks and partial failures. Brownell, Marlatt, Lichtenstein, and Wilson (1986) differentiated between the terms lapse and relapse. A lapse refers to a process, such as a behavioral slip, that may or may not portend a negative outcome. A negative outcome would be a relapse. In the area of the treatment of children's anxiety disorders, this distinction appears useful. For example, certain aspects of the FEAR plan may, at times, be forgotten, inappropriately or ineffectively applied, or even undermined by others despite the child's best efforts. Left unchecked, a temporary lapse of this sort can, among other things, lead children to question their ability to carry out the steps of the FEAR program. With time, the child may—because of earlier failures—enter new situations with a resultant decrease in a sense of self-efficacy (e.g., "I failed before when this happened, I just know I'll blow it again"). The risk of relapse, at this point, increases as the child may begin to abandon the use of problem solving with the accumulation of too many unchecked failures. Intervention following such a sequence of events may be difficult in correcting a child's cumulative loss of self-confidence and resultant half-hearted attempts at problem solving (e.g., "See, I tried but it just can't work for me"). On the other hand, proactive efforts that directly address the inevitability of slips, mistakes, and failures allow the child to anticipate lapses and, as we see it, greatly reduce the potential of relapse and possible collapse. Importantly, parents must be informed that a lapse is not equal to collapse.

We consider relapse prevention particularly crucial in preparing children for the end of formal therapy sessions. By focusing therapeutic efforts on the cognitive and behavioral coping skills necessary to overcome lapses, we work with the child in therapy to process errors when they occur naturally. In rather routine fashion, the therapist assists the child in "handling" day-to-day difficulties (errors). Coping modeling is particularly useful in demonstrating to the child that mistakes and failures are all part of the learning process. The therapist, by making errors and correcting them in systematic fashion, invites the child to become a "mistake-handling" partner. Particularly appropriate contexts for this training are imaginal role plays, STIC reviews, and *in-vivo* exposures.

The main goal in relapse prevention is to have the child be able to label and accept a setback as a setback and then, as quickly as possible, return to problem solving. Or, in other words, "get back to the drawing board." The therapist actively discourages the child from attributing the setback to global, internal characteristics (e.g., "It didn't work—I can't do it"). Mistakes—being part of everyone's life—are not taken as excuses to "throw in the towel." The occasional slip can, instead, present the opportunity to set new goals and start again.

SHOWING OFF

A specific and crucial element of maintenance and generalization begins with the final sessions of therapy. These final sessions are geared toward consolidating successes and fine-tuning the coping template. The child can—being familiar by now with the FEAR steps—begin to demonstrate these coping strengths to others. Framing select situations as opportunities to *SH*ow *O*thers ho*W* (SHOW off) allows the child to SHOW off or put on a SHOW, all in the service of demonstrating to others his or her personal ownership of the FEAR plan. For example, the therapist and child may switch roles toward the end of treatment. The child assumes the role of the coping advocate and coaches the somewhat distressed therapist through the steps of the FEAR plan. Role plays are suitable for this exercise, and naturally occurring "unplanned" stressors present the "anxious" therapist with the opportunity to solicit help from his or her new young coach. The child's owning the plan and telling others how to use it contributes meaningfully to maintenance.

Therapist: I'm sorry I seem a little out of it today. I have to give a talk tonight that is making me kind of nervous. I've got to calm down a little bit. What can I do?

Child: Use the FEAR plan, duh.

Therapist: Yeah, I could do that, but I can't concentrate very well because I'm scared about the speech. Could you help me, Coach?

Child: Sure, just remember the steps. Are you "Feeling Frightened?"

Therapist: (Nods.) My stomach has butterflies and my muscles are tight.

Child: Okay, take some deep breaths to calm down.

Therapist: Okay, that's a little better.

Child: Wait, we gotta do all the steps. Are you "Expecting Bad Things to Happen?"

Therapist: Well, yeah, I'm afraid I'll make mistakes and everyone will laugh.

Child: You can use "Attitudes and Actions" to help. Like, you can study to make sure you know the speech. Even if you make a mistake, you can take a deep breath and just start over. You could even chuckle to yourself or make a joke. When you're done, give yourself something for the things that went well. It doesn't have to be perfect to give yourself a pat on the back, you know.

Putting the child in the role of problem-solving advocate will help in the generalization and maintenance of coping skills. Two strategies further facilitate maintenance: (a) paradox and (b) public statements of commitment (see Meichenbaum & Turk, 1988). Both are illustrated in the following brief transcript.

Therapist: (In the presence of both parents.) You really mean to say that you know the FEAR plan, and you actually use it when you're nervous?

Child: Yeah, I know it.

Therapist: You mean you really know the FEAR plan and you use it when you're nervous?

Child: Sure, my mom has seen me use the FEAR plan.

Therapist: You're kidding me.

Child: No, really, I'm getting pretty good at it.

Therapist: Wow, you know, I believe you're not kidding with me. Let's take a situation and you can SHOW me how you use the FEAR plan.

In the last session of treatment the child and therapist work to produce a video commercial—a commercial designed by the child to tell others how to cope. This activity is another splendid opportunity for the child to put on a SHOW. The commercial allows each child to put a personal signature on the steps of the FEAR plan and, as a result, can help to strengthen the vital link between the simple learning of skills and their actual assimilation and use in everyday, anxiety-provoking situations. The child is involved in making the commercial and owns the ideas that are presented. The following two brief case examples are illustrative of the link between putting on a SHOW and the real-life application of the FEAR plan.

Case Illustration 1

Treatment with Jeffrey, a 10-year-old, avoidant boy, focused on helping him cope in social interactions whether small (e.g., approaching an adult with a minor request) or large (e.g., going to a party with peers present). Jeffrey avoided contact with others, often preferring to play alone. He had only one friend and was teased by peers about his social awkwardness. His dysfunctional expectations included "people will yell at me if I ask them something." Jeffrey made progress in treatment—he gained increased confidence in his ability to dispute his irrational expectations and began to use more facilitative self-cognitions in anxiety-producing situations. However, during the last weeks of treatment it was learned that Jeffrey would be moving across state due to family circumstances. Transferring to a new school is a challenge for any child, but particularly for a socially anxious child. Final sessions were spent role playing and practicing the situations that Jeffrey might face at the new school. This practice was useful in helping Jeffrey anticipate stressful situations and in devising appropriate coping strategies. However, in terms of maintenance of gains, perhaps the most important aspect became apparent during the making of Jeffrey's commercial at the end of treatment.

Jeffrey made the decision to do an ad-libbed commercial. First, he got up in front of the camera and began to sing about the clinic to the tune of the popular "Ghost Busters" theme, renamed "Nerve Busters." Next, he did an interview show about the program, discussing how the program can help children and the "great" facilities and staff that he had encountered. He then paused for a commercial break to advertise "Nerve Busters Cereal." Jeffrey's creativity and lack of inhibition were evident during this and two additionally improvised commercials. Singing and acting were clearly activities in which Jeffrey showed talent. The therapist congratulated Jeffrey's budding dramatic talents and suggested that he might benefit from joining the drama club and/or chorus in his new school. These groups were seen as providing settings that could help Jeffrey maintain treatment gains (i.e., constructive peer relations, positive self-attributions). For Jeffrey, the commercial provided him with a new way of seeing himself—what he had formerly thought of as just goofing around with songs was instead reframed as a talent worth pursuing. Jeffrey's SHOW and new-found talent also seemed to have an effect on his parents. Their pride in his accomplishment was evident, and they appeared to share Jeffrey's enthusiasm about helping their son seek out extra-curricular acting and singing clubs in his new school.

Case Illustration 2

The commercial created by a 10-year-old boy essentially re-created the event that was the reason for referral to our clinic. This boy had been involved in a confrontation with another boy on his way home from school and had been unable to walk to school for six months. The commercial represented his impression of the confrontation with some of the original characters acting out the drama. However, this time "Super Can" (the child) was ready for the bully with a variety of techniques he learned while in treatment. (See Figure 9.1.)

Super Can: "There's a bully I know called Louie the Lemon. He beat me up once and this is the way I dealt with it. This is the first time I met up with Louie. I was walking along and accidentally bumped Louie.

FIGURE 9.1. One client's super-hero. Drawing by Devin Clark. Reprinted with permission.

"He said: 'Why you pushing me, you want to start a fight?!'
"I said: 'No.'
"He said: 'Too bad' and bonked me on the head.

"The next day my dad asked me to go to the store and buy some milk. I didn't want to go because I didn't want to bump into Louie again. I thought to myself, 'Oh no, I'm going to get bonked again.' I started trembling and refused to go alone.

"Then I went to Temple's Child Anxiety Clinic and there I learned the FEAR steps. Here's what they mean:
   Feeling frightened?
   Expecting bad things to happen?
   Attitudes and actions that will help.
   Results and rewards.
"For me, that meant some other things I could do:

1.   Taking deep breaths to relax.
2.   Thinking 'I'll be all right' and that 'Nothing will happen.'
3.   Remember that X-man is along with me on my walk.
4.   Or, going into my favorite store.
5.   My reward is me being able to go anywhere I want.

"The next time I ran into Louie, this is what happened. I decided to go into my favorite store and Louie walked right on by. I breathed a sigh of relief. Once I dealt with him once, it got easier and easier to do. Now I can go anywhere I want.
   "Another victory for Super Can!"

As evident in his own commercial, the young client now clearly sees himself as competent to handle this kind of situation should it confront him again in the future.

POSTTREATMENT THERAPEUTIC CONTACT

In addition to taping the commercial during the last session of treatment, the child should be assured the support offered by therapy will not be abruptly terminated. As might seem obvious, let the child know directly that termination of therapy does not mean the end of contact. Setting up a regular check-in time can remind the child that the therapist is still working on his or her behalf. Additionally, as emphasized herein, not all initial efforts to exercise the FEAR plan will be successful. Depending on the magnitude of the problem, simply refocusing on certain aspects of the

FEAR plan may be successful in helping the child process a situation, whereas other situations may require a "check-in." Leaving the door open for further contact whenever appropriate reassures the child that the therapist is only a phone call away.

BOOSTER SESSIONS

Moving beyond informal contact, we recommend structured booster sessions in two general cases (see also Kendall & Braswell, 1985). First, booster sessions are appropriate when the child has encountered a particularly difficult situation that has not gone well. This type of booster session involves looking back at the problem and, in systematic fashion, reframing it with the use of the FEAR plan. Specifically, retracing cognitive and behavioral alternatives and actions and their consequences can help the child better understand that the difficult situation might be more adaptively managed when encountered in the future. Structured booster sessions include the components necessary to readdress the problem, including coping modeling, role plays, homework, and further *in-vivo* experiences.

The second general case in which booster sessions are recommended can be viewed as preventive in nature. That is, when an anxiety-arousing problem looms for the child or family, a booster session can be effective in helping the child anticipate potential difficulties that may arise. For example, switching schools, being exposed to a new group of peers, going into the hospital, or dealing with an impending parental separation or divorce are all cases where a booster session(s) can be scheduled to help the child cope in a proactive, anticipatory fashion. These booster sessions are geared proactively toward the actual or anticipated problem.

Booster sessions—whether they are used to anticipate a difficult situation or process a lapse—are an integral component of our cognitive-behavioral treatment model. Follow-up contacts allow the therapist to assess a child's progress, remind the child of the problem-solving steps of the FEAR plan, assure the child of continued therapist interest and involvement, and, importantly, to continue the establishment of the links between the problem-solving process and real-life problems. With such efforts, the child gains valuable exposure to the philosophy underlying the treatment program and the coping template: The continued use of the FEAR plan via hard work, repeated practice, and even the occasional lapse will have a tangible payoff in the push toward adaptive functioning.

Appendix

Sample scripts for child or adolescent participation in the relaxation training; the first is for the younger child (from Koeppen, 1974), the second is for an older child (from Ollendick & Cerny, 1981.)

RELAXATION TRAINING SCRIPTS

1. For the younger child

Hands and Arms

Pretend you have a whole lemon in your left hand. Now squeeze it hard. Try to squeeze all the juice out. Feel the tightness in your hand and arm as you squeeze. Now drop the lemon. Notice how your muscles feel when they are relaxed. Take another lemon and squeeze it. Try to squeeze this one harder than you did the first one. That's right. Real hard. Now drop your lemon and relax. See how much better your hand and arm feel when they are relaxed. Once again, take a lemon in your left hand and squeeze all the juice out. Don't leave a single drop. Squeeze hard. Good. Now relax and let the lemon fall from your hand. (Repeat the process for the right hand and arm.)

Arms and Shoulders

Pretend you are a furry, lazy cat. You want to stretch. Stretch your arms out in front of you. Raise them up high over your head. Way back. Feel the pull in your shoulders. Stretch higher. Now just let your arms drop back to your side. Okay, kitten, stretch again. Stretch your arms out in front of you. Raise them over your head. Pull them back, way back. Pull hard. Now let them drop quickly. Good. Notice how your shoulders feel more relaxed. This time let's have a great big stretch. Try to touch the ceiling. Stretch your arms way out in front of you. Raise them way up high over your head. Push them way, way back. Notice the tension and pull in your arms and shoulders. Hold tight, now. Great. Let them drop very quickly and feel how good it is to be relaxed. It feels good and warm and lazy.

Shoulder and Neck

Now pretend you are a turtle. You're sitting out on a rock by a nice, peaceful pond, just relaxing in the warm sun. It feels nice and warm and safe here. Oh-oh! You sense danger. Pull your head into your house. Try to pull your shoulders up to your ears and push your head down into your shoulders. Hold in tight. It isn't easy to be a turtle in a shell. The danger is past now. You can come out into the warm sunshine, and, once again, you can relax and feel the warm sunshine. Watch out now! More danger. Hurry, pull your head back into your house and hold it tight. You have to be closed in tight to protect yourself. Okay, you can relax now. Bring your head out and let your shoulders relax. Notice how much better it feels to be relaxed than to be all tight. One more time, now. Danger! Pull your head in. Push your shoulders way up to your ears and hold tight. Don't let even a tiny piece of your head show outside your shell. Hold it. Feel the tenseness in your neck and shoulders. Okay. You can come out now. It's safe again. Relax and feel comfortable in your safety. There's no more danger. Nothing to worry about. Nothing to be afraid of. You feel good.

Jaw

You have a giant jawbreaker bubble gum in your mouth. It's very hard to chew. Bite down on it. Hard! Let your neck muscles help you. Now relax. Just let your jaw hang loose. Notice how good it feels just to let your jaw drop. Okay, let's tackle that jawbreaker again now. Bite down. Hard! Try to squeeze it out between your teeth. That's good. You're really tearing that gum up. Now relax again. Just let your jaw drop off your face. It feels so good just to let go and not have to fight that bubble gum. Okay, one more time. We're really going to tear it up this time. Bite down. Hard as you can. Harder. Oh, you're really working hard. Good. Now relax. Try to relax your whole body. You've beaten the bubble gum. Let yourself go as loose as you can.

Face and Nose

Here comes a pesky old fly. He has landed on your nose. Try to get him off without using your hands. That's right, wrinkle up your nose. Make as many wrinkles in your nose as you can. Scrunch your nose up real hard.

Good. You've chased him away. Now you can relax your nose. Oops, here he comes back again. Shoo him off. Wrinkle it up hard. Hold it just as tight as you can. Okay, he flew away. You can relax your face. Notice that when you scrunch up your nose that your cheeks and your mouth and your forehead and your eyes all help you, and, they get tight, too. So when you relax your nose, your whole face relaxes too, and that feels good. Oh-oh. This time that old fly has come back, but this time he's on your forehead. Make lots of wrinkles. Try to catch him between all those wrinkles. Hold it tight, now. Okay, you can let go. He's gone for good. Now you can just relax. Let your face go smooth, no wrinkles anywhere. Your face feels nice and smooth and relaxed.

Stomach

Hey! Here comes a cute baby elephant. But he's not watching where he's going. He doesn't see you lying there in the grass, and he's about to step on your stomach. Don't move. You don't have time to get out of the way. Just get ready for him. Make your stomach very hard. Tighten up your stomach muscles real tight. Hold it. It looks like he is going the other way. You can relax now. Let your stomach go soft. Let it be as relaxed as you can. That feels so much better. Oops, he's coming this way again. Get ready. Tighten up your stomach. Real hard. If he steps on you when your stomach is hard, it won't hurt. Make your stomach into a rock. Okay, he's moving away again. You can relax now. Kind of settle down, get comfortable, and relax. Notice the difference between a tight stomach and a relaxed one. That's how we want it to feel—nice and loose and relaxed. You won't believe this, but this time he's really coming your way and no turning around. He's headed straight for you. Tighten up. Tighten hard. Here he comes. This is really it. You've got to hold on tight. He's stepping on you. He's stepped over you. Now he's gone for good. You can relax completely. You're safe. Everything is okay, and you can feel nice and relaxed.

This time imagine that you want to squeeze through a narrow fence and the boards have splinters on them. You'll have to make yourself very skinny if you're going to make it through. Suck your stomach in. Try to squeeze it up against your backbone. Try to be as skinny as you can. You've got to get through. Now relax. You don't have to be skinny now. Just relax and feel your stomach being warm and loose. Okay, let's try to get through that fence now. Squeeze up your stomach. Make it touch your backbone. Get it real small and tight. Get as skinny as you can. Hold tight now. You've got to squeeze through. You got through that skinny little fence and no splinters. You can relax now. Settle back and let your stomach come back out where it belongs. You can feel really good now. You've done fine.

Legs and Feet

Now pretend that you are standing barefoot in a big, fat mud puddle. Squish your toes down deep into the mud. Try to get your feet down to the bottom of the mud puddle. You'll probably need your legs to help you push. Push down, spread your toes apart, and feel the mud squish up between your toes. Now step out of the mud puddle. Relax your feet. Let your toes go loose and feel how nice that is. It feels good to be relaxed. Back into the mud puddle. Squish your toes down. Let your leg muscles help you push your feet down. Push your feet. Hard. Try to squeeze that mud puddle dry. Okay. Come back out now. Relax your feet, relax your legs, relax your toes. It feels so good to be relaxed. No tenseness anywhere. You feel kind of warm and tingly.

2. For the older child

Hands and Arms

Make a fist with your left hand. Squeeze it hard. Feel the tightness in your hand and arm as you squeeze. Now let your hand go and relax. See how much better your hand and arm feel when they are relaxed. Once again, make a fist with your left hand and squeeze hard. Good. Now relax and let your hand go. (Repeat the process for the right hand and arm.)

Arms and Shoulders

Stretch your arms out in front of you. Raise them high up over your head. Way back. Feel the pull in your shoulders. Stretch higher. Now just let your arms drop back to your side. Okay, let's stretch again. Stretch your arms out in front of you. Raise them over your head. Pull them back, way back. Pull hard. Now let them drop quickly. Good. Notice how your shoulders feel more relaxed. This time let's have a great big stretch. Try to touch the ceiling. Stretch your arms way out in front of you. Raise them way up high over your head. Push them way, way back. Notice the tension and pull in your arms and shoulders. Hold tight, now. Great. Let them drop very quickly and feel how good it is to be relaxed. It feels good and warm and lazy.

Shoulder and Neck

Try to pull your shoulders up to your ears and push your head down into your shoulders. Hold in tight. Okay, now relax and feel the warmth. Again, pull your shoulders up to your ears and push your head down into your shoulders. Do it tightly. Okay, you can relax now. Bring your head out and let your shoulders relax. Notice how much better it feels to be relaxed than to be all tight. One more time now. Push your head down and your shoulders way up to your ears. Hold it. Feel the tenseness in your neck and shoulders. Okay. You can relax now and feel comfortable. You feel good.

Jaw

Put your teeth together real hard. Let your neck muscles help you. Now relax. Just let your jaw hang loose. Notice how good it feels just to let your jaw drop. Okay, bite down again hard. That's good. Now relax again. Just let your jaw drop. It feels so good just to let go. Okay, one more time. Bite down. Hard as you can. Harder. Oh, you're really working hard. Good. Now relax. Try to relax your whole body. Let yourself go as loose as you can.

Face and Nose

Wrinkle up your nose. Make as many wrinkles in your nose as you can. Scrunch your nose up real hard. Good. Now you can relax your nose. Now wrinkle up your nose again. Wrinkle it up hard. Hold it just as tight as you can. Okay. You can relax your face. Notice that when you scrunch up your nose that your cheeks and your mouth and your forehead all help you and they get tight, too. So when you relax your nose, your whole face relaxes too, and that feels good. Now make lots of wrinkles on your forehead. Hold it tight, now. Okay, you can let go. Now you can just relax. Let your face go smooth. No wrinkles anywhere. Your face feels nice and smooth and relaxed.

Stomach

Now tighten up your stomach muscles real tight. Make your stomach real hard. Don't move. Hold it. You can relax now. Let your stomach go soft. Let it be as relaxed as you can. That feels so much better. Okay, again. Tighten your stomach real hard. Good. You can relax now. Kind of settle down, get comfortable, and relax. Notice the difference between a tight stomach and a relaxed one. That's how we want it to feel. Nice and loose and relaxed. Okay. Once more. Tighten up. Tighten hard. Good. Now you can relax completely. You can feel nice and relaxed.

This time, try to pull your stomach in. Try to squeeze it against your backbone. Try to be as skinny as you can. Now relax. You don't have to be skinny now. Just relax and feel your stomach being warm and loose. Okay, squeeze in your stomach again. Make it touch your backbone. Get it real small and tight. Get as skinny as you can. Hold tight now. You can relax now. Settle back and let your stomach come back out where it belongs. You can really feel good now. You've done fine.

Legs and Feet

Push your toes down on the floor real hard. You'll probably need your legs to help you push. Push down, spread your toes apart. Now relax your feet. Let your toes go loose and feel how nice that is. It feels good to be relaxed. Okay. Now push your toes down. Let your leg muscles help you push your feet down. Push your feet. Hard. Okay. Relax your feet, relax your legs, relax your toes. It feels so good to be relaxed. No tenseness anywhere. You feel kind of warm and tingly.

Conclusion

Stay as relaxed as you can. Let your whole body go limp and feel all your muscles relaxed. In a few minutes I will ask you to open your eyes and that will be the end of the session. Today is a good day, and you are ready to go back to class feeling very relaxed. You've worked hard in here and it feels good to work hard. Shake your arms. Now shake your legs. Move your head around. Slowly open your eyes. Very good. You've done a good job. You're going to be a super relaxer.

References

Abe, K., & Masui, T. (1981). Age-sex trends of phobic and anxiety symptoms. *British Journal of Psychiatry, 138,* 297–302.

Abramson, L. Y., Seligman, M. E. P., & Teasdale, J. D. (1978). Learned helplessness in humans: Critique and reformation. *Journal of Abnormal Psychology, 87,* 49–74.

Achenbach, T. M. (1985). *Assessment and taxonomy of child and adolescent psychopathology.* Beverly Hills: Sage Publications.

Achenbach, T. M., & Edelbrock, C. S. (1978). The classification of child psychopathology: A review and analysis of empirical efforts. *Psychological Bulletin, 85,* 1275–1301.

Achenbach, T. M., & Edelbrock, C. S. (1983). *Manual for the Child Behavior Checklist and Revised Child Behavior Profile.* Burlington: University Associates in Psychiatry.

Achenbach, T., McConaughty, S., & Howell, C. (1987). Child/adolescent behavioral and emotional problems: Implication of cross-informant correlations for situational specificity. *Psychological Bulletin, 101,* 213–232.

Agras, S., Sylvester, D., & Oliveau, D. (1969). The epidemiology of common fears and phobias. *Comprehensive Psychiatry, 10,* 151–156.

American Psychiatric Association. (1980). *Diagnostic and statistical manual of mental disorders—Third edition.* Washington, DC: Author.

American Psychiatric Association. (1987). *Diagnostic and statistical manual of mental disorders—Third edition revised.* Washington, DC: Author.

Angelino, H., Dollins, J., & Mech, E. V. (1956). Trends in the "fears and worries" of school children as related to socioeconomic status and age. *Journal of Genetic Psychology, 89,* 263–276.

Ayllon, T., Smith, D., & Rogers, M. (1970). Behavioral management of school phobia. *Journal of Behavior Therapy and Experimental Psychiatry, 1,* 125–138.

Baldwin, A. L., Cole, R. E., & Baldwin, C. (1982). Parental pathology, family interaction, and the competence of the child in school. *Monographs of the Society of Research in Child Development, 47*(5).

Ball, W., & Tronick, E. (1971). Infant responses to impending collision: Optical and real. *Science, 171,* 818–820.

Bandura, A. (1969). *Principles of behavior modification.* Englewood Cliffs, NJ: Prentice-Hall.

Bandura, A. (1986). *Social foundation of thought and action: A social cognitive theory.* Englewood Cliffs, NJ: Prentice-Hall.

Bandura, A., Grusec, J. E., & Menlove, F. L. (1967). Vicarious extinction of avoidance behavior. *Journal of Personality and Social Psychology, 5,* 16–23.

Barker, P. (1976). *Basic Child Psychiatry.* Staples, London. Crosby Lockwood.

Barlow, D. H. (1988). *Anxiety and its disorders.* New York: Guilford Press.

Barlow, D. H., & Cerny, J. A. (1988). *Psychological treatment of panic.* New York: Guilford Press.

Barlow, D. H., & Wolfe, B. E. (1981). Behavioral approaches to anxiety disorders: A report on the NIMH-SUNY, Albany Research Conference. *Journal of Consulting and Clinical Psychology, 49,* 448–454.

Barrios, B. A., & Hartmann, D. P. (1988). Fears and anxieties. In E. J. Mash & L. G. Terdal (Eds.), *Behavioral assessment of childhood disorder,* Second edition (pp. 196–264). New York: Guilford Press.

Barrios, B. A., & Shigetomi, C. C. (1979). Coping skills training for the management of anxiety: A critical review. *Behavior Therapy, 10,* 491–522.

Baucom, D. H., Bell, W. G., & Duhe, A. G. (1982, November). *The measurement of couples attributions for positive and negative dyadic interactions.* Paper presented at the 16th Annual Convention of the Association for the Advancement of Behavior Therapy, Los Angeles.

Bauer, D. H. (1976). An exploratory study of developmental changes in children's fears. *Journal of Child Psychology and Psychiatry, 17,* 69–74.

Beck, A. T., Brown, G., Steer, R. A., Eidelson, J. I., & Riskind, J. H. (1987). Differentiating anxiety and depression: A test of the cognitive specificity hypothesis. *Journal of Abnormal Psychology, 96,* 179–183.

Beck, A. T., & Emery, G. (1985). *Anxiety disorders and phobias: A cognitive perspective.* New York: Guilford Press.

Beck, A. T., Rush, A. J., Shaw, B. F., & Emery, G. (1979). *Cognitive therapy of depression.* New York: Guilford Press.

Beidel, D. C. (1988). Psychophysiological assessment of anxious emotional states in children. *Journal of Abnormal Psychology, 97,* 80–82.

Berg, I., Butler, A., & Pritchard, J. (1974). Psychiatric illness in the mothers of school-phobic adolescents. *British Journal of Psychiatry, 125,* 466–467.

Bernard, M. E., & Joyce, M. R. (1984). *Rational emotive therapy with children and adolescents: Theory, treatment strategies, preventive motives.* New York: John Wiley & Sons.

Bertalanffy, L. von (1968). *General systems theory.* New York: Braziller.

Block, J. H., Block, J., & Morrison, A. (1981). Parental agreement-disagreement on child rearing orientations and gender-related personality correlates in children. *Child Development, 52,* 965–974.

Borkovec, T., Weerts, T., & Bernstein, D. (1977). Assessment of anxiety. In A. Ciminero, K. Calhoun, & H. Adams (Eds.), *Handbook of behavioral assessment.* New York: John Wiley & Sons.

Bowlby, J. (1961). Childhood mourning and its implications for psychiatry. *American Journal of Psychiatry, 118,* 481–498.

Bowlby, J. (1969). *Attachment and loss* (Vol. 1: *Attachment*). New York: Basic Books.

Bradbury, T. N., & Fincham, F. D. (1990). Attributions in marriage: Review and critique. *Psychological Bulletin, 107*(1), 3–33.

Brady, E. U., & Kendall, P. C. (1991). *Comorbidity of anxiety and depression in children and adolescents.* Manuscript submitted for publication.

Brent, D. A., Kalas, R., Edelbrock, C., Costello, A. J., Duncan, M. K., & Conover, N. (1986). Psychopathology and its relationship to suicidal ideation in childhood and adolescence. *Journal of the American Academy of Child Psychiatry, 25,* 666–673.

Bronson, G. W. (1972). Infants' reactions to unfamiliar persons and novel objects. *Monographs of the Society for Research in Child Development, 37,* (3, Serial No. 148).

Brownell, K.D., Marlatt, G.A., Lichtenstein, E. & Wilson, G.T. (1986). Understanding and preventing relapse. *American Psychologist, 41,* 765–776.

Campbell, S. B. (1986). Developmental issues. In R. Gittelman (Ed.), *Anxiety disorders of childhood* (pp. 24–57). New York: Guilford Press.

Carey, G., & Gottesman, I. (1981). Twin and family studies of anxiety, phobic, and obsessive disorders. In D. F. Klein & J. Rabkin (Eds.), *Anxiety: New research and changing concepts* (pp. 117–133). New York: Raven Press.

Chambers, W. J., Puig-Antich, J., Hirsch, M., Paez, P., Ambrosini, P. J., Tabrizi, M. A., & Davies, M. (1985). The assessment of affective disorders in children and adolescents by semistructured interview. *Archives of General Psychiatry, 42,* 696–702.

Chandler, M. J. (1973). Egocentrism and antisocial behavior: The assessment and training of social perspective taking skills. *Developmental Psychology, 9,* 326–332.

Cicchetti, D. (1984). The emergence of developmental psychopathology. *Child Development, 55,* 1–7.

Cloninger, C. R., Martin, R. L., Clayton, P., & Guze, S. B. (1981). A blind follow-up and family study of anxiety neurosis: Preliminary analysis of the St. Louis 500. In D. F. Klein & J. Rabkin (Eds.), *Anxiety: New research and changing concepts* (pp. 137–148). New York: Raven Press.

Conners, C. K. (1969). A teacher rating scale for use in drug studies with children. *American Journal of Psychiatry, 126,* 884–888.

Coolidge, J. C., & Brodie, R. D. (1974). Observations of mothers of 49 school phobic children. *Journal of the American Academy of Child Psychiatry, 13,* 275–285.

Costello, A. J., Edelbrock, C., Kalas, R., Dulcan, M. K., & Klaric, S. H. (1984). *Development and testing of the NIMH diagnostic interview schedule for children (DISC) in a clinic population: final report* (Contract No. RFP-DB-81-0027). Rockville, MD: Center for Epidemiological Studies, NIMH.

Craighead, W. C., Meyers, A. W., Craighead, L. W., & McHale, S. M. (1983). Issues in cognitive behavior therapy with children. In M. Rosenbaum, C. B. Franks, & Y. Jaffe (Eds.), *Perspectives on behavior therapy in the 80's* (pp. 234–261). New York: Springer.

Crowe, R. R., Noyes, R., Pauls, D. L., & Slymen, D. (1983). A family study of panic disorder. *Archives of General Psychiatry, 40,* 1065–1069.

Crowe, R. R., Pauls, D. L., Slymen, D. J., & Noyes, R. (1980). A family study of anxiety neurosis. *Archives of General Psychiatry, 37,* 77–79.

Darley, S., & Katz, I. (1973). Heart rate changes in children as a function of test versus game instructions and test anxiety. *Child Development, 44,* 784–789.

Davidson, S. (1961) School phobia as a manifestation of family disturbance: Its structure and treatment. *Journal of Child Psychology and Psychiatry, 1,* 270–287.

Dobson, K. S., & Shaw, B. F. (1988). The use of treatment manuals in cognitive therapy: Experience and issues. *Journal of Consulting and Clinical Psychology, 56,* 673–680.

Dodge, K. (1985). Attributional bias in aggressive children. In P. C. Kendall (Ed.), *Advances in cognitive-behavioral research and therapy.* (V. 4). New York: Academic Press.

D'Zurilla, T. J. (1986). *Problem-solving therapy: A social competence approach to clinical intervention.* New York: Springer.

D'Zurilla, T. J., & Goldfried, M. R. (1971). Problem-solving and behavior modification. *Journal of Abnormal Psychology, 73,* 107–126.

Earls, F. (1980). The prevalence of behavior problems in three year old children. A cross-cultural replication. *Archives of General Psychiatry, 37,* 1153–1157.

Edelbrock, C., & Costello, A. J. (1988). Structured psychiatric interviews for children. In M. Rutter, A. H. Tuma, & I. S. Lann (Eds.), Assessment and diagnosis of child psychopathology. (pp. 87–112). New York: Guilford Press.

Edelbrock, C., Costello, C. J., Duncan, M. K., Conover, N. C., & Kalas, R. (1986). Parent-child agreement on child psychiatric symptoms assessed via structured interview. *Journal of Child Psychology and Psychiatry, 27,* 181–190.

Edelbrock, C., Costello, A. J., Duncan, M. K. Kalas, R., & Conover, N. C. (1985). Age differences in the reliability of the psychiatric interview of the child. *Child Development, 56,* 265–275.

Eisenberg, L. (1958a). School phobia: Diagnosis, genesis and clinical management. *American Journal of Psychiatry, 4,* 645–666.

Eisenberg, L. (1958b). School phobia: A study in the communication of anxiety. *American Journal of Psychiatry, 114,* 712–718.

Epstein, N., Schlesinger, S. E., & Dryden, W. (1988). Concepts and methods of cognitive-behavioral family treatment. In N. Epstein, S. E. Schlesinger, & W. Dryden (Eds.), *Cognitive-Behavioral Therapy with Families* (pp. 5–83). New York: Brunner/Mazel.

Evans, I. M., & Nelson, R. O. (1986). Assessment of children. In A. R. Ciminero, K. S. Calhoun, & H. E. Adams (Eds.), *Handbook of behavioral assessment,* Second edition, (pp. 601–630). New York: John Wiley & Sons.

Faravelli, C., Webb, T., Ambonetti, A., Fonnesu, F., & Sessarego, A. (1985). Prevalence of traumatic early life events in 31 agoraphobic patients with panic attacks. *American Journal of Psychiatry, 142,* 1493–1494.

Finch, A.J., Lipovsky, A.J., & Casat, C.D. (1989). Anxiety and depression in children and adolescents: Negative affectivity or separate constructs? In P.C. Kendall & D. Watson (Eds.), *Anxiety and depression: Distinctive and overlapping features.* New York: Academic Press.

Finch, A. J., Fryer, L. L., Saylor, C. F., Carek, D. J., & McIntosh, J. A. (1990). Anxiety & depression in children: Negative affectivity or separate constructs? Manuscript submitted for publication.

Finch, A. J., & Montgomery, L. E. (1973). Reflection-impulsivity and information seeking in emotionally disturbed children. *Journal of Abnormal Child Psychology, 1,* 358–362.

Fincham, F., & O'Leary, K. D. (1983). Causal inferences for spouse behavior in maritally distressed and nondistressed couples. *Journal of Social and Clinical Psychology, 1,* 42–57.

Foa, E. B., Steketee, G., & Grayson, J. B. (1985). Imaginal and in vivo exposure: A comparison with obsessive-compulsive checkers. *Behavioral Therapy, 16,* 292–302.

Foster, S., & Cone, J. (1986). Observational methods. In A. Ciminero, K. Calhoun, & H. Adams (Eds.), *Handbook of behavioral assessment,* Second edition. New York: John Wiley & Sons.

Francis, G. (1988). Assessing cognitions in anxious children. *Behavior Modification, 12,* 267–280.

Gassner, S., & Murray, E. J. (1969). Dominance and conflict in the interactions between parents of normal and neurotic children. *Journal of Abnormal and Social Psychology, 74,* 33–41.

Gittelman, R. (1984). Anxiety disorders in children. *Psychiatry Update, 3,* 410–418.

Gittelman, R. (1985). Anxiety disorders in children. In B. B. Lahey & A. E. Kazdin (Eds.), *Advances in clinical child psychology,* Volume 8, (pp. 53–79). New York: Plenum Publishing.

Gittelman, R. (1986). Childhood anxiety disorders: Correlates and outcome. In R. Gittelman (Ed.), *Anxiety disorders of childhood* (pp. 101–125). New York: Guilford Press.

Gittelman, R., & Koplewicz, H. S. (1986). Pharmacotherapy of childhood anxiety disorders. In R. Gittelman (Ed.), *Anxiety disorders of childhood.* New York: Guilford Press.

Gotlib, I. H., & Cane, D. B. (1989). Self-report assessment of depression and anxiety. In P. C. Kendall & D. Watson (Eds.), *Anxiety and depression: Distinctive and overlapping features.* New York: Academic Press.

Gottman, J. M. (1979). *Marital interactions: Experimental investigations.* New York: Academic Press.

Graziano, A. M., DeGiovanni, I. S., & Garcia, K. A. (1979). Behavioral treatment of children's fears: A review. *Psychological Bulletin, 86,* 804–830.

Grotevant, H. D., & Carlson, C. I. (1989). *Family Assessment: A guide to methods and measures.* New York: The Guilford Press.

Harris, S. L., & Ferrari, M. (1983). Developmental factors in child behavior therapy. *Behavior Therapy, 14,* 54–72.

Harris, E. L., Noyes, R., Crowe, R. R., & Chaudery, M. D. (1983). A family study of agoraphobia. *Archives of General Psychiatry, 40,* 1061–1064.

Hartup, W. W. (1984). Peer relations. In P. Mussen (Ed.), *Handbook of child psychology*. New York: John Wiley & Sons.

Hatzenbuehler, L. C., & Schroeder, H. E. (1978). Desensitization procedures in the treatment of childhood disorders. *Psychological Bulletin, 85,* 831–844.

Hauser, S. T., Powers, S. I., Weiss-Perry, B., Follansbee, D., Rajapark, D. C., & Greene, W. M. (1987). *Family constraining and enabling coding system (CECS) manual.* Unpublished manuscript, Harvard Medical School, Adolescent and Family Development Project.

Heide, F. J., & Borkovec, T. D. (1983). Relaxation-induced anxiety: Paradoxical anxiety enhancement due to relaxation training. *Journal of Consulting and Clinical Psychology, 51*(2), 171–182.

Heide, F. J., & Borkovec, T. D. (1984). Relaxation-induced anxiety: Mechanisms and theoretical implications. *Behavioral Research and Therapy, 22*(1), 1–12.

Herjanic, B., & Reich, W. (1982). Development of a structured psychiatric interview for children: Agreement between child and parent on individual symptoms. *Journal of Abnormal Child Psychology, 10,* 307–324.

Hersov, L. A. (1960). Persistent non-attendance at school. *Child Psychology and Psychiatry, 1,* 130–136.

Hetherington, E. M., Stouwie, R., & Ridberg E. H. (1971). Patterns of family interaction and child rearing attitudes related to three dimensions of juvenile delinquency. *Journal of Abnormal Psychology, 77,* 160–176.

Hill, J. P., & Holmbeck, G. H. (1986). The role of conflict in the adaptation to pubertal change: A research proposal. In S. T. Hauser (Chair), *Family relations during adolescence.* Preconference workshop at the meeting of the Society for Research on Adolescence, Madison, WI.

Himadi, W. G., Boice, R., & Barlow, D. H. (1985). Assessment of agoraphobia: Triple response measurement. *Behavior Research and Therapy, 23,* 311–323.

Hodges, K., McKnew, D., Burback, D. J., & Roebuck, L. (1987). Diagnostic concordance between the Child Assessment Schedule (CAS) and the Schedule for Affective Disorders and Schizophrenia for School-Age Children (K-SADS) in an outpatient sample using lay interviews. *Journal of the American Academy of Child and Adolescent Psychiatry, 26,* 654–661.

Hollon, S. D., & Beck, A. T. (1979). Cognitive therapy of depression. In P. C. Kendall & S. D. Hollon (Eds.), *Cognitive-behavioral interventions: Theory, research, and procedures.* New York: Academic Press.

Holtzworth-Munroe, A., & Jacobson, N. S. (1985). Causal attributions of married couples: When do they search for causes? What do they conclude when they do? *Journal of Personality and Social Psychology, 48,* 1398–1412.

Houston, B. K., Fox, J. E., & Forbes, L. (1984). Trait anxiety and children's state anxiety, cognitive behaviors, and performance under stress. *Cognitive Therapy and Research, 8,* 631–641.

Ingram, R. E., & Kendall, P. C. (1986). Cognitive clinical psychology: Implications of an information processing perspective. In R. E. Ingram (Ed.), *Information processing approaches to clinical psychology* (pp. 3–21). New York: Academic Press.

Ingram, R. E., & Kendall, P. C. (1987). The cognitive side of anxiety. *Cognitive Therapy and Research, 1,* 331–341.

Izard, C.E. (1971). *The face of emotion.* New York: Appleton-Century-Crofts.

Jacob, T. (1975). Family interaction in disturbed and normal families: A methodological and substantive review. *Psychological Bulletin, 82,* 33–65.

Jacob, T., & Tennenbaum, D. L. (1988). *Family assessment: Rationale, methods, and future directions.* New York: Plenum Publishing.

Jacobson, N. S. (1984). A component analysis of behavior marital therapy: The relative effectiveness of behavior exchange and communication problem solving. *Journal of Consulting and Clinical Psychology, 52,* 295–305.

Jacobson, N. S., & Margolin, G. (1979). *Marital therapy: Strategies based on social learning and behavior exchange principles.* New York: Brunner/Mazel.

Jannoun, L., Munby, M., Catalan, J., & Gelder, M. (1980). A home-based treatment program for agoraphobia: Replication and controlled evaluation. *Behavior Therapy, 11,* 294.

Jersild, A. T., & Holmes, F. B. (1935). *Children's fears.* New York: Teachers College, Columbia University.

Johnson, T., Tyler, V., Thompson, R., & Jones, E. (1971). Systematic desensitization and assertive training in the treatment of speech anxiety in middle school students. *Psychology in the Schools, 8,* 263–267.

Justice, B., & Justice, R. (1976). *The abusing family.* New York: Human Sciences Press.

Kane, M. T., & Kendall, P. C. (1991). Anxiety disorders in children: A multiple-baseline evaluation of a cognitive-behavioral treatment. *Behavior Therapy, 20,* 499–508.

Kastrup, M. (1976). Psychic disorders among pre-school children in a geographically delimited area of Aarhus county, Denmark. *Acta Psychiatrica Scandinavia, 54,* 29–42.

Kendall, P. C. (1984). Behavioral assessment and methodology. In G. T. Wilson, C. M. Franks, K. D. Brownell, and P. C. Kendall (Eds.), *Annual review of behavior therapy: Theory and practice* (Vol. 9). New York: Guilford Press.

Kendall, P. C. (1985). Toward a cognitive-behavioral model of child psychopathology and a critique of related interventions. *Journal of Abnormal Child Psychology, 13*(3), 357–372.

Kendall, P. C. (1989). *Stop and think workbook.* Available from the author, 238 Meeting House Lane, Merion, PA 19066.

Kendall, P. C. (1990). *Coping cat workbook.* Available from the author, 238 Meeting House Lane, Merion, PA 19066.

Kendall, P. C. (1991). Guiding theory for therapy with children and adolescents. In P. C. Kendall (Ed.), *Child and adolescent therapy: Cognitive-behavioral procedures.* New York: Guilford Press.

Kendall, P. C., & Braswell, L. (1985). *Cognitive-behavioral therapy for impulsive children.* New York: Guilford Press.

Kendall, P. C., & Braswell, L. (1986). Medical applications of cognitive-behavioral interventions with children. *Developmental and Behavioral Pediatrics, 7,* 257–264.

Kendall, P. C., & Chansky, T. E. (1991). Considering cognition in anxiety disordered youth. *Journal of Anxiety Disorders, 5,* 167–185.

Kendall, P. C., & Grove, W. (1988). Normative comparisons in therapy outcome. *Behavioral Assessment, 10,* 147–158.

Kendall, P. C., & Hollon, S. D. (Eds.). (1979). *Cognitive-behavioral interventions: Theory, research, and procedures.* New York: Academic Press.

Kendall, P. C., & Hollon, S. D. (1981). Assessing self-referent speech: Methods in the measurement of self-statements. In P. C. Kendall & S. D. Hollon (Eds.), *Assessment strategies for cognitive-behavioral interventions.* New York: Academic Press.

Kendall, P. C., & Hollon, S. D. (1989). Anxious self-talk: Development of the Anxious Self-Statements Questionnaire (ASSQ). *Cognitive Therapy and Research, 13,* 81–93.

Kendall, P. C., Howard, B. L., & Epps, J. (1988). The anxious child: Cognitive-behavioral treatment strategies. *Behavioral Modification, 12,* 271–319.

Kendall, P. C., Howard, B. L., & Hays, R. C. (1989). Self-referent speech and psychopathology: The balance of positive and negative thinking. *Cognitive Therapy and Research, 13,* 583–598.

Kendall, P. C., & Ingram, R. E. (1987). The future for cognitive assessment of anxiety: Let's get specific. In L. Michelson & M. Ascher (Eds.), *Stress and anxiety: Cognitive-behavioral assessment and therapy.* New York: Guilford Press.

Kendall, P. C., & Ingram, R. E. (1989). Cognitive-behavioral perspectives: Theory and research on depression and anxiety. In P. C. Kendall & D. Watson (Eds.), *Anxiety and depression: Distinctive and overlapping features*. New York: Academic Press.

Kendall, P. C., Kane, M., Howard, B., & Siqueland, L. (1989). *Cognitive-behavioral therapy for anxious children: Treatment manual*. Available from the first author, Department of Psychology, Temple University, Philadelphia, PA 19122.

Kendall, P. C., & Korgeski, G. (1979). Assessment and cognitive-behavioral interventions. *Cognitive Therapy and Research, 3,* 1–21.

Kendall, P. C., & Kriss, M. R. (1983). Cognitive-behavioral interventions. In C. Eugene Walker (Ed.), *Handbook of clinical psychology*. Homewood, IL: Dow Jones-Irwin.

Kendall, P. C., Lerner, R. M., & Craighead, W. E. (1984). Human development and intervention in childhood psychopathology. *Child Development, 53,* 71–82.

Kendall, P. C., & Ronan, K. R. (1990). Assessment of children's anxieties, fears, and phobias: Cognitive-behavioral models and methods. In C. R. Reynolds, & R. W. Kamphaus (Eds.), *Handbook of psychological and educational assessment of children* (pp. 223–244). New York: Guilford Press.

Kendall, P. C., Ronan, K., & Epps J. (1989). Aggression in children/adolescents: Cognitive-behavioral treatment perspectives. In D. Pepler & K. Rubin (Eds.), *Development and treatment of childhood aggression*. Hillsdale, NJ: Lawrence Erlbaum Associates.

Kendall, P. C., & Siqueland, L. (1989). Child and adolescent therapy. In A. M. Nezu & C. M. Nezu (Eds.), *Clinical decision making in behavior therapy: A problem-solving perspective* (pp. 321–337). Champaign, IL: Research Press.

Kendall, P. C., Stark, K., & Adam, T. (1990). Cognitive distortion or cognitive deficit in childhood depression. *Journal of Abnormal Child Psychology, 18,* 255–270.

Kendall, P. C., Vitousek, K. B., & Kane, M. (in press). Thought and action in psychotherapy: Cognitive-behavioral interventions. In M. Hersen, A. Kazdin, & A. Bellack (Eds.), *The clinical psychology handbook,* (second edition). New York: Pergamon Press.

Kendall, P. C., & Watson, D. (Eds.). (1989). *Anxiety and depression: Distinctive and overlapping features*. New York: Academic Press.

King, N. J., Hamilton, D. I., & Ollendick, T. H. (1988). *Children's phobias: A behavioral perspective*. Chichester: John Wiley & Sons.

Kleiner, L., Marshall, W. L., & Spevack, M. (1987). Training in problem-solving and exposure treatment for agoraphobics with panic attacks. *Journal of Anxiety Disorders, 1,* 219.

Kleinknecht, R. A. (1985). *The anxious self: Diagnosis and treatment of fears and phobias*. New York: Human Sciences Press.

Klinnert, M. D., Campos, J. J., Sorce, J. F., Emde, R. N., & Svegda, M. (1983). Emotions as behavior regulators: Social referencing in infancy. In R. Plutchik & H. Kellerman (Eds.), *Emotion: Theory, research and experience* (Vol. 2, p. 57). New York: Academic Press.

Koeppen, A. S. (1974). Relaxation training for children. *Elementary School Guidance & Counseling, 9,* 14–21.

Kovacs, M. (1981). Rating scales to assess depression in school-aged children. *Acta Paedopsychiatria, 46,* 305–315.

Lang, P. J. (1968). Fear reduction and fear behavior: Problems in treating a construct. In J. M. Schleen (Ed.), *Research in Psychotherapy*. Washington, D.C.: American Psychological Association.

Lapouse, R., & Monk, M. A. (1958). An epidemiologic study of behavior characteristics in children. *American Journal of Public Health, 48,* 1134–1144.

Last, C. G. (1988). Anxiety disorders in childhood and adolescence. In C. G. Last & M. Hersen (Eds.), *Handbook of anxiety disorders* (p. 531). New York: Plenum Publishing.

Last, C. G., Hersen, M., Kazdin, A. E., Finkelstein, R., & Strauss, C. C. (1987a). Comparison of DSM-III separation anxiety and overanxious disorders: Demographic characteristics and patterns of comorbidity. *Journal of the American Academy of Child and Adolescent Psychiatry, 26,* 527–531.

Last, C. G., Hersen, M., Kazdin, A. E., Francis, G., & Grubb, H. J. (1987b). Psychiatric illness in the mothers of anxious children. *American Journal of Psychiatry, 144*(12), 1580–1583.

Last, C. G., Phillips, J. E., Statfield, A. (1987). Childhood anxiety disorders in mothers and their children. *Childhood Psychiatry and Human Development, 18,* 103–112.

Last, C. G., Strauss, C. C., & Francis, G. (1987). Comorbidity among childhood anxiety disorders. *Journal of Nervous and Mental Disease, 175,* 726–730.

Leckman, J. F., Weissman, M., Merikangas, K. R., Pauls, D. L., & Prusoff, B. (1983). Panic disorder and major depression. *Archives of General Psychiatry, 40,* 1055–1060.

Leslie, L. A. (1988). Cognitive-behavioral and systems models of family therapy: How compatible are they? In N. Epstein, S. E. Schlesinger, & W. Dryden (Eds.), *Cognitive-Behavioral Therapy with Families* (pp. 49–83). New York: Brunner/Mazel.

Lewis, S. A. (1974). A comparison of behavior therapy techniques in the reduction of fearful avoidance behaviors. *Behavior Therapy, 5,* 648–655.

Ley, R. (1987). Panic disorder: A hyperventilation interpretation. In L. Michelson & L. M. Ascher (Eds.), *Anxiety and stress disorders: Cognitive behavioral assessment and treatment* (pp. 191–112). New York: Guilford Press.

Lick, J., & Katkin, E. (1976). Assessment of anxiety and fear. In M. Hersen & A. Bellack (Eds.), *Behavioral assessment: A practical handbook.* New York: Pergamon Press.

Little, V., & Kendall, P. C. (1979). Cognitive-behavioral interventions with delinquents: Problem solving, role-taking, and self-control. In P. C. Kendall & S. D. Hollon (Eds.), *Cognitive-behavioral interventions: Theory, research, and procedures* (pp. 81–116). New York: Academic Press.

Livingston, R., Nugent, H., Rader, L., & Smith, R. G. (1985). Family histories of depressed and severely anxious children. *American Journal of Psychiatry, 142*(12), 1497–1499.

Luiselli, J. K. (1978). Treatment of an autistic child's fear of riding a school bus through exposure and reinforcement. *Journal of Behavior Therapy and Experimental Psychiatry, 9,* 169.

Lynch, M. (1976). Risk factors in the child. A study of abused children and their siblings. In H. P. Martin (Ed.), *The abused child: A multidisciplinary approach to developmental issues and treatment* (pp. 43–56). Cambridge: Ballinger.

Mahoney, M. J. (1977). Reflections on the cognitive-learning trend in psychotherapy. *American Psychologist, 32,* 5–13.

Mahoney, M. J., & Arnkoff, D. B. (1978). Cognitive and self-control therapies. In S. L. Garfield & A. E. Bergin (Eds.), *Handbook of psychotherapy and behavior change* (2nd ed.). New York: John Wiley & Sons.

Mannuzza, S., & Klein, R. (1987). *Schedule for the assessment of conduct, hyperactivity, anxiety, mood and psychoactive substances (CHAMPS).* Children's Behavior Disorders Clinic, Long Island Jewish Medical Center, New Hyde Park, NY 11042.

Margolin, G. (1987). Marital therapy: A cognitive-behavior-affective approach. In N. S. Jacobson (Ed.), *Psychotherapists in clinical practice* (p. 283), New York: Guilford Press.

Marks, I. M. (1975). Behavioral treatments of phobic and obsessive-compulsive disorders: A critical appraisal. In M. Hersen, R. M. Eisler, & P. M. Miller (Eds.), *Progress in behavior modification.* New York: Academic Press.

Matson, J. L. (1989). *Treating depression in children and adolescents.* New York: Pergamon Press.

Maurer, A. (1965). What children fear. *Journal of Genetic Psychology, 106,* 265–277.

McFarlane, A. C. (1987). The relationship between patterns of family interaction and psychiatric disorder in children. *Australian and New Zealand Journal of Psychiatry, 21,* 383.

McFarlane, J. W., Allen, L., & Honzik, M. P. (1954). *A developmental study of the behavior problems of normal children between 21 months and 14 years.* Berkeley: University of California Press.

Meichenbaum, D. (1977). *Cognitive-behavior modification: An integrative approach.* New York: Plenum Publishing.

Meichenbaum, D. (1986). *Stress inoculation training.* New York: Pergamon Press.

Meichenbaum, D., & Turk, D. (1988). *Facilitating treatment adherence: A practitioner's handbook.* New York: Plenum Publishing.

Melamed, B. G., & Siegel, L. J. (1975). Reduction of anxiety in children facing hospitalization and surgery by way of filmed modeling. *Journal of Consulting and Clinical Psychology, 43,* 511–521.

Melamed, B. G., Yurcheson, R., Fleece, E. L., Hutcherson, S., & Hawes, R. (1978). Effects of film modeling on the reduction of anxiety-related behaviors in individuals varying in levels of previous experience in the stress situation. *Journal of Consulting and Clinical Psychology, 46,* 1357–1367.

Mezzich, A. C., & Mezzich, J. E. (1985). Reliability of DSM-III versus DSM-II in child psychopathology. *Journal of the American Academy of Child Psychiatry, 24,* 273–280.

Michelson, L., & Marchione, K. (1991). Behavioral, cognitive, and pharmacological treatments of panic disorder with agoraphobia: Critique and synthesis. *Journal of Consulting and Clinical Psychology, 59,* 100–114.

Miller, L. C. (1983). Fears and anxieties in children. In C. E. Walker & M. C. Roberts (Eds.), *Handbook of clinical child psychology,* (pp. 337–380). New York: John Wiley & Sons.

Miller, L. C., Barrett, C. L., & Hampe, E. (1974). Phobias of childhood in a prescientific era. In S. Davids (Ed.), *Child personality and psychopathology* (pp. 89–134). New York: John Wiley & Sons.

Miller, L. C., Barrett, C. L., Hampe, E., & Noble, H. (1972). Factor structure of childhood fears. *Journal of Consulting and Clinical Psychology, 39,* 264–268.

Morris, R. J., & Kratochwill, T. R. (1983). *Treating children's fears and phobias.* New York: Pergamon Press.

Morris, R. J., & Kratochwill, T. R. (1985). Behavioral treatment of children's fears and phobias: A review. *School Psychology Review, 14,* 84–93.

Morton, T. L., Twentyman, C. T., & Azar, S. T. (1988). Cognitive-behavioral assessment and treatment of child abuse. In N. Epstein, S. E. Schlesinger, & W. Dryden (Eds.), *Cognitive-Behavioral Therapy with Families* (pp. 87–117). New York: Brunner/Mazel.

Munjack, D. J., Howard, B., & Moss, H. B. (1981). Affective disorder and alcoholism in families of agoraphobics. *Archives of General Psychiatry, 38,* 869–871.

Neisworth, J. T., Madle, R. A., & Goeke, K. E. (1975). Errorless elimination of separation anxiety: A case study. *Journal of Behavioral Therapy and Experimental Psychiatry, 6,* 79–82.

Nelles, W. B., & Barlow, D. H. (1988). Do children panic? *Clinical Psychology Review, 8,* 359–372.

Nezu, A. M., Nezu, C. M., & Perri, M. G. (1989). *Problem-solving therapy for depression: Theory, research, and clinical guidelines.* New York: John Wiley & Sons.

Noyes, R., Clancy, J., Crowe, R., Hoenk, P. R., & Slymen, D. J. (1978). The familial prevalence of anxiety neurosis. *Archives of General Psychiatry, 35,* 1057–1059.

Ollendick, T. H. (1979). Behavioral treatment of anorexia nervosa: A five year study. *Behavior Modification, 3,* 124–135.

Ollendick, T. H. (1983). Reliability and validity of the Revised Fear Survey Schedule for Children. *Behavior Research and Therapy, 21,* 685–692.

Ollendick, T. H. (1986). Behavior therapy with children and adolescents. In S. L. Garfield & A. E. Bergen (Eds.), *Handbook of psychotherapy and behavior change* (3rd ed.). New York: John Wiley & Sons.

Ollendick, T. H., & Cerny, J. A. (1981). *Clinical behavior therapy with children.* New York: Plenum Publishing.

Ollendick, T. H., & Francis, G. (1988). Behavioral assessment and treatment of childhood phobias. *Behavior Modification, 12,* 165–204.

Ollendick, T. H., Matson, J. L., & Helsel, W. J. (1985). Fears in children and adolescents: Normative data. *Behaviour Research and Therapy, 23,* 465–467.

Orvaschel, H., & Weissman, M. M. (1986). Epidemiology of anxiety disorders in children: A review. In R. Gittelman (Ed.), *Anxiety disorders of childhood* (pp. 58–72). New York: Guilford Press.

Parker, G. (1983). *Parental overprotection: A risk factor in psychosocial development.* New York: Grune and Stratton.

Pratt, K. C. (1945). The study of the "Fears" of rural children. *Journal of Genetic Psychology, 67,* 179–194.

Prince, G. S. (1968). School phobia. In E. Miller (Ed.), *Foundations of Child Psychiatry* (pp. 413–434). London: Pergamon Press.

Prins, P. J. M. (1986). Children's self-speech and self-regulation during a fear-provoking behavioral test. *Behavior Research and Therapy, 24,* 181–191.

Puig-Antich, J., & Chambers, W. (1978). *The Schedule for Affective Disorders and Schizophrenia for School-aged Children.* New York State Psychiatric Institute: Authors.

Quay, H. C. (1972). Patterns of aggression, withdrawal, and immaturity. In H. C. Quay & J. S. Werry (Eds.), *Psychophysiological disorders of childhood* (pp. 1–29). New York: John Wiley & Sons.

Quay, H. C. (1977). Measuring dimensions of deviant behavior: The Behavior Problem Checklist. *Journal of Abnormal Child Psychology, 5,* 277–289.

Quay, H. C. (1979). Classification. In H. C. Quay & J. S. Werry (Eds.), *Psychopathological disorders of childhood,* Second edition (pp. 1–42). New York: John Wiley & Sons.

Quay, H. C. (1986). DSM-III as a taxonomy of psychopathology in childhood and adolescence. In T. Millon & G. Klerman (Eds.), *Contemporary directions in psychopathology: Toward the DSM-IV.* New York: Guilford Press.

Quay, H. C., & Peterson, D. R. (1983). *Interim manual for the Revised Behavior Problem Checklist.* Coral Gables, FL: University of Miami.

Rachman, S. (1968). *Phobias: Their nature and control.* Springfield, IL: Charles C Thomas.

Rachman, S. J., & Hodgson, R. J. (1980). *Obsessions and compulsions.* Englewood Cliffs, NJ: Prentice-Hall.

Rapoport, J. L. (1986). Childhood obsessive-compulsive disorder. *Journal of Child Psychology and Psychiatry, 27,* 289–295.

Reynolds, C. R., & Richmond, B. O. (1978). What I think and feel: A revised measure of children's manifest anxiety scale. *Journal of Abnormal Child Psychology, 6,* 271–280.

Richman, N., Stevenson, J. E., & Graham, P. J. (1975). Prevalence of behavior problems in three-year old children: An epidemiologic study in a London borough. *Journal of Child Psychology and Psychiatry, 16,* 277–287.

Rimm, D. C., & Masters, J. C. (1974). *Behavior therapy: Techniques and empirical findings.* New York: Academic Press.

Rines, W. B. (1973). Behavior therapy before institutionalization. *Psychotherapy: Theory, Research, and Practice, 10,* 281–283.

Roehling, P. V., & Robin, A. L. (1986). Development and validation of the Family Beliefs Inventory: A measure of unrealistic beliefs among parents and adolescents. *Journal of Consulting and Clinical Psychology, 54,* 693–697.

Ronan, K., Rowe, M., & Kendall, P. C. (1988, November). Children's anxious self-statement questionnaire (CASSQ): Development and validation. Paper presented at Association for Advancement of Behavior Therapy Convention, New York.

Ross, A. O. (1981). *Child behavior therapy: Principles, procedures, and empirical basis* (pp. 251–289). New York: John Wiley & Sons.

Ross, D., Ross, S., & Evans, T. A. (1971). The modification of extreme social withdrawal by modification with guided practice. *Journal of Behavior Therapy and Experimental Psychiatry, 2,* 273–279.

Saal, F. E., Downey, R. G., & Lahey, M. A. (1980). Rating the ratings: Assessing the psychometric qualities of rating data. *Psychological Bulletin, 88,* 413–428.

Saylor, C., Finch, A. J., Spirito, A., & Bennett, B. (1984). The Children's Depression Inventory: A systematic evaluation of psychometric properties. *Journal of Consulting and Clinical Psychology, 52,* 955–967.

Scherer, M. W., & Nakamura, C. Y. (1968). A Fear Survey Schedule for Children (FSS-FC): A factor analytical comparison with manifest anxiety (CMAS) *Behavior Research and Therapy, 6,* 173–182.

Schlesinger, S. E. (1988). Cognitive-behavioral approaches to family treatment of addictions. In N. Epstein, S. E. Schlesinger, & W. Dryden (Eds.), *Cognitive-Behavioral Therapy with Families* (pp. 254–291). New York: Brunner/Mazel.

Schlesinger, S. E., & Epstein, N. (1986). Cognitive-behavioral techniques in marital therapy. In P. Keller & L. Ritt (Eds.), *Innovations in clinical practice: A source book* (Vol. 5, pp. 137–155). Sarasota, FL: Professional Resource Exchange.

Schwartz, R. M., & Garamoni, G. L. (1989). Cognitive balance and psychopathology: Evaluation of an information processing model of positive and negative states of mind. *Clinical Psychology Review, 9,* 271–294.

Schwarz, J. C., & Getter, H. (1980). Parental conflict and dominance in late adolescent maladjustment: A triple interaction model. *Journal of Abnormal Psychology, 89,* 573–580.

Sheslow, D. V., Bondy, A. S., & Nelson, R. O. (1982). A comparison of graduated exposure, verbal coping skills, and their combination in the treatment of children's fear of the dark. *Child and Family Behavior Therapy, 4,* 33–45.

Silverman, W. K. (1987). *Anxiety Disorders Interview Schedule for Children.* Unpublished manuscript. (Available from author, State University of New York, Albany, NY.)

Silverman, W. K. (1991). *Anxiety disorders interview schedule for children.* Albany, NY: Graywind Publications.

Silverman, W. K., Cerny, J. A., & Nelles, W. B. (1988). Familial influence in anxiety disorders: Studies on the offspring of patients with anxiety disorders. In B. B. Lahey & A. E. Kazdin (Eds.), *Advances in child clinical psychology: Vol. 16* (pp. 223–248). New York: Plenum Publishing.

Skinner, B. F. (1966). *Cumulative record.* New York: Appleton-Century-Crofts.

Solyom, M. D., Beck, P., Solyom, C., & Hugel, R. (1974). Some etiological factors in phobic neurosis. *Canadian Psychiatric Association Journal, 19*(1), 69–78.

Speilberger, C. (1973). *Manual for State-Trait Anxiety Inventory for Children.* Palo Alto, CA: Consulting Psychologists Press.

Spitzer, R. L., Endicott, J., & Robin, E. (1978). Research diagnostic criteria: Rationale and reliability. *Archives of General Psychiatry, 35,* 773–782.

Sroufe, L. A. (1983). Infant-caregiver attachment and patterns of adaptation in preschool: The roots of maladaptation and competence. In M. Perlmutter (Ed.), *Minnesota symposium on child psychology, 16.* Minneapolis: University of Minnesota Press.

Sroufe, L. A., & Rutter, M. (1984). The domain of developmental psychopathology. *Child Development, 55,* 17–29.

Stampfl, T., & Levis, D. (1967). Essentials of implosive therapy: A learning theory-based psychodynamic behavioral therapy. *Journal of Abnormal Psychology, 72,* 496–503.

Stark, K. (1990). *Childhood depression: School-based intervention.* New York: Guilford Press.

Stein, A. B., Finch, A. J., Hooke, J. F., Montgomery, L. E., & Nelson, W. M. (1975). Cognitive tempo and the mode of representation in emotionally disturbed children and normal children. *Journal of Psychology, 90,* 197–201.

Strauss, C. C. (1987). Anxiety. In M. Hersen & V. B. Van Hasselt (Eds.), *Behavior therapy with children and adolescents.* New York: John Wiley & Sons.

Strauss, C. C. (1988). Behavioral assessment and treatment of overanxious disorder in children and adolescents. *Behavior Modification, 12,* 234–250.

Strauss, C. C., Lease, C. A., Last, C. G., & Francis, G. (1988). Overanxious disorder: An examination of developmental differences. *Journal of Abnormal Child Psychology, 16,* 433–443.

Strober, M., Green, J., & Carlson, G. (1981). Reliability of psychiatric diagnosis in hospitalized adolescents. *Archives of General Psychiatry, 38,* 141–145.

Suinn, R. M. (1984). Generalized anxiety disorder. In S. M. Turner (Ed.), *Behavior theories and treatment of anxiety.* New York: Plenum Publishing.

Sylvester, C., Hyde, T. S., & Reichler, R. J. (1987). The Diagnostic Interview for Children and Personality Interview for Children in studies of children at risk for anxiety disorders and depression. *Journal of the American Academy of Child and Adolescent Psychiatry, 26,* 668–675.

Thyer, B. A., & Sowers-Hoag, K. M. (1988). Behavior therapy for separation anxiety disorder. *Behavior Modification, 12*(2), 205–233.

Torgesen, S. (1983). Genetic factors in anxiety disorders. *Archives of General Psychiatry, 40,* 1085–1089.

Turner, S. M., & Beidel, D. C. (1988). *Treating obsessive-compulsive disorder.* New York: Pergamon Press.

Turner, S. M., Beidel, D. C., & Costello, A. (1987). Psychopathology in the offspring of anxiety disorders patients. *Journal of Consulting and Clinical Psychology, 55,* 229–235.

Vaughn, C. E., & Leff, J. P. (1976). The influence of family and social factors on the course of psychiatric illness. *British Journal of Psychiatry, 129,* 125–137.

Verlhulst, F. C., Althaus, M., & Berden, G. F. M. G. (1987). The child assessment schedule: Parent-child agreement and validity measures. *Journal of Child Psychology and Psychiatry, 28,* 455–466.

Waldron, S., Shrier, D. K., Stone, B., & Tobin, F. (1975). School phobia and other childhood neuroses: A systematic study of the children and their families. *American Journal of Psychiatry, 132,* 802–808.

Watson, D., & Clark, L. A. (1984). Negative affectivity: The disposition to experience aversive emotional states. *Psychological Bulletin, 96,* 465–490.

Weisman, D., Ollendick, T. H., & Horne, A. M. (1978). *A comparison of mental relaxation techniques with children.* Unpublished manuscript, Indiana State University.

Weissman, M. M., Leckman, J. F., Merikangas, K. R., Gammon, G. D., & Prusoff, B. (1984). Depression and anxiety disorders in parents and children. *Archives of General Psychiatry, 41,* 845–852.

Wells, K. C., & Virtulano, L. A. (1984). Anxiety disorders in childhood. In S. E. Turner (Ed.), *Behavioral theories and treatment of anxiety.* New York: Plenum Publishing.

Werry, J. S. (1986). Diagnosis and assessment. In R. Gittelman (Ed.), *Anxiety disorders of childhood.* New York: Guilford Press.

Werry, J. S., & Quay, H. C. (1971). The prevalence of behavior symptoms in younger elementary school children. *American Journal of Orthopsychiatry, 41,* 136–143.

Wilson, G. T. (1984). Fear reduction methods and the treatment of anxiety disorders. In G. T. Wilson, C. M. Franks, K. D. Brownell, & P. C. Kendall, *Annual review of behavior therapy: Theory research and practice,* (Vol. 9), (pp. 95–131). New York: Guilford Press.

Wilson, G. T. (1990). Fear reduction methods and the treatment of anxiety disorders. In C. M. Franks, G. T. Wilson, P. C. Kendall, & J. Foreyt, *Review of behavior therapy: Theory, research, and practice,* (Vol. 12), (pp. 72–102). New York: Guilford Press.

Wolpe, J. (1961). The systematic desensitization treatment of neuroses. *Journal of Nervous and Mental Disease, 132,* 189–203.

Zatz, S., & Chassin, L. (1985). Cognitions of test-anxious children. *Journal of Consulting and Clinical Psychology, 51,* 526–534.

Author Index

Abe, K., 7–8
Abramson, L. Y., 16
Achenbach, T. M., 31, 48, 49
Adam, T., 17, 65, 133
Agras, S., 7
Allen, L., 8
Althaus, M., 42
Ambonetti, A., 149
Ambrosini, P. J., 41, 42
American Psychiatric Association, 4, 7, 31, 33
Angelino, H., 140
Arnkoff, D. B., 13
Azar, S. T., 154, 161

Baldwin, A. L., 51
Baldwin, C., 51
Ball, W., 8
Bandura, A., 24, 68, 151
Barker, P., 151
Barlow, D. H., 11, 49, 50, 57, 138, 139
Barrett, C. L., 8, 10, 35, 40
Barrios, B. A., 2, 3, 31, 36, 40, 42, 57, 134, 151
Baucom, D. H., 154
Bauer, D. H., 8, 10
Beck, A. T., 16, 39, 57, 133
Beck, P., 146, 147
Beidel, D. C., 49, 136, 147
Bell, W. G., 154
Berden, G. F. M. G., 42
Berg, I., 148

Bernstein, D., 49, 58
Bertalanffy, L. von, 159
Block, J., 150
Block, J. H., 150
Boice, R., 49
Bondy, A. S., 37
Borkovec, T., 49, 58, 134
Bowlby, J., 10, 149
Bradbury, T. N., 154
Brady, E. U., 131
Braswell, L., 63, 65, 134, 179
Brent, D. A., 39
Bronson, G. W., 10
Brown, G., 133
Burback, D. J., 41, 42
Butler, A., 148

Campbell, S. B., 8, 10
Campos, J. J., 151
Carek, D. J., 131
Carey, S., 146
Carlson, C. I., 50, 51, 52, 53, 54
Carlson, G., 34
Casat, C. D., 39
Catalan, J., 63
Cerny, J. A., 58, 59, 84, 139, 147, 151, 183
Chambers, W., 41
Chambers, W. J., 41, 42
Chandler, M. J., 71
Chansky, T. E., 45, 139
Chassin, L., 45
Chaudery, M. D., 145, 146

Cicchetti, D., 35
Clancy, J., 146, 147
Clark, L. A., 132
Clayton, 145, 146
Cloninger, C. R., 145, 146
Cole, R. E., 51
Cone, J., 47–48
Conover, N., 39
Conover, N. C., 41, 42
Costello, A., 147
Costello, A. J., 39, 40, 41
Costello, C. J., 41, 42
Craighead, L. W., 37
Craighead, W. C., 37
Craighead, W. E., 34
Crowe, R., 146, 147
Crowe, R. R., 145, 146

Darley, S., 50
Davies, M., 41, 42
DeGiovanni, I. S., 7, 35
Dobson, K. S., 130
Dodge, K., 16
Dollins, J., 140
Dryden, W., 159, 161
Duhe, A. G., 154
Duncan, M. K., 39, 41, 42
D'Zurilla, T. J., 62, 63

Earls, F., 7
Edelbrock, C., 39, 40, 41, 42
Edelbrock, C. S., 31, 48, 49
Eidelson, J. I., 133
Eisenberg, L., 145, 149, 160
Emde, R. N., 151
Emery, G., 16, 39, 57, 133
Endicott, J., 41
Epps, J., 1, 45, 115
Epstein, N., 154, 159, 161
Evans, I. M., 37
Evans, T. A., 68

Faravelli, C., 149
Ferrari, M., 8, 37
Finch, A. J., 37, 39, 131
Fincham, F., 154
Finkelstein, R., 39

Fleece, E. L., 49
Foa, E. B., 72
Follansbee, D., 52
Fonnesu, F., 149
Forbes, L., 8
Foster, S., 47–48
Fox, J. E., 8
Francis, G., 34, 36, 39, 41, 45, 46, 70, 148
Fryer, L. L., 131

Gammon, G. D., 147
Garamoni, G. L., 28
Garcia, K. A., 7, 35
Gassner, S., 150
Gelder, M., 63
Getter, H., 150
Gittelman, R., 6, 31, 149
Goeke, K. E., 64
Goldfreid, M. R., 62, 63
Gotlib, I. H., 131
Gottesman, I., 146
Gottman, J. M., 51
Graham, P. J., 7
Grayson, J. B., 72
Graziano, A. M., 7, 35
Green, J., 34
Greene, W. M., 52
Grotevant, H. D., 50, 51, 52, 53, 54
Grove, W., 129
Grubb, H. J., 34, 148
Guze, S. B., 145, 146

Hamilton, D. I., 11, 58, 71
Hampe, E., 8, 10, 35, 40
Harris, E. L., 145, 146
Harris, S. L., 8, 37
Hartmann, D. P., 2, 3, 31, 36, 40, 42, 134, 151
Hartup, W. W., 14
Hatzenbuehler, L. C., 71
Hauser, S. T., 52
Hawes, R., 49
Hays, R. C., 28
Heide, F. J., 134
Helsel, W. J., 8, 10
Herjanic, B., 41, 42

Hersen, M., 34, 39, 148
Hersov, L. A., 149
Hetherington, E. M., 150
Hill, J. P., 35
Himadi, W. G., 49
Hirsch, M., 41, 42
Hodges, K., 41, 42
Hoenk, P. R., 146, 147
Hollon, S. D., 13, 60, 133, 162
Holmbeck, G. H., 35
Holmes, F. B., 8
Holtzworth-Munroe, A., 154
Honzik, M. P., 8
Hooke, J. F., 37
Horne, A. M., 59
Houston, B. K., 8
Howard, B., 77, 146, 147
Howard, B. L., 1, 28, 45
Hugel, R., 146, 147
Hutcherson, S., 49
Hyde, T. S., 147

Ingram, R. E., 15, 16, 22, 46, 57

Jacob, T., 50, 51, 53
Jacobson, N. S., 154
Jannoun, L., 63
Jersild, A. T., 8

Kalas, R., 39, 41, 42
Kane, M., 13, 77
Kastrup, M., 7, 8
Katkin, E., 49
Katz, I., 50
Kazdin, A. E., 34, 39, 148
Kendall, P. C., 1, 3, 10, 12, 13, 15,
    16, 22, 27, 28, 34, 39, 43, 45, 46,
    48, 57, 60, 63, 65, 71, 77, 115,
    129, 131, 132, 133, 134, 135,
    139, 144, 162, 179
King, N. J., 11, 58, 71
Klaric, S. H., 41
Klein, R., 6, 41
Kleiner, L., 63
Kleinert, M. D., 151
Kleinknecht, R. A., 72
Koeppen, A. S., 58, 59, 84, 180

Koplewicz, H. S., 6
Kovacs, M., 55, 131
Kratochwill, T. R., 1, 35, 40, 48, 64
Kriss, M. R., 12

Lang, P. J., 3, 40, 50
Lapouse, R., 7
Last, C. G., 1, 6, 34, 36, 39, 148
Lease, C. A., 36
Leckman, J. F., 147
Leff, J. P., 52
Lerner, R. M., 34
Leslie, L. A., 160
Levis, D., 72
Lewis, S. A., 69
Ley, R., 138
Lick, J., 49
Lipovsky, A. J., 39
Little, V., 71
Livingston, R., 147
Luiselli, J. K., 64
Lynch, M., 155

McFarlane, A. C., 151, 152
McFarlane, J. W., 8
McHale, S. M., 37
McIntosh, J. A., 131
McKnew, D., 41, 42
Madle, R. A., 64
Mahoney, M. J., 13
Mannuzza, S., 41
Marchione, K., 57
Margolin, G., 154, 162, 164
Marks, I. M., 71
Marshall, W. L., 63
Martin, R. L., 145–46
Masters, J. C., 58, 72
Masui, T., 7–8
Matson, J. L., 8, 10, 132
Maurer, A., 10, 35
Mech, E. V., 140
Meichenbaum, D., 14, 171
Melamed, B. G., 46, 49, 69
Merikangas, K. R., 147
Meyers, A. W., 37
Mezzich, A. C., 34
Mezzich, J. E., 34

Michelson, L., 57
Miller, L. C., 8, 10, 35, 40
Monk, M. A., 7
Montgomery, L. E., 37
Morris, R. J., 1, 35, 40, 48, 64
Morrison, A., 150
Morton, T. L., 154, 161
Moss, H. B., 146, 147
Munby, M., 63
Munjack, D. J., 146, 147
Murray, E. J., 150

Nakamura, C. Y., 10
Neisworth, J. T., 64
Nelles, W. B., 11, 138, 147, 151
Nelson, R. O., 37
Nelson, W. M., 37
Nezu, A. M., 62
Nezu, C. M., 62
Noble, H., 10
Noyes, R., 145, 146, 147
Nugent, H., 147

O'Leary, K. D., 154
Oliveau, D., 7
Ollendick, T. H., 8, 10, 11, 35, 41, 43,
    58, 59, 61, 68, 70, 71, 79, 84, 183
Orvaschel, H., 7, 9

Paez, P., 41, 42
Parker, G., 152
Pauls, D. L., 145–46, 147
Perri, M. G., 62
Peterson, D. R., 48
Phillips, J. E., 1
Powers, S. I., 52
Pratt, K. C., 8
Prince, G. S., 145
Prins, P. J. M., 45
Pritchard, J., 148
Prusoff, B., 147
Puig-Antich, J., 41, 42

Quay, H. C., 7, 31, 48

Rachman, S., 35
Rader, L., 147

Rajapark, D. C., 52
Rapoport, J. L., 136
Reich, W., 41, 42
Reichler, R. J., 147
Reynolds, C. R., 43, 44
Richman, N., 7
Richmond, B. O., 43, 44
Ridberg, E. H., 150
Rimm, D. C., 58, 72
Riskind, J. H., 133
Robin, A. L., 162
Robin, E., 41
Roebuck, L., 41, 42
Roehling, P. V., 162
Ronan, K., 46, 115
Ronan, K. R., 3, 10, 43, 46, 48
Ross, A. O., 68
Ross, D., 68
Ross, S., 68
Rowe, M., 46
Rush, A. J., 133
Rutter, M., 35, 151

Saylor, C. F., 131
Scherer, M. W., 10
Schlesinger, S. E., 154, 159, 161
Schroeder, H. E., 71
Schwartz, J. C., 150
Schwartz, R. M., 28
Seligman, M. R. P., 16
Sessarego, A., 149
Shaw, B. F., 130, 133
Sheslow, D. V., 37
Shigetomi, C. C., 57
Shrier, D. K., 149, 150, 158
Siegel, L. J., 69
Silverman, W., 41
Silverman, W. K., 147, 151
Siqueland, L., 63, 77
Skinner, B. F., 64
Slymen, D., 145, 146
Slymen, D. J., 146, 147
Smith, R. G., 147
Solyom, C., 146, 147
Solyom, M. D., 146, 147
Sorce, J. F., 151
Sowers-Hoag, K. M., 6

Speilberger, C., 43, 44
Spevack, M., 63
Spitzer, R. L., 41
Sroufe, L. A., 11, 35
Stampfl, T., 72
Stark, K., 17, 65, 133
Statfield, A., 1
Steer, R. A., 133
Stein, A. B., 37
Steketee, G., 72
Stevenson, J. E., 7
Stone, B., 149, 150, 158
Stouwie, R., 150
Strauss, C. C., 1, 6, 34, 36, 39, 42,
    46, 58, 64, 68
Strober, M., 34
Suinn, R. M., 6
Svegda, M., 151
Sylvester, C., 147
Sylvester, D., 7

Tabrizi, M. A., 41, 42
Teasdale, L. D., 16
Tennenbaum, D. L., 50, 51, 53
Thyer, B. A., 6
Tobin, F., 149, 150, 158

Torgesen, S., 146
Tronick, E., 8
Turner, S. M., 136, 147
Twentyman, C. T., 154, 161

Vaughn, C. E., 52
Verlhulst, F. C., 42
Virtulano, L. A., 50

Waldron, S., 149, 150, 158
Watson, D., 39, 131, 132
Webb, T., 149
Weerts, T., 49
Weisman, D., 59
Weissman, M., 8, 147
Weissman, M. M., 7, 147
Weiss-Perry, B., 52
Wells, K. C., 50
Werry, J. S., 2, 7, 50
Wilson, G. T., 72
Wolfe, B. E., 50

Yurcheson, R., 49

Zatz, S., 45

Subject Index

Academic evaluation, 94, 97, 117, 132
Actions and attitudes, 89, 133, 139.
    See also FEAR steps
Agoraphobia, 57, 148, 151
Anger:
    difficulty with, case illustration,
        102, 113, 116
Anxiety:
    and attention deficit disorder, 36,
        39
    defined, 1–7
    and depression, 36, 39, 42, 55,
        126, 147
    distinction between normal and
        clinical, 1–2
    provoking cognition, 85
    and single phobia, 36
    symptoms, 2–4
Anxiety Disorders Interview
    Schedule for Children
    (ADIS-C), 41, 54–55, 102
Assessment:
    considerations, 34–40
    developmental 34–37, 40, 42, 44,
        54
    diagnostic changes, 39
    referral by others, 37–38
    methods, 40–54
    behavioral observations, 46–47
    family assessment, 50–54,
        162–164
    mapping out cognition and
        behavior, 164

Assessment *(continued)*
    parent & teacher ratings, 48–49
    physiological assessment, 49–50
    pictorial assessment, 37
    self-report scales, 42–46
    structural interviews, 40–42
    multimethod Approach, 54–56
    of cognitions, 45–46
    sample battery, 55
    strategies, 30–56
Attention-Deficit Hyperactivity
    Disorder:
    as alternative diagnosis, 20
    case study, with OAD/SAD,
        School phobia, Avoidant
        disorder, Oppositional
        disorder, 112–116
    comorbidity with anxiety
        disorders, 36, 39
Attitudes and actions, 89, 133, 139.
    See also FEAR steps
Attributions, 22, 84, 133, 144, 153,
        154, 165
    attributional processes, 160
    case study example, 109
    depressogenic, 133
    effort, 172
    interplay of parent and child
        attributions, 159–160
Avoidant disorder
    behavioral indicators, 4
    case study with Overanxious
        disorder, Separation anxiety,

Avoidant disorder *(continued)*
    School phobia,
    Attention-Deficit
    Hyperactivity Disorder,
    Oppositional disorder,
    112–116
  cognitive features, 5, 6
  described, 6
  overlap with Social phobia, 6–7
  primary diagnosis, 122
Avoidant parenting style, 150–153

Behavioral Avoidance Tasks (BATs).
    See Behavioral observations
Behavioral events:
  role in theory, 22–24
Behavioral experiments, 168
Behavioral observations, 46–48, 55
  Behavioral Avoidance Tasks
    (BATs), 46
  Behavior Profile Rating Scale, 46
  families, 51–53
  Observer Rating Scale of Anxiety,
    46
Beliefs, 24, 165. *See also* parental
    beliefs
Booster sessions, 99, 179

Cartoons, 47, 85, 86
Catastrophic perceptions:
  case illustration, 108
Challenging expectations, 166. *See
    also* cognitive procedures
Check-in times in maintenance of
    gains, 178, 179
Child Behavior Checklist (CBCL),
    48, 49, 54–55
  in case illustrations, 102, 105, 113,
    116, 118, 121, 148
  means and standard deviations,
    123
Children of anxious parents,
    147–149
Children's Anxious Self Statement
    Questionnaire, 46, 48, 55
Children's Depression Inventory
    (CDI), 55, 113, 116, 123, 131

Classification of anxiety disorders,
    31–33
Clinical case illustrations, 100–121
  9 year old male, 112–116
  10 year old male, 101–105
  12 year old female, 105–112
  13 year old male, 117–121
Clinical interviews, 40–42
  Anxiety Disorders Interview
    Schedule for Children, 41,
    54–55
  Diagnostic Interview for Children
    and Adolescents, 41
Diagnostic Interview Schedule for
    Children, 41
  Schedule for Affective Disorders
    & Schizophrenia for
    School-Aged Children, 41
  Schedule for the Assessment of
    Conduct, Hyperactivity,
    Anxiety, Mood, and
    Psychoactive Substances, 41
Clinical Significance, 129
Cognitive-behavioral interventions:
  coping template, 58–67
  core principles, 13
  with families, 156–170
  strategies, 57–73
  and systems theory, 160
Cognitive-behavioral perspective,
    12–29
  childhood anxiety, model, 21–25
  cognition, 15–18
  definition, 14–15
  tenets, 12–14
  therapeutic posture, 18–21
  treatment goals, 25–29
Cognitive development, 10, 36–37,
    60. *See also* developmental
    factors
Cognitive features:
  content, 16
  deficiency, 17, 18
  distortion, 17, 18
  information processing, 13
  parental cognition, 153–155
  processes, 16

Cognitive features *(continued)*
  products, 16
  structures, 16, 17, 66
Cognitive restructuring, 60, 166
Collaboration, 18–19, 67, 133, 165.
  See also therapeutic posture
Commercials, 98, 175, 176, 177, 178.
  See also SHOWING OFF
  My Commercial, 98
  "Nerve Busters," 176
  "Super Can," 177
Comorbidity, 27, 36, 39, 42, 55, 130,
  131–139, 142
  anxiety and depression, 36, 39, 42,
    55, 126, 147
Compliance, 131, 175
  with STIC tasks, 79
  See also over-compliance and
    noncompliance
Connors' Teacher Rating Scale, 48
Coping Cat Workbook, 57, 74, 99
Coping Model, 68–71, 75, 86, 94,
  135, 140, 172, 174,
  case illustration, 110, 119
Coping problem-solving template,
  165
Coping Questionnaire:
  child form, 43, 45, 54–55, 123
  parent form, 43, 45, 54–55, 123
Coping skills, 26, 67, 172
Coping statements, 85, 87–89
Coping steps, 93–94. *See also* FEAR
  plan
Coping strategies. *See* coping
  template
Coping template, 58–67, 168, 171
  building a coping template, 66–67
  imagery, 59–60
  maladaptive self-talk, correcting,
    60–62
  problem-solving, 62–63
  relaxation, 58–59
  rewards, 63–65
  superhero characters, 65–66

Deep breathing, 82, 84, 89, 97
Denial, 130, 139–140

Depression, 17, 65, 130, 131–133,
  136, 142, 148, 151
  case illustration, 113, 115, 116
  implications for the treatment of
    anxiety, 132
Depressogenic cognition, 133
Developmental factors, 11, 57, 70
  changes in childhood fears, 8–11
  in clinical interviews, 42
  in child self-report, 44
  cognitive development, 36–37
  process in anxiety, 34–37
Diagnosis of anxiety disorders,
  31–33
  issues, 30–56
  reliability, 33–34, 42
  validity, 33–34
Diagnostic Interview for Children
  and Adolescents, 41
Diagnostic Interview Schedule for
  Children, 41
Diathesis-Stress Model, 155–156
Dealing with potential difficulties;
  Problems, 131–143, 179
  comorbidity, 131–139
  depression, 131–133
  hyperactivity, 134–135
  hypercriticality, 134
  obsessive-compulsive patterns,
    135–137
  panic attacks, 138–139
  denial of anxiety, 139–140
  over- and noncompliance, 130,
    141–142
  realistic fears, 140–141
DSM-III-R diagnoses, 4–7, 19,
  31–32, 130, 136, 138
  Avoidant disorder, 32
  Overanxious disorder, 32, 39
  Separation anxiety disorder,
    31
  Simple phobia, 33
  Social phobia, 32

Effort attributions, 172
Electrodermal recording, 48, 56. *See
  also* physiological assessment

Electromyography, 49. *See also*
    physiological assessment
Embarrassing situations, 90
Emotions, 13, 22–24
    intensity, 22, 24
Empty thought bubbles, 47, 85,
    86
Environmental factors, 156. *See also*
    social context; stressful family
    events
Ethological approach, 10–11
    adaptation, 10
    attachment, 10
    separation anxiety, 10
Evaluation-reward, 169. *See also*
    FEAR plan
Expectations, 20, 23, 24, 84, 93, 133,
    135, 144, 153, 165, 176
    challenging expectations, 166
Expecting bad things to happen, 93.
    See also FEAR plan
Exposure, 94, 95, 97, 137
    features of, 94
    imaginal, 94
Externalizing symptoms, 141
Extinction, 64, 72, 137

Family, 11, 15, 20, 26, 29,
    144–170
    assessment, 50–54, 160–162
        cognitive-behavioral, 53–54
        observations, 51–53
        self-report, 51–54
    behavioral interventions, 167–169
    brainstorming, 168–169
    cognitive-behavioral treatment,
        144–170
    context, 170
    environment of family, 149–153
    predispositions, 145–159
    problem solving, 168–169
    relaxation, 169
    role-play, 168
    stressful events, 149–150
    treatment, 156–159, 164–169
Family Beliefs Inventory, 162

Family factors contributing to the
    disorder, 145–152
    attributions:
        beliefs, 153–155
        expectations, 153–155
    parenting styles, 150–153
    predispositions, 145–149
FEAR plan, 133, 136, 138, 139, 171,
    172, 173, 174–175, 178, 179
    in case illustration, 103–105
    See also Feeling frightened;
        Expectations; Actions and
        attitudes; Results and
        rewards; FEAR steps
Fears:
    as an adaptive response, 1
    developmental changes in, 8–11
    gender differences in, 8
    as part of a normal developmental
        process, 1, 8
FEAR steps (acronym), 92–93, 98,
    133, 134, 137, 138, 158
    actions and attitudes, 89
    case study example, 104, 110, 112,
        120
    example of child using FEAR
        steps, 178
    expecting bad things to happen,
        93
    explanation of, 93
    feeling frightened, 93
    results and rewards, 93
    See also FEAR plan
Fear Survey Schedule for
    Children—Revised, 43, 54–55,
    123
Feeling frightened, 93. *See* FEAR
    plan

Generalized anxiety, 57, 148
Goal of the program, 74–75, 134,
    171
    for parental involvement, 161–164

Hierarchy, 94, 97
Home environment, 130, 140

Homework assignments. *See* STIC
    tasks
Humor, 132, 169
    case illustration, 108, 112, 118
Hyperactivity, 17–18, 134–135, 136,
    143. *See also* Attention-Deficit
    Hyperactivity Disorder
Hyperventilation, 138

Impulsive children, 17–18, 65, 134
Information processing, 17
Intervention strategies, 67–73
    coping modeling, 68–70, 71, 75,
        86, 94, 135, 140, 172, 174
    exposure 71–73
    role plays, 70–71, 174
    therapeutic relationship 67–68
In vivo experiences, 13, 25, 63, 94, 95,
    97, 98, 157
    in case illustrations, 103–104,
        109–111, 115–116, 120, 124
    See also exposure
Irritable distress, 152
    parenting style, 150–153

Maintaining gains, 171–185
    booster sessions, 179
    effort attributions, 172–173
    posttreatment therapeutic
        contacts, 178–179
    relapse prevention, 173–174
    SHOWing off, 174–176
        case illustration 1 of SHOWing
            off (Nervebusters
            commercial), 176–177
        case illustration 2 of SHOWing
            off (Supercan commercial),
            177–178
        transcript of SHOWing off (role
            switching with therapist),
            175–176
        transcript of SHOWing off
            (talking about FEAR plan
            in front of parents), 175
Management of anxiety, 27, 75, 98.
    See also goals of treatment

Marital conflict, 149–150
Mechanisms:
    of change, 28–29
    of transmission, 145–152
Modeling, 68, 135, 150–151
    "tag along," 70, 79, 86
Multimethod assessment, 54–56

Negative thinking, 61
Noncompliance, 130, 141–142
Normal limits, 7–8, 20, 140
Normative comparisons, 129
Nonnegative thinking, 27

Obsessive-compulsive patterns, 85,
    130, 135–137, 142
Overanxious disorder (OAD):
    anxiety problems in school, 128
    behavioral indicators, 4
    case illustration, 10 year old male
        with Simple phobia, 101–105
    case illustration, 12 year old
        female with Separation
        anxiety, 105–112
    case illustration, 9 year old male
        with Separation anxiety,
        School phobia, Avoidant
        disorder, ADHD, and
        Oppositional disorder,
        112–116
    case illustration, 13 year old male
        with Separation anxiety,
        117–121
    cognitive features, 5
    described, 4–5, 74
    diagnostic criteria, 32, 39, 130
    mothers of, 148
Overcompliance, 130, 141–142
Overprotectiveness, 150–155

Panic attacks, 130, 138–139
Panic disorder, 145, 148
Paradox, 175
Parent–child:
    agreement in assessment, 36–38,
        41–42
    interactions, 167

Parent reports:
  Child Behavior Checklist (CBCL),
    48–49, 54–55, 126, 127
  Coping Questionnaire-Parent
    (CQ-P), 126, 127
  Parent-State-Trait Anxiety
    Inventory for Children-Trait
    (P-STAIC-T), 126, 127
  Rating scales, 48–49
  Revised Behavior Problem
    Checklist, 48
Parents' attributions, beliefs, and
    expectations, 98, 132, 140–141,
    147–149, 153–155
  as consultants, 156–159
  disorder, 158
  involvement, 98, 156–159, 170
  modeling, 150–151
  sessions, 99
  styles, 151–153
  support, 131, 140
Perceptions, families, 53–54
Perfectionism, 131, 134, 136, 137
  case illustration, 106, 107, 109, 111
Performance-based interventions, 13,
    94
Personal experiments, 69, 133
Physical symptoms, 76, 79–82, 138,
    139
  as cues, 138
Physiological assessment, 49–50, 56
Positive thinking, 27
Posture of the cognitive-behavioral
    therapist, 21
Practice at home, 84. See also STIC
    tasks
Predispositions:
  children of anxious parents,
    147–149
  family patterns in anxiety and
    depression, 145, 147
  panic disorder, 145
  parents of anxious children,
    147–149
  patterns of problems among
    relatives of anxiety disorder,
    146–147

Prevalence of childhood anxiety
    disorders, 7–9
  prevalence study summaries, 9
Prevention, 25, 173–174
Problem solving, 13, 19, 26, 63,
    172
  approach, 171, 173
  coping strategies, 103, 111, 120
  dependency on adults, 112
  difficulties with (case illustration
    example), 109
  skills, 76, 89–91
  steps, 63

Realistic fears, 140–141
Reframing, 179
Relapse, 27, 173
  lapse, 173, 179
  relapse prevention, 173–174
Relationship, 18–21, 161–162
Relaxation, 58–60, 71, 82–84, 89,
    134–135, 138–139
  case illustration, 84, 119
  robot-rag doll, 134
  scripts, 58, 84, 180–185
Relaxation-induced anxiety
  case illustration, 108
Research results, 121–129
  parent reports, 126
  self-report measures, 122–126
  structured interview diagnoses,
    128–129
  teacher reports, 126–128
Resistance to treatment, 77
Results and rewards, 93, 133, 134.
    See also FEAR plan
Rewards, 64, 76, 79, 91, 92, 93, 94,
    97, 99, 133
Revised Behavior Problem Checklist,
    48
Revised Children's Manifest Anxiety
    Scale (RCMAS), 43, 44, 54–55,
    106, 113, 116, 123, 129
Risk-taking, 97
Role-playing, 79, 86, 103, 119,
    174–176
  with families, 167–168

Schedule for Affective Disorders and
Schizophrenia for School-aged
Children, 41
Schedule for the Assessment of
Conduct, Hyperactivity,
Anxiety, Mood, and
Psychoactive Substances
(CHAMPS), 41
Schema, 16, 66, 153
School based anxiety, case
illustration, 105, 118
School phobia, case illustration,
112–116
School report, 37–38
Self-efficacy expectancies, 24
Self-evaluation, 65, 76, 91, 93, 97
case illustration, 103, 109
negative, 84
Self-explanations, 24
Self-report measures:
Children's Anxious Self-statement
Questionnaire (CASSQ), 46,
48, 54–55
Coping Questionnaire (CQ), 43,
45, 54–55, 123
Fear Survey Schedule for
Children-Revised (FSSC-R),
43, 54–55, 123
Revised Children's Manifest
Anxiety Scale (RCMAS), 43,
44, 54–55, 106, 113, 116, 123,
129
State-Trait Anxiety Inventory for
Children-Trait (STAIC-T), 43,
54–55, 123
Self-talk, 17, 24, 46, 60, 76, 84, 85,
87, 103, 108, 119, 153, 165, 166
case illustration, 103, 108, 119
negative, 61
Separation anxiety, 4–6, 11, 31, 130,
136, 148, 164
case illustration with Overanxious
disorder, 105–112, 117–121
case illustration with Overanxious
disorder, Avoidant disorder,
School phobia, Attention
deficit hyperactivity disorder,

Separation anxiety (continued)
Oppositional disorder,
112–116
primary diagnosis of, 122
Session descriptions, 75–98
first 8 sessions, 76–94
session 1, 76–79
session 2, 79–80, 82
session 3, 80–82
session 4, 82–84
session 5, 84–87
session 6, 87–91
session 7, 91–92
session 8, 92–94
second 8 sessions (9–16), 94–99
Sex differences, 8
Shaping, 64
Shared experience, 69, 133
SHOWing off, 174–178
Show-That-I-Can (STIC) Tasks, 132,
134, 135, 141, 142, 173
case illustrations, 103, 107, 109, 121
Simple phobia, 33
Sleep difficulties, case illustrations,
106
Social context, 13, 26, 29, 144, 153.
See also family
Social phobia, 32
State-Trait Anxiety Inventory for
Children (STAIC), 43, 54, 123
case illustrations, 102, 104, 106,
113, 116
clinical significance, 129
STIC (See "Show-That-I-Can"
Tasks)
Stop and Think Workbook, 135
Stressors, 130
family events as, 149–150
Structured interview diagnoses,
40–42, 128–129
"Super Can", 177
Superhero, 66, 91
Systems theory, 159–160

Teacher reports, 37–38, 48–49, 54–55
changes in ratings pre- to
posttreatment, 128

Teacher reports *(continued)*
  Child Behavior Checklist-Teacher
    Report Form (CBCL-T), 128
Temporal model, 21, 23
Termination, 98–99
Therapeutic posture, 18–21, 165
  consultant, 18–19
  diagnostician, 18–20
  educator, 18, 20–21
  therapist, collaborative—
    nonconfrontive posture,
    78
Therapy process, 165
"Think Aloud" tasks, 45
Thought listing, 45, 55
Transcripts:
  Session 1, 77–78
  Session 3, 80–82
  Session 4, 83
  Session 5, 85, 86
  Session 6, 87–89
  Session 7, 92
  Session 8, 93
  session 9–16, 95–97
  anxiety provoking cognitions,
    87–89

Transcripts *(continued)*
  cartoons, 86
  coping statements, 87–89
  establishing rapport, 77–78
  in vivo experience, 95–97
  negative self-talk, 61–62
  physical symptoms, 80–82
  relaxation, 83
  reward, 92
  self-talk, 84–86
  superhero as model, 66
  using FEAR plan, 174–175
Treatment referral, 37–38
  treatment strategies, 164–169
    cognitive procedures, 165–167
    behavioral interventions,
      167–169
  treatment goals, 25–29
    models of change, 28–29
    normal development, 25–26
    rational therapist expectations,
      26–28
  treatment manual, 121
  treatment outcomes, 121–129
Triple column assessment, 87
  example of, 90

About the Authors

Philip C. Kendall, Ph.D., ABBP, is professor of psychology, Head of the Division of Clinical Psychology, and Director of the Child and Adolescent Anxiety Disorders Clinic at Temple University. Dr. Kendall serves as the editor of the journal *Cognitive Therapy and Research,* associate editor of the *Journal of Consulting and Clinical Psychology,* and serves on the editorial board of numerous other professional journals (e.g., *Behavior Therapy*). In 1977, and from 1980 to 1981 he was a fellow at the Center for Advanced Study in the Behavioral Sciences, Stanford, California. The author of numerous research papers and monographs, Dr. Kendall coauthored *Clinical Psychology: Scientific and Professional Dimensions* (with J. Ford) and *Cognitive-Behavioral Therapy for Impulsive Children* (with L. Braswell), coedited *Anxiety and Depression: Distinctive and Overlapping Features* (with Dr. Watson) and *Cognitive-Behavioral Interventions: Theory, Research, and Procedures* (with S. Hollon), edited *Child and Adolescent Therapy: Cognitive-Behavioral Procedures,* and is one of the coauthors of the *Annual Review of Behavior Therapy* (with Franks, Wilson, and Foreyt). Dr. Kendall is a fellow of the American Psychological Association and the American Association for the Advancement of Science. He was president of AABT (Association for Advancement of Behavior Therapy). His research and clinical interests lie in cognitive-behavioral assessment and treatment, especially with children and adolescents. He has lectured throughout the United States, Canada, Europe, and South America.

Tamar Ellsas Chansky, M.A., is a therapist at the Child and Adolescent Anxiety Disorders Clinic and a graduate student in the doctoral training program in Clinical Psychology at Temple University. Her interests include issues in assessment of cognition and family treatment modalities.

Martha T. Kane, M.A., is a student in the doctoral program in Clinical Psychology at Temple University. She has been involved in the Child and Adolescent Anxiety Disorders Clinic since its inception and is currently a

214   About the Authors

senior therapist as well as the coordinator of community contact. Her research interests focus on information processing in anxiety disorders.

Ray S. Kim, M.A., is a doctoral student in clinical psychology at Temple University, and was a therapist and research assistant in the Child and Adolescent Anxiety Disorders Clinic.

Elizabeth Kortlander, M.S., is a doctoral student in clinical psychology at Temple University. She is a therapist at the Child and Adolescent Anxiety Disorders Clinic as well as the Temple University Psychological Services Center. Her research interests include parental perception of their children's anxious behavior.

Kevin R. Ronan, M.A., is a doctoral candidate in the Clinical Psychology division at Temple University. He has served as a therapist and research associate in the area of childhood anxiety, and is currently investigating the cognitive features of negative affect in children.

Frances M. Sessa, M.A., a student in the doctoral program in Clinical
Psy   liagnostician
of t   rders Clinic.
Her   on child and
ado

Lyr   ;ram in Clinical   h diagnosti-
ciar   Anxiety Dis-
ord   n factors in
inte